NOISE OF THE WORLD

NOISE OF THE WORLD

NON-WESTERN MUSICIANS IN THEIR OWN WORDS

BY HANK BORDOWITZ

SOFT SKULL PRESS
BROOKLYN, NY • 2004

Noise of the World
ISBN: 1-932360-60-3
©2004 Hank Bordowitz

Published by Soft Skull Press
www.softskull.com

Distributed by Publishers Group West
800.788.3123 | www.pgw.com

Book Design by David Janik

Printed in Canada

Cataloging in Publication Data for this title
is available from the Library of Congress

ACKNOWLEDGEMENTS

Mega-thanks to my agent, Jim Fitzgerald, for negotiating this deal with very little up front involved for him, and for constantly expressing that he "has a good feeling about this book." This project is very important to me, and Jim knew it.

Thanks to:

David and Richard at Soft Skull who believed from the beginning, but more importantly who understood.

Dr. Michael Fagin, who early in my tenure at *Jazziz*, when I pitched him a piece on Fela, asked if I would like to do a column about non-Western music. The column, which I took over, was called Cosmopolitan, which demonstrated both of our attitudes toward these old new sounds that were finally drifting over the oceans and washing up on our shores.

Rob Hambrecht, Esq., my translator for many of these adventures, particularly the ones that involved French and Spanish. The man speaks a dozen languages, an amazing gift.

To Carolyn, who translated the Gipsy Kings interview,

J. Rajasekaran who translated for Vijay Anand.

To Lynn Adalist (where have you disappeared to, Lynn?) who translated the Anouar Brahem interview.

I'm sure I'm forgetting someone who helped facilitate the language gap that my English presents.

Randal Grass at Shanachie, who has always encouraged my interest, from that first piece he wrote on Fela for *Musician*, through his sojourn at *Shanachie*. Long may he reign!

The publicists who put all of these together over the years.

CONTENTS

FOREWORD IX

NORTH AMERICA

  REGGAE 3

    WILLIE STEWART | THIRD WORLD 5
    DUCKIE SIMPSON | BLACK UHURU 11
    JIMMY CLIFF 15
    WINSTON "BURNING SPEAR" RODNEY 19
    COXSONE DODD 25
    ERNEST RANGLIN 29

  SOCA, CALYPSO, KOMPAS, RARA, AND ZOUK 35

    AUGUST DARNELL | KID CREOLE & THE COCONUTS 37
    JOCELYNE BEROARD | KASSAV 41
    FRED PAUL 47
    JONATHAN DEMME 53
    CLIFFORD SYLVAIN | RARA MACHINE 57

  ACADIAN AND ZYDECO 63

    MICHAEL DOUCET | BEAUSOLIEL 65
    TERRANCE SIMIEN 71

  LATIN AMERICA/SALSA 75

    EMILIO ESTEFAN | MIAMI SOUND MACHINE 77
    GLORIA ESTEFAN | MIAMI SOUND MACHINE 81
    JOE GALDO, RAFAEL VIGIL,
        LARRY DERMER | THE JERKS 83
    JON SECADA 89
    EMMANUEL 93
    YOMO TORO 95
    WILLIE COLÓN 99
    RUBEN BLADES 105
    OSCAR HERNANDEZ | CARABALI/SON DE SOLAR 117
    DANILO PEREZ 123

SOUTH AMERICA

BRAZIL AND ARGENTINA 127
    NANA VASCONCELOS 129
    AL DI MEOLA 131
    DINO SALUZZI 135

AFRICA

NORTH AFRICA 139
    ANOUAR BRAHEM 141
    HASSAN HAKMOUN 143

WEST AND CENTRAL AFRICA 151
    KING SUNNY ADE 153
    ISMAIL TOURE | TOURE KUNDA 159
    PACO YE | FARAFINA 161
    FELA ANIKULAPO KUTI 167
    YOUSSOU N'DOUR 173
    WALLY BADAROU 181
    MARIE DAULNE, SABINE KABONGO,
        SYLVIE NAWASADIO | ZAP MAMA 187

EAST AFRICA 193
    ASTER AWEKE 195
    HENRY KAISER 199

SOUTH AFRICA 205
    PAUL SIMON 207
    JOSEPH SHABALALA | LADYSMITH BLACK MAMBAZO .. 213
    WEST NKOSI 221
    HILDA TLOUBATLA | THE MAHOTELLA QUEENS 225
    ROBBI ROBB | TRIBE AFTER TRIBE 227
    MZWAKHE MBULI 235
    MIRIAM MAKEBA 245
    HUGH MASEKELA 249

EUROPE

FLAMENCO 263

CHICO BALIARDO | THE GIPSY KINGS............ 265
JORGE PARDO.. 269
CARLES BENAVENT 273
JOSE MIGUEL CARMONA, ANTONIO CARMONA, JUAN CARMONA, JOSE SOTO | KETAMA 275
PACO DE LUCIA... 279
EDUARDO BAUTISTA GARCIA........................ 283
MARIO PACHECO | PATA NEGRA/ NUEVOS MEDIOS RECORDS 287
JORGE STRUNZ & ARDASHIR FARAH............. 291

EASTERN EUROPE/KLEZMER........................ 299

HENRY SAPOZNIK | KAPELYE 301
HANKUS NETSKY | THE KLEZMER CONSERVATORY BAND . 307
FRANK LONDON | THE KLEZMATICS 313
ANDY STATMAN 319
BEN "HIJAZ MUSTAPHA" MANDELSON | 3 MUSTAPHAS 3 323
VLADIMIR IVANOFF & TANJA ADREEVA | LES MYSTERE DES VOIX BULGARES 329
ALEXANDER (SASHA) LIPNITSKY | ZVUKI MU 337
MARCEL | DUTCH ROCK MUSIC FOUNDATION 341

ASIA

JAPAN, THE INDIAN SUBCONTINENT AND "THE ORIENT" .. 345

OSAMU KITAJIMA.. 347
DAVID LEWISTON.. 351
RAVI SHANKAR 361
VIJAY ANAND 363

MIDDLE EAST 369

OFRA HAZA 371
SIMON SHAHEEN.. 377

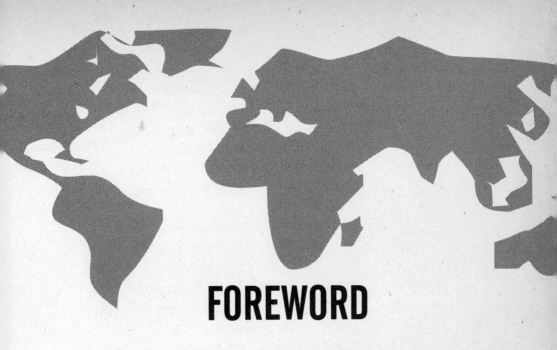

FOREWORD

If you walk up to troubadours on the Nile River and ask them what they were playing, they wouldn't say "world music." My understanding of what "world music" is doing in the marketplace is to defocus real ethnic music. Also, when we call something 'world music' we're obviously saying it's not our world. If it were our world, it would include all the music in the store, the rest of the stuff from our culture. When we say this is "world music," what we really mean is it's out there and it's not to do with us.

—Keith Jarrett

Before anything, there was the drum. For some Africans as recently as six decades ago, the word spread by drum, the drum communicated. Like the drum communicates, music communicates, often where words cannot. Arabs and Israelis do not agree on much, but young Israelis crowd the streets of Tel Aviv to hear the new jack Arabic rappers.

Few things in contemporary music get the blood racing like the sound of the drum. That's why the tiny dancefloor at SOB's—New York City's premier club for non-Western artists—and similar clubs throughout the Western world, steam like Trinidad and other locations whence they book talent. The air conditioning doesn't stand a chance with all the heat generated by the bands and the bodies undulating on the dancefloor, in the aisles, by the bar and wherever they can find a patch of floor.

On the other hand, human nature says go with what you know. Far more people have seen *The Magnificent Seven* and *Star Wars* than *The Seven Samurai* or *Yojimbo*. Yet, the American movies merely put these classic Japanese films into a more familiar package. More people study the art Picasso based on African masks than appreciate the artistry of the masks themselves.

These days, we truly live in a global village, where at any given moment a person can see what's going on in Iraq or Tel Aviv or the House of Commons without leaving the living room. As information becomes a commodity, cross-cultural pollination naturally occurs. Nearly anywhere you go in the world, you can find a McDonald's and Western pop music.

But what's this we're hearing? A pop star from Queens playing South African sheshwe? A founder of New York new wave recording with Latin artists and reissuing Brazilian records? A jazz singer leading an American choir in South African mbube? A vocalist from Senegal singing with an English rock star?

Not long ago, very few Americans knew anything about African, Caribbean, Arabic, or Asian music. Listening to Cuban music was just short of seditious. You might hear Celtic music on St. Patrick's Day. Flamenco music was something you saw in movies, where men made more noise with their heels than with guitars and the vocals didn't matter at all. You might hear Indian film music on a quick flip through the UHF channels in a major urban area. The Western attitude toward non-Western music is well summed up in the Jamaican film *Rockers*, where a white couple is sitting in an outdoor café listening to a reggae band and the man leans over to the woman and says, "This isn't calypso."

Clearly, more people own *Graceland* than know of Mahlathini and the Mahotella Queens. Bobby McFerrin's version of South African choral music has a somewhat better chance in the Western marketplace than Ladysmith Black Mambazo—even post-*Graceland*—if only because he performs it in English.

David Byrne's excursions into Afro-Spanish and Portuguese culture carry cachet because they carry his name, as did Talking Heads's forays into African rhythms. Far more people know Youssou N'Dour for the Peter Gabriel *So* tour than for his superstar status in Senegal. Even Bob Marley never enjoyed the Western acceptance with his music that Eric Clapton did. Kid Creole's calypso pan-Americanisms stay better known than Arrow's Brooklyn-based socas, which stay better known than island-bound Blue Boy. Artists ranging from groundbreaking jazz saxophonist Ornette Coleman to Rolling Stones guitarist Brian Jones went to the far reaches of Morocco's Atlas Mountains to record with the Master Musicians of Jajouka. The indigenous artists, the originators, rarely enjoy the fame and fortune of the imitators.

On the other hand, this exposure is important. In the way that people started digging for the roots of the blues when the Rolling Stones and Blues Breakers rode to fame on that music, people "discovered" the joy of Bob Marley and reggae; of isicathamiya music and its foremost purveyors, Ladysmith Black Mambazo; the fusion of traditional Spanish music and artists like the Gipsy Kings and Paco de Lucia. And the world became a smaller, more rhythmic place.

Musicologists ventured into the central African jungles to record the drummers of Burundi. These recordings found favor with English new-wave musicians like Bow Wow Wow and Visage who used it as the basis of their work. Even the DJ at the late, lamented Peppermint Lounge in Manhattan used to close the place down with the music of the late, great Nigerian drummer Olatunji and his *Drums of Passion*.

These musicians came from deep traditions. Gnawa musicians like Hassan Hakmoun spent years training in the healing ceremonies of their musical and cultural tradition, as do the South

African Malombo drummers with whom Dr. Philip Tabane performs and records.

Stores like Sterns Records in London and others in Paris started offering records from Africa to the many expatriates gathered in these metropolitan hot-spots of Europe. When Jamaica became independent of England, expatriate Jamaicans flooded the country, seeking a better life than their infant nation promised. They brought their music with them, and smart entrepreneurs like Chris Blackwell started to import it as well.

The sound spread through the English art schools like rhythm and blues had reached out to white musicians a generation earlier. Mainstream record stores began to stock the music, often putting it into a small section of the store with the label "World Music." Here, Adam Ant, Bow Wow Wow's Dave Barbarossa, and Rusty Egan of Visage discovered the drummers of Burundi.

The musicians among the expatriates had as large an influence as the records. They started to work with English musicians. The seventies jazz-rock band Traffic, formed by Steve Winwood, employed several African drummers. Later, Winwood would record on their albums. Western musicians from renowned jazz trumpeter Lester Bowie to Rock and Roll Hall of Famer Ginger Baker, one of Eric Clapton's partners in the seminal British blues band Cream, went to Nigeria to work with Fela. Baker eventually set up a studio in Nigeria. Gloria and Emilio Estefan couched their Cuban roots in a pop sound accessible to everyone.

Western artists draw on the music of developing nations, either to kick start their own muses or when those muses take a leave of absence. Discounting the black roots of contemporary Western pop (the subject for theses rather than mass-market books), musicians from the industrialized world frequently extract elements of "emerging nations" music into their own art, sometimes championing it, sometimes merely exploiting it.

"I'm an addict for that soca beat," August "Kid Creole" Darnell remarks. "My ex-wife is Haitian. She used to play this calypso, reggae music all the time. That is a strong element in my music today, the island, Latin, calypso feel."

Nothing new about this. Jelly Roll Morton often used the syncopated rhythms from the Spanish Caribbean to give his music "a Latin tinge." During the 1930s and 1940s, bands from Cuba and Puerto Rico spawned dance crazes across America. The mambo, one of the biggest, is loosely based on Afro-Cuban religious rites, likely via Angola. American dance bands adopted and adapted these rhythms into their sets. One of the Ellington band's best-known tunes remains "Caravan," a Latinesque composition by his Puerto Rican trombonist, Juan Tizol. By 1947, Dizzy Gillespie put together his own Afro-Cuban jazz band. In the early fifties, drummer and band leader Desi Arnaz brought the sound to television on *I Love Lucy*. Since the mid-fifties, Sonny Rollins has infused his bop with calypso rhythms. The sixties saw Stan Getz and Charlie Byrd adapting rhythms from Brazil. In the seventies and eighties, artists as diverse as Oliver Lake and Stevie Wonder reggaefied recordings.

While indigenous, primarily black, musics from developing nations have become a cult phenomenon in recent years, major labels regard it as a loss leader. Virgin's expectations of a Paula Abdul album differ from anything they put out on their Earthworks or Real World sub-labels. Promoted to the existing core of fans, reviews are read by the converted rather than the convertible, albums danced to in specialty clubs rather than appreciated for their general dancabilty. While Paul Simon might garner hits with mbaqanga and foros, the artists who created and continue these traditions are regarded as too ethnic or earthy to appeal to a mainstream audience.

And even the music that gets released in America has to conform with a mainstream musical agenda. When he was alive, few major Western labels would deal with Fela, despite the fact that he recorded more or less in English. Frequently the themes of his songs were intra-African politics, accurate or nasty enough that they landed him in prison for over two years on a trumped up charge. Beyond that, he has a reputation for personal wildness, with twenty-seven ex-wives ("They are now just mothers of my children," he once explained) and a fondness for herb. *The beat may be infectious*, you can hear the record companies thinking, *but is it worth the risk?* Then there's King Sunny Ade who indulges in few of these excesses, but also finds corporate Western acceptance a problem since he failed to replace Bob Marley as the great non-Western hope, a role his record company at the time had hoped he would fill.

Many artists from these developing countries assimilate aspects of the West into their musical traditions. While the Nazis failed to take over the world in the Second World War, Western media did. Armed Forces Radio spread American popular music across the planet. In Nigeria, palm wine musicians, who played a simple music on drums, soda bottles and traditional stringed instruments, adapted the sound to horns and electric guitars giving birth to highlife. Yet, the roots of palm wine music remained intact under the Western trappings. Something vital might have passed on (though it is preserved in recordings), but something vibrant, new and unique bloomed out of it.

Some indigenous culture and music manages to survive, and even occasionally thrive, in the wake of the onslaught of Western culture. Marketed as "world music" or "worldbeat," this music retains a purity, heart, and soul missing in so much of today's prefabricated pop.

Pioneers like David Lewiston took their tape recorders to exotic places like Bali with a mission to capture the indigenous music before it disappeared into the maw of mass culture. But a strange thing happened. Through the efforts and field recordings of people like Lewiston and Alan Lomax, the music didn't disappear. Even in its native environment, the music got passed on from generation to generation. Sometimes it transformed as palm wine had, taking on aspects of Western music but remaining completely distinctive. Other times it maintained a purity and integrity matched only by the musicians who played it.

While some of the indigenous artists found an audience at home for a music regarded as quaint and folkloric, many only found ridicule. But in the West, they found fellow artists and fans who understood why they chose to keep this music alive. They recognized the passion, magic, and ecstasy in these sounds.

The influential "world beat" doesn't usually come from field recordings but from the popular musics of these developing nations, from Cuban son to Zibabwean jive. Fela's Afro-beat had deep Nigerian roots, but it also tapped into James Brown and John Coltrane. King Sunny Ade uses a great deal of traditional Juju in his music, but also invokes Jimmy Reed, especially with his idiosyncratic use of slide guitar. Brenda Fassi, "South Africa's Madonna," carries more currency than Stella Chiweshe, at home and abroad.

"When the television was introduced," noted South African record producer West Nkosi pointed out, "they did not have regular material to show the audience. What they did was get videos from all over the world. That alone has got a very, very big influence to the people. You press your button and on the screen, there's Michael Jackson. Then everybody thought, if you want to appear on that box, you have to dance like Michael Jackson or sing like him."

Yet traditions all over the world survive, despite the onslaught of Western cultural imperialism. In truth, *Graceland* exposed many of these artists to an audience that might otherwise never have known. The same thing that helped Paul Simon out of his slump also vastly expanded the audience for the a cappella purity of Ladysmith Black Mambazo. But some of the accompanied funk tracks on their last album raise the question of the cost in artistic corruption. Wonderful music from Haiti and the Caribbean still knocks 'em dead at home. Gutsy sounds continue to power the clubs from Dakar to Durban. Even though a relatively small audience checks it out in America, there are pleasures in rai, zouk, and soukous that have yet to be exploited. But without this music, where would the next big beat come from?

The noise of the world is exciting. It's exotic. It moves people in a way that Western pop music has forgotten, reaches down for the kernel of why man started making music in the first place. It's primitive and cosmopolitan. It speaks to people, even if they don't know the language. It reaches people in their guts and their butts as well as their brains.

This book does not aim to explain this musical phenomenon that has spread like wildflowers in the wind, piquing the imaginations of several generations of music fans. Rather, through oral histories gathered over the course of the past twenty years, it allows the creators of this music to discuss their own motivations, methods, and passions in making their musical statements.

Never before has the interest in these artists been so keen or the diversity of music from around the globe become so generally available. Most of the people who record in developing countries, or make non-Western roots music have a viewpoint unlike ours, whether it was the way Paul Simon was changed after recording with musicians from South Africa or the way the Gipsy Kings lives changed after they fell into the mainstream.

The world of music continues to get smaller as more artists discover non-Western sounds and take their fans along with them. This book features dozens of non-Western artists (and a few Western ones) presenting the world of music from their own perspective, solely in their own words.

Through twenty years of oral histories, the musicians at the heart of these sounds discuss their enthusiasm, their means, and their methods, capturing the non-Western music scene through the ideas of the musicians who create it. Musicians from South Africa talk openly and frankly about making music in pre-Mandela days, when apartheid still ruled. Expatriate artists talk about the pain of separation from their homeland. Gypsies discuss the prejudices against their people that exist even in cosmopolitan places like Barcelona. Through this book, I hope to offer the Western fan of non-Western music a unique insight into the source and soul behind the music, and what leads their favorite artists to create it.

As pop music encompasses the smooth instrumentals of Kenny G and the high velocity rap of Eminem, the noise of the world is even more diverse, embracing music from such fundamentally different locations as the Spanish countryside and the jungles of the Congo, the movie theaters of Bombay to the streets of Bali and even the swamps of Louisiana. It is all manna to Western ears bored with the pablum of pop. Because this music is so varied, I have sectioned the book off by cultural and geographical borders. The music of Western Africa, with its urban sounds, massive drums, and performers sometimes even working in English, is vastly different from the loping music of South Africa, performed in all manner of the more than a dozen tribal dialects spoken in that country. They deserve to be dealt with as such.

This approach allows the points of view of the artists in each section the chance to resonate with each other. Not that all will agree. There is as much dissent between the artistic and holistic outlooks of Nigerian artists like Sunny Ade and Fela as there is between a Christian rock band and a satanic metal band. That goes with any creative territory.

The oral histories include artists who left a massive musical legacy, like Fela, and artists who continue to make crucial recordings, like Winston "Burning Spear" Rodney. They feature artists whose music has become part of the "mainstream," like the Gipsy Kings and Gloria Estefan, talking about their tradition and that transition from the fringes of acceptance to the pop culture consciousness. They feature artists like Hugh Masekela and Miriam Makeba, who managed to cross over and garner that rarest of things, a pop hit, while retaining their roots, talking about making music in their native country and in exile.

These open and honest portraits offer the opportunity for a greater appreciation of what is behind these sounds, the suffering many of these artists have endured and triumphs they have enjoyed. I hope you find *Noise of the World* inspirational and informational, offering an extraordinary point of view on what people would have you believe are alien cultures—the viewpoint of the person whose artistic goal is to bring that culture to the world. I further hope this book will help to create a better understanding and appreciation of the artists who make the music by letting them explain how and why they do what they do in their own words.

This book aspires to capture the essence of communication that allows music to transcend borders and cultures and speak to humans on a level somewhere between their gonads, their behinds, their hearts, and their brains. Perhaps this is the location of the soul.

NORTH AMERICA

REGGAE

Certainly the most popular genre among the noises of the world, reggae may well be Jamaica's biggest export outside of bauxite, the raw material for making aluminum. Several reggae stars have "crossed over" into the mainstream, with pop hits of their own. Groups like Inner Circle and Aswad as well as dancehall artists like Beenie Man, Sean Paul, and Wayne Wonder have scored on charts and sold lots of records outside of Jamaica as well as on the island.

There are several ironies here. Many, when their career goes "international," move off the island and live in the U.S. or England. Both Burning Spear and Coxsone Dodd call Queens, New York, home.

Further, many complain that they are overshadowed by the man with whom they all have a love/hate relationship, the late Robert Nesta Marley. Ras Bob became a worldwide icon, and both the Western record business and the Jamaican music scene have sought "the next" Bob Marley even twenty years after his passing. From the Western perspective, the artist doesn't have to even be Jamaican or reggae: King Sunny Ade was touted as the next great hope of music from developing nations as Marley's favorite singer, Dennis Brown, went major label as the next logical superstar of reggae. Only there really has not been another artist of Marley's magnitude in terms of consistency, impact, and quite frankly, artistry.

WILLIE STEWART | THIRD WORLD

When New York's Newsday *reviewed Third World's 1985 album,* Sense Of Purpose, *they called it "the most successful attempt yet by a Jamaican band to fuse its native roots with pop, soul and rock." Third World began changing the rules of reggae over twenty-five years ago, though the members have been playing together for even longer, having met while still in school. They went on to play with successful bands like Inner Circle, Byron Lee and the Dragonaires, and the Slickers (who had a number one English hit, "Johnny Too Bad"). In 1973, they formed Third World, and by 1975 they were opening concerts for the Jacksons, without benefit of an album or even a recording contract. They continued this trend, playing on bills with Stevie Wonder and others, before going to England as an opening act for Bob Marley and the Wailers at the Lyceum in 1975. Third World blew the music worldwide open with* Journey To Addis *(1978) and the hit reggae version of the O'Jays's "Now That We've Found Love." The song had unprecedented success, topping European pop charts, the U.S. black and dance charts, hitting number ten pop in England and even cracking the American pop charts (number forty-seven). They had a major worldwide dance hit, "Dancing On The Floor" (number ten U.K.). On the next album,* You've Got The Power, *they cut two songs with Stevie Wonder. "Try Jah Love" became another major worldwide hit. That album was one of the first reggae records to go platinum in Japan. They continue to rock audiences worldwide.*

From when we were kids, we played every music. When you play a dance in Jamaica, you're playing a set from eight o'clock at night to four in the morning. You took four breaks and you played around the clock. You had to play the top forty. So, at that time we played Santana, "Black Magic Woman," Tower of Power, Philly soul, all the sounds. This gave us a background to move forward from. That provided a base of practicing.

When we were kids, we played with a group called Inner Circle. It was the greatest time in our life. At all the big festivals, we used to back up all the artists, like Toots, Bob, everybody.

Later we splintered off and became Third World. We went to London with Bob Marley to play the Lyceum, and while they were there, auditioned for a club called Mister B.'s. If they liked you in the afternoon, you played that night. They liked Third World, and they invited Chris Blackwell to the show. He wasn't very excited about it, but he went anyway. He signed us that evening.

With everything we are going to do, not just we as Third World, but the third world as a whole, we have to take our lives seriously, from a spiritual point of view, to your business, to your way of life, to your attitude. Everything! The world is in a serious turmoil.

Getting through a storm like Hurricane Gilbert changed everyone's life. At that point we were halfway through the album *Serious Business*. From the whole thing we got a very important message. Your home is within you. You can't get a physical structure and say, that's your home, because that can be broken up. The houses that went through that storm have been incredible. God saved us, and we have to give thanks to that force and that element that we got through. It should have killed more people. I say we give thanks that we came out of it alive. It is an experience that, once in a lifetime like that, shows there is a God.

It also shows material things don't matter. People lost everything. A lot of people lost their cars. We had to do without light and water for about a month. You light a fire outside, and that's how you have to live for a time, ten of you or fifteen of you in one room. The whole place was under water. You can imagine staying under water for fifteen hours. Trying to prevent the water from flooding out the children downstairs. And the whole roof coming off. You can't imagine anything like that.

I was down the road when the storm hit. I ran through the storm. When the eye hit, I ran over to see if my house was still intact and when I was about halfway there, the second part of the storm came. I had to wait two hours, stuck in this house, and when it eased up a little bit, I ran through the storm about a mile and a half.

It was crazy. Sinks were flying like guillotines. Trees just took off. There were jokes about people sitting around in their houses and saying, "My god, I've lost my roof!" and another roof coming on from next door.

It changed everybody's lives

It was a serious time for us. There is a love. Even though there were a lot of negatives, there were a lot of positives. People helped people. I know people who were on the roof for four or five days. I went in to help different homes, joined with the Salvation Army, went up into the hills to deliver food. It was a vibe of "Come, let us rebuild." Jamaica is going to rebuild the country fully.

The world has to take that structure from Jamaica. Say that we are going to rebuild a new musical sound, a new message. We cannot continue with the slackness the world is going through, where everything is based on sex and drugs. We're not setting an example for tomorrow's children. What's going to happen to the kids of tomorrow? What kind of principles are we setting? What standards are we building? We're not building anything this way. We have to start to realize that we have a serious responsibility. Musicians of the world have to take on that responsibility that they are the forerunners.

Good music can transcend every boundary. Music can hit every nerve center in the world that not even a prime minister has the power to touch. Musicians have to know that their job is to play music to feed the people, to give them that hope for tomorrow, to give them that aspect that, yes, there is a future. With all diseases, with all the problems, we can make this world a better place. In this, when storms come and a lot of other things, is a time of rebirth.

We went to Nigeria after *You've Got The Power*, in 1982. It was really incredible. Touching the motherland was an experience that we cherish to this day. Fela came. We talked to Fela, went to his house, met all his wives. We met Sunny Ade, met all the great musicians.

Music is our lives. To me, my motto is invest fully in music. Because if you don't, tomorrow you are out of it.

We have, instead of spending money on ourselves, especially in the early days, when we got money, we preferred to buy equipment. We believed you must invest in your craft.

In my house, I have an Akai twelve track with a DAT, so I can actually record at home and cut it. I have a supply of tapes. I go through a dozen. I have an Akai/Roger Linn MPC60, so I can store, sequence and sample. Incredible. So I can store ninety-nine sequences on it. I can store everything on disc, so I don't have to record everything. The key is to keep everything on disc and just use vocals on the recording studio, use a SMPTE time code and tie in everything. I have automatic mixers, so I can get twenty-eight channels. Then I go straight down to DAT. That means the quality is incredible. That means you can compete with a studio sound, because you are going straight down to digital. Ibu (Cooper, keyboards) has a sixteen track at home.

I remember when drums were just acoustic. Now, I'm using an MPC60 drum machines. I never knew anything about computers. But now I know everything. Everything about music programming, checking out everything. It's a whole different train.

I was one of the first in Jamaica to get into the electronic drums. After Sly got the Simmons, I was the next to get it. Just like the MP 360s and the D-drum. I use a D-drum on stage.

If you want to compete with the world, it doesn't make sense to use an outdated thing. Especially today. Every second, you have to get new equipment, you have to be studying.

I trained with Billy Moore, at the Billy Moore percussion school which I'm finishing. I have a final exam. I'm going to take it. I really want to teach later on. I want to pass on some information, other than, just be as great a player from a natural source, but then you must have a form of writing so you understand it.

A lot of musicians, who are young, have not studied. They have not had a chance to play live. They have studied at the university, and are great on paper and in theory, but when it comes to playing, some of them can't even keep time. That's an experience you cannot avoid. You have to go to the school of playing. Either you play for a dance band, or you have to learn the hard way up. It's not easy on the stamina to play all night, and I find that some of the younger musicians are wizards on sound, but not playing live, because they program. But when people come to see you in concert, they don't want to hear what's on the album alone, they want to see a show. I find there are very few show bands now, and they are becoming less and less every day. They play exactly what they play on the record. And they get away with it! People are starving for good entertainment. You want to see the drummer do stuff. You have to try to give it your best, and it has to come from the heart.

The moment you start repeating yourself, your creativity is over. And that's serious for a musician. You should be able to create new every day. This is why the music scene is very serious. Even though you have a lot of electronic, the most important thing is the natural, the drums and the voice. That is the creation. You can never give that up. The electronics are tools. What the music business is using now, which is wrong to a certain extent, is that they are putting too much stress on the electronics. What you find is that the true musicians that used to play can still play, and people are going after a lot of jazz records.

We all have a reason to be on earth. Music is my reason. We all have to pass something on. You can't come and live in the world and keep your gifts. You must give your gifts away. Suppose you have ten dinners here, and you eat the ten dinners right away. You're just going to get fat and get sick from it.

When you die, people will say, "Yes, he left this music for us. He was a good man." You have to pass something on. You cannot leave with it. We are here to set an example and leave a legacy for tomorrow.

We got awards from the United Nations, for the African Crisis. Each one of us got medals for that. We are still dedicated. Before "We Are The World," we did a song called "Land Of Africa" with Aswad, Steel Pulse, Dean Frazier, Freddy McGregor and other artists. That also helps Ethiopian kids.

We as Third World still represent love throughout the world. We will continue as ambassadors, doing our job. We still have a commitment to the people, we still love music, and we hope that the people will accept our music for the sincerity that we've put into it.

Photograph: Mesa / Bluemoon Recordings

DUCKIE SIMPSON | BLACK UHURU

Black Uhuru has had as many permutations as, say, the Rolling Stones, with personnel changes defining the era. The one constant has been Derrick "Duckie" Simpson. Built on the classic reggae vocal trio (think the Wailers or the early Burning Spear), they mixed fiery Rastafarian vibes and heavy politics-of-developing-nations rhetoric with incandescent harmonies and the bad-assed bottom of Sly Dunbar and Robbie Shakespeare, who came out of one of the hottest (and most rhetorical) bands in the land, Peter Tosh's group. Every version of the group formed extraordinary vocal ensembles. Stunning harmonies punctuated the lyrics. The group began with Euvin "Don Carlos" Spencer, Rudolph "Garth" Dennis, and Simpson in the early seventies. Dennis went on to a better opportunity (at the time) with the Wailing Souls, Carlos tried to make it as a solo. Michael Rose came in and after a while he was joined by Sandra "Puma" Jones, a Brooklyn social worker (with a master's from Columbia, no less) who had come to ply her trade in Jamaica, and wound up working with Ras Michael and the Sons of Negus. This trio hooked up with Sly and Robbie and cut four incen-

diary albums for Island. Rose went solo, and was replace by Junior Reid, who by 1987 also went solo. Jones left the band in 1987, due to poor health (she would die of breast cancer in 1990). In 1987, the group went full circle, with Dennis, Carlos, and Simpson singing brilliant harmonies with a political edge. Songs like "Bloodshed" and "Youth of Eglington" portray vivid scenes of downtrodden people on the brink of revolution.

Me, Don and Garth, we all came from the same neighborhood, Waterhouse, Kingston 11. It's west Kingston. We've all been in contact with each other, even when we were doing separate things. So, after Junior went on without us, we just decided to reunite the original Black Uhuru.

It just automatically happened. As it was in the beginning, so shall it be. After Junior went solo, I just figured that that was the right move, to go back with Don and them, because they were the originals.

Sly was the one who recorded us. He was the one who had confidence in us and gave us our first major break. So all respect due to Sly. And Sly is a neighbor. We grew up together, we come from the same neighborhood.

I'm not a third world singer. I've been coming for decades, so I'm not the type who goes for DJ music. I strictly go for lyrics. I'm a songwriter, so when I hear stuff that's not put together properly, then I don't really go for it. It don't matter how much it sells or how popular it is.

In Jamaica these days, DJ is on the top. DJ is on the top in Jamaica. It's the mentality of the people. The mentality of the people has changed over the decades. It's more gimmicks for their money. People are more into gimmicks in this time than reality and life. Singers like us, and Burning Spear and Culture and those singers, we mostly stay on the reality trends, or revolution or militant. In Jamaica, their mind is more for, like hip-hop and love songs, x-rated songs and DJ stuff. Whatever. Nothing conscious.

Dancehall has a market. That's what's going on down here. The music down here is mostly that type of music. It's not like in the eighties. Singers like Black Uhuru, and other singers who sing cultural, political lyrics don't really go across in Jamaica now. They're more for the gimmicks.

That's not raggamuffin stuff. Raggamuffin is anything that is hardcore. Shabba Ranks is a DJ. So you can be raggamuffin if you're a DJ, and you can also be raggamuffin if you're a singer. It depends on the lyrics that you put out, that makes you be raggamuffin. Raggamuffin would be hardcore lyrics, not about sex and like that. That would be, we call that lover rock. Raggamuffin is like rebel, militant, revolutionary-wise. Ragamuffin. It's rough and tough. It's not like Shabba Ranks. That's not raggamuffin. That's like GQ.

No reggae artists had album sales, apart from Bob Marley. He was the only one who ever had album sales. He was the only one who slipped through the system and they weren't aware. After that era, the American tycoons, the American companies, all those big tycoons were so aware, they made sure no one else slipped through the system.

All the evidence is there. No Jamaican artist has ever benefitted from that level from reggae, apart from Bob. And I know a lot of other artists who do good songs. But it goes with the marketing strategy and the promotion and the input that they put into it. They're not going to put a certain amount of input in a reggae artist's songs. You notice, whoever sings reggae, apart from the reggae singers, it sells. But when the guys from Jamaica do it, it never sells. When UB40 or the Police do it, it's great.

The problem is, anyone can be signed. I've been signed so many times in my life. Signing is not the key. That's just the first step. The other stages never even manifested.

I'm trying to break into the American market, and I know the way they think and the way they operate. We are trying to get across to the black market. The people up there have a broader mind. You see, the media plays a lot of tricks on the people down here. The music business has switched from in the eighties, from this drug problem starts arising, and they started putting the stigma on Jamaica, that all Jamaicans are druggies, murderers.

People get killed everywhere in the world. Even Malcolm X and Martin Luther got shot in America, man. The president of America. They've killed so many presidents compared to Peter Tosh. So, people get killed everywhere in the world. But maybe some people have the right to do it. That's the way that it seems. What's happening in Jamaica is petty compared to what's happening in America.

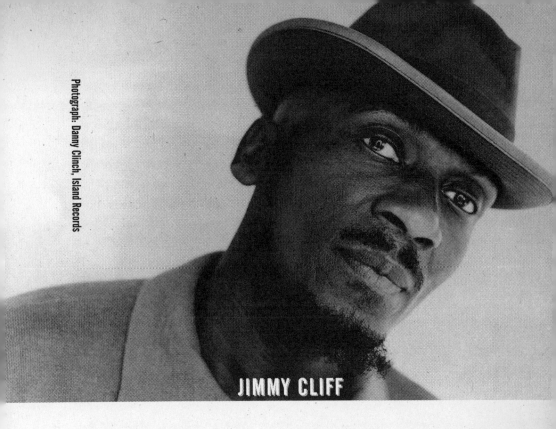

Photograph: Danny Clinch, Island Records

JIMMY CLIFF

Even before Bob Marley broke through in the seventies, Jimmy Cliff brought Jamaican rocksteady to the States as the star of the cult classic film, The Harder They Come. *The soundtrack to this record became the reggae primer for many listeners. This included Cliff's many musical contributions, like "Many Rivers To Cross" and the title track. This established Cliff on several fronts. He earned respect as an actor, which has led to many other roles. He also earned respect outside of Jamaica as a singer, one of the first Jamaican artists to do this and maintain it. In Africa, where reggae has a following that has spawned stars like Lucky Dube and Majek Fashek, Cliff is a major star. However, even having a reputation has its downside, especially something as indelible as* The Harder They Come. *Very little could be as diametrically opposed as the outlaw character that Cliff played in the film and the gentle man Cliff actually is. About all that is similar are the dynamic performances.*

There was a point in my career when I was trying to break out of *The Harder They Come*, but I realized somewhere along the line that at least it's good to have an anchor, something that you can be identified with.

Every few months I get a few new scripts, and I read them. I have my music to fall back on, so if the scripts aren't what I like, I don't do them. I was offered a part in *Crocodile Dundee 2*. They wanted me to play a drug pusher around New York. I can't play that. It would ruin my image. Luckily, I have my music to fall back on, so acting . . . I don't have to rely on that totally for my livelihood. So I don't have to take something I don't want.

That anchor, that image from *The Harder They Come,* was a positive image. It was the image of the fighter in society, which we all are. All of us are trying to get ahead as human beings in society, regardless of whether you are born rich or born poor. Some of us have it easier, yeah. But everyone likes a fighter. I think that's a positive image.

That's why a movie like *The Harder They Come* has become a cult classic. Because it comes to the point of telling what is happening in this music business, like the character that I played.

Actually, "Many Rivers To Cross" has kept me going through the lean and mean times. But I don't own the copyright. It was one of those stages of my life when I didn't realize that show business was show and business. You think about the show, but you don't think about the business, I guess.

Island Publishing owns the publishing on those songs I did at the time. I was bitter about that at one stage of my life, but you can't go around carrying bitterness. It only affects the individual. It was a stage of my life when I did something in my ignorance and it's gone, so I have to move on.

I was at a party at Chris Blackwell's home in Jamaica not long ago. Two or three groups played. It was okay. Chris Blackwell has to be respected for who he is. He was the person who was there at the time, to see that this music could do something. He has a good ear, he knows the business well, he has a good sense of image and that sort of thing, so yes, I heard about it and I went.

People have accused me of sounding too pop. On all of my albums, there's always at least one track that identifies me with the roots of what people are expecting. But being a creative person, I like to expand and do other things. If it turns out to be pop, to put a label on it, then that's what it is. Dance music is most popular, all over Africa, whether they are English speaking or French speaking Africa. It's something that I've always wanted to do, because I love Zairian dance music.

I was listening to South African music long ago. I have stacks of tapes from the seventies. I've been listening to that. Tape swapping is a typical third world thing, a so-called third world thing. You'll find a situation like that also in Nigeria and Zaire or Sierra Leone, or in Bahia in Brazil.

There was a time when I dropped off touring for a while, but when I go on the road, I carry a lot of African music from all over. That's what I listen to on the road. I only listen to the radio to hear what's happening commercially, but for my pleasure, that's what I listen to. I don't even know some of their names, but when I go to Africa I say, "Play me something." They'll play me some records, and I say, "I'll take that."

I always wanted to work with African music, but I didn't go to Zaire to record. I went there just to do this tour of Zaire for two weeks and then go home. But I got intrigued. I've been listening to it for years, and I got intrigued. I went to these clubs, and everywhere you go, you hear this music. I'd just hang out every night, start talking to the musicians, and suggestions of recording come up. So I started to find out how, and I had some songs.

It's difficult to record there. You have to go across the river to the Congo to record. It's a hassle. You hire a boat to take you across the river. If you miss that boat you have to go on the regular big boat. It's a different mentality. It's like Jamaica in the fifties, the musician mentality. Meaning, it's a happy-go-lucky, "I play my music because I like it" sort of thing. I found that I went through hell to record two songs. I do have the complete tape, and eventually I'll release it for people who love music.

Of course, all of these countries are on a different rhythm, the rhythm of the people is different. The rhythm in Africa is a very happy, carefree type of thing. It's loose and it's tight. The rhythm in America is similar to the rhythm of France and England, because people are more into I-tech, and they become a little more sensitive to how that is going to sound. So, whereas like Jamaica and Africa, you just go for the feel, and if the feel is good, everything is all right, whereas here, you're focusing a lot on what it sounds like.

When I studied African music, in West Africa there's a different feel, a different type of rhythms, in South Africa there's a different feel, a different type of rhythms, in West Africa there's a different feel, and in North Africa there's a different feel. And in Central Africa, like Zaire and the Congo, there's a different feel.

No matter where I record, I haven't changed my theme about struggle, which is what a lot of my songs are all about. Over the years, I sing about struggle.

I put out an album almost every year. If it doesn't make a big impression in America and England, which are the music centers of the world, it still makes an impression on the countries that matter to me, like Africa or Brazil, so whatever I put out still makes an impression. Reggae is always here.

WINSTON "BURNING SPEAR" RODNEY

In the close to three decades that he has been performing as Burning Spear, Winston Rodney has managed to slide that razor's edge between entertaining and challenging, capturing creative magic with a conscious message. Those who only know Burning Spear's scabrous seventies reggae classics Marcus Garvey *and* Man in the Hills *can still enjoy the original, horn driven reggae sound of Spear and his burning band. However, the years have smoothed a lot of Spear's rough edges. His political messages have become subtler, his music and voice more refined. He has started to sing love songs, not just to Rastafari but to women. The conscious, political Spear perseveres, but the scabrous Spear vanished in a cloud of tight, soulful, contemporary rock steady. This tightness reflects the economy of performing—in the seventies, Spear used whatever band he could pick up. Through the eighties and nineties, he has maintained the Burning band, tight, professional and his when he wants them. He sums this up musically in his early nineties song "Mi Gi Dem": "Gi dem what dey want, reggae music in Jamaica, reggae music in America, reggae music in Africa." He and his band play well over one hundred shows a year to thousands of people. If interest might be waning in Jamaica, Europe and the U.S. remain strong and his audience in Africa continues to grow.*

To be honest, my sound will always change. I will always be creative within and around my sound, always maintaining that original flavor and that original standard.

The current direction of music in Jamaica is a direction I myself did expect. In the fifties, sixties, and seventies, I knew the music wouldn't be the same way. I knew that you would have a younger generation coming through from that time where it would require a different flavor of music, a different taste. There is not a problem, really, with the music that we're listening to today, but I think people need to take time out and get their lyrics more properly together. But, this approach, musically, is very good as long as they can keep it intelligent and keep it clean and create a little more education within it and around it. But, it's a good step. People showing what they can do, but as I say, some people intend, at times, to show people the wrong side. Wherein, I don't think the music needs that kind of side. This music we're listening to today, it's good. It's plain to see it's another strain coming around from the original section of the music.

In a sense, they actually sound the same way. It's like the brothers who are doing the rapping in America. You have to listen good, otherwise they are all sounding the same way. After a while all these people start sounding the same way because they are actually doing the same thing. It's not like somebody trying to be creative in a different direction. Everyone is trying to be creative in one direction. Pretty early, people are going to get more confused. They just can't understand what they're listening to.

I wouldn't want to take that direction. It's not dealing with too much of a constructiveness. It's more like a money making direction. That's not saying that we shouldn't be paid or we shouldn't like making money. Of course, that's necessary. But that direction has no protection, there's no guide from that direction for the music. It's not like the people who are in control of that direction doing something to help the music, to lift it up, to have it going places, presenting the music to people who need music.

It's not like that. It's a money-making thing. It's like a real estate business. Some people get involved in the real estate business, not because they like real estate business, but because they can put in x amount of money and triple up their money. They're not doing it to help people to have houses to live. It's like the music. It's a big, wide commercial thing. It's a money thing. It's not like in the seventies, when people would get involved in the music to strengthen it because they knew what we were doing was constructive, what we were saying was the right thing. It's not like that.

Many years ago, for a company to sign a brother who was doing DJ work, it was like you're crazy, signing people like those. Today, if you're not dealing with stuff like that, that is the first thing you're going to say, "You're not going to make money." I think you can make money, but promotion is the key, and proper marketing.

Outside Jamaica, people look up more to the music that Burning Spear puts out today. When I say "outside Jamaica," I mean Europe and other places. America today, and the day before today, is very tight in terms of getting what you'd like to get done, and get it done properly. America has so many different types of music that for reggae music to come through and be on top of all these musics that were here before, it's just not possible. The closest artist up to now, who really got so close, is Bob Marley. And Bob Marley was the only reggae artist promoted properly and that they did market properly. Since that, it's like they created a barrier around that standard of music, that kind of flavor music, preventing it from going places that it usually went before. But there is a market for the music that I'm dealing with, that other people are dealing with, the same kind of quality music. We always have a market, and we always will have a market for that music.

When I played with the Clash, the Talking Heads, UB40, to me, that is fun, you know. That is like mystic, more than exciting, playing for those people who were never really into reggae that much. I start playing and I see how much the people are into what I was dealing with. That is very good. That just goes to show you that the quality of music that I and I are dealing with, people are there for it. People want it. And any time we go up there, people accept what we're dealing with.

Along the way you grow, and that maturing starts to spread itself out. Each time we go into the studio, we try to get deeper and deeper with our arrangements. Tightness. Mixing has a lot to do with it too. You can lay the tracks, and all the tracks can lay properly, but if it's not mixed properly, you end up having a problem. It's a wide combination of everything.

I want the people to know that the kind of music I stand up for today, which is the original section of the whole, we have a wide level of support, of people who support my concerts and people who keep buying the records. Today, I will go places and I will work and I will perform and I will draw more people than any young person today will draw. You can pick out the places where this kind of music is strong, and you can pick out the place where, when performers go to perform this kind of music today, you can see the kind of people who attend. It depends on the kind of artist.

What we try to do with the arranging is bring in every little thing, a little African song cutting across, a little jazz cut in there, a little blues cut in there. You know, we try to be that kind of creative and blend in everything. Music is not just one thing or one sound. A lot of different things create the sound, and you get that kind of taste, that sweetness. We intend to maintain that sweetness within and around the music, by not preventing with the original.

Out of toughness can bring sweetness and sweetness can become toughness. It's a combination. Something is rough but it's sweet. Something is sweet, but it's rough. But it's not dangerous. Dangerous can be some thing good and it can be something bad.

I listen to African music, I listen to Fela, I listen to Sunny Ade, I listen to Thomas Mapfumo. I listen to a wide variety of Africans. I listen to a little blues now and again. I, Fela, and Sunny Ade, we worked together in 1989. We did a tour in West Africa, Nigeria, places like that, Liberia, Zaire, places like those. I've been to Africa a couple of times. Reggae is big. Africa has many people to buy any amount of records once the business is settled over there.

After a period of time, many of us get pretty big in the business. Not big in terms of rich, but big in terms of matureness. So, we get more capable to do a lot of things with the music, especially in our section of the music, this type of music, we can do a lot of things. I'm here to show people that our first step towards presenting quality like that, an album like this carrying a lot of different quality flavors and tastes.

I've learned a lot. I had no understanding pertaining to the business. I made sure I got as much understanding as I could about the business. When I found out how the business is supposed to be run, I handled it. I took care of it. You've got to have a good attorney.

You've got to have an accountant. You've got to have people around you who are not there only to achieve a weekly salary. They have to be there to strengthen the whole foundation and deepen it. There are a lot of artists in the reggae business who don't set themselves up properly. I think the first step in the business is to know the business.

You don't have as much bands working like a couple of years ago. People don't deal with bands. Even in the studio. Now when some brother goes into the studio to make a record, it's not like a musician goes into the studio and tunes their instrument and get down and does some line check and make sure everything is working and be creative and work out some form of arrangement. It's not like that no more. The brother today, they go to the studio with their little machines, and they program whatsoever they want to program and that's it.

Some of these brothers, when they tour, it's not like they tour with a band. They do it more with people doing dancing and stuff like that. They're just singing with the rhythm and stuff like that. Some of these guys are doing the fake. A guy make fake with his guitar, fake around his keyboard, fake with his drummer or his brass or whatsoever. The real thing is not here like at one time. I think when you can see the brother or the sister on the stage, playing that instrument, and it's going through from the board to the monitor, you know, you can see that playing on his face, that expression that he's playing something, and what he's doing is getting across to some people. When you look in the audience, you can see the people responding like they're feeling something. That is how it should be.

The original will always be the original. I will always maintain that original standard. You've got to be strong. From 1969 until today, if I wasn't a strong man, I wouldn't be here talking to you.

COXSONE DODD

If Clement "Coxsone" Dodd didn't invent reggae, he certainly midwifed the birth and nurtured it. Originally running the Studio One sound system, a dancehall on the back of a flatbed truck that literally brought the party to the people, by 1959 Dodd had started recording artists so that he would have fresh music that couldn't be heard any other way than attending one of his parties. When the sound systems were outlawed (and in Dodd's case, even a little before), he fell back into recording full time as a producer and an engineer, turning Studio One from a sound system company to one of the most influential record companies of its time. At the time, the only other big studio in Jamaica was called Federal, and they mostly recorded calypso, uptown music. Dodd's Studio One Records dealt with the Jamaican people's popular music at the time, ska. Toots and the Maytals, the Skatalites, Alton Ellis, Roland Alphonso, Lee Perry, Lone Ranger, Delroy Wilson, Sugar Minott, and literally hundreds of other greater and lesser lights in ska, rock steady, and reggae passed through Studio One, often making their greatest mark there. But they all pale beside a group Dodd signed in 1963 and nurtured through the sixties. He was the first producer to work with the Wailers. All of their early Jamaican hits were on Studio One. For these contributions to the Jamaican export that rivals aluminum, Dodd was awarded the Order of Distinction by the Jamaican government.

In the West Indies, Coxsone means music. I had adopted the name from an English cricketer by the name of Coxsone. I was playing a lot of cricket. I used it for good luck and got good scores, so I followed through hoping that would be a good name for me in the music business.

I used to have a sound system, what they now call a discotheque, playing all over. I started when I was about ninteen years of age. Really fresh, full of ideas. I started recording when I was about twenty-two, twenty-three. Then, when we started recording, we weren't certain that it was salable. We loved it, but we didn't know if it was possible to go internationally. "When the Well Runs Dry," "He's a Snappin'," "My Baby." We did a lot of instrumentals. People loved instrumentals.

More or less, I was the only producer out there building the artists up from the ground floor. The other producers wanted somebody who was strong already and in the limelight. I would take a no-name guy by just auditioning and hearing his voice. I understood what it took to put it together. I took a little time. The more an artist heard themselves playing back, the more confident they'd become. And when they sing a certain way and it sounds good, he knows to stick to that method. Actual rehearsing and regular recording of the artist and he'll back himself. It just came naturally.

At that time, apart from Graham Goodall, who was from Australia, there was no other engineer in Jamaica. This was quite new in Jamaica. Federal Records was there. The first studio would be Stanley Motta. That was down Hanover Street, below Lourdes Street. That was really early, say 1951, 1952. Then Khouri acquired his studio. So, actually, the first big studio would be Federal Records. Then, I'd be next. All the early Wailers records were done by me. I engineered the whole thing.

I had my fans and when we started recording locally, I had guys rooting for me. Whenever they would hear a good artist, they would bring them. This chap, Seeco, he was the one who brought them. He said, "Boss, I have a good group here." Seeco Patterson. He was a close friend of mine. He loved the music that I played on my sound system. Every weekend, he'd be where we had our session. So, it started from the rhythm blues, and we played a little jazz, until we started recording our own in Jamaica. Seeco knew these guys and brought them for an audition. They were four boys and two girls. All singing. He was with them until Bob died. He played conga for them.

What really happened, when they started, it was Junior, the lead singer on "Urge to Be Alone" and a couple of more songs, he was definitely the leader because he had that beautiful, strong voice, that high-pitched tenor. Then he left Jamaica and joined his family abroad. So, by then, we were there with the group and I knew that Bob was the right person to really take his place and be the leader of the group.

After a couple of months, I realized that giving them a guitar would allow them to build their harmony and rehearse by themselves. Peter was more inclined to be a musician than even Bob was. He could play before Bob.

The freedom that they had in the studio, hearing themselves over time, they got that confidence to say, well this is working. And they stuck with it.

Bob and Rita met each other by my studios. When I found out she was pregnant, being old-fashioned, I said, "You've really got to get married." I didn't want the people outside to think I was a careless man, letting the kids get together and have kids. So I said they should get married. At that time, there was no other means of income for either of them. Their only means of income was by me. They weren't working otherwise.

When he caught with the Rasta scene, he'd say "We're not married, she's just my little sister." Then Rita got scared, and she came by saying, "Would you have our marriage picture?" I always had one, and I'd loan it to her and she could bring it by the record store they ran and straighten him out.

Dealing with the Wailers was a trip. What made it difficult was the company they kept. It was a rough kind. But being with the sound system from the early days, most of the people who came around had that kind of respect. It kept them from getting out of line.

Studio One in Jamaica is still operating. It's open when I return to Jamaica for production. Two days a week, it's open for regular singles, export, and local sales offices. The studio itself is open only when I go to Jamaica, four, five, six times a year. Sometimes I'll stay there for two months trying to get things together. Trying to cash in on the current artists, the new artists. I do a lot of auditions while I'm in Jamaica for whatever available new artists there are.

Actually, we really started—when I say we, I mean Studio One—started toasting [precursor to dancehall and rap]. The first rapping on a record, I did that on the sound system. That was like "Go Down King Pharaoh, Go Down." I did that. That was like 1955, 1956. Then in the early sixties, I went in and did "Ball of Fire" and I did toasting with another chap on "Phoenix City." I can't remember all of it.

Currently, we're not too happy with the lyrics. A lot of people in Jamaica are not too happy with the dancehall slackness. The promotion is not around the best of their material. In Jamaica, a great deal of people don't like that sort of stuff. I don't know if I'm getting old-fashioned, but thing has got to be clean and aboveboard, so we deal mostly with the grown-up artists. Whenever we come in contact with a new artist, we give them an idea of what direction we want them to go in.

The cultural aspect is part of our stance, but the rude part of it, the violence, mentioning guns and whatever, we stay away from that. We think that music should be a happy thing. We are talking about great love and great hopes. Stick to that.

We find ourselves with a lot of back stuff that we thought, at that time, wasn't good enough for the market. Going back to this stuff here, we can't find the fault that we heard earlier. It sounds good.

If you experiment on a song, and it works, you try to stick with it as close as possible, thinking that it will work every time. I think if you love it, you dream about what would help to do better.

ERNEST RANGLIN

Aficionados generally regard one of Ernest Ranglin's early records, the 1959 Federal single "Shuffling Bug," recorded with Clue J & His Blues Blasters, as one of the first ska records. That same year, a young music business entrepreneur named Chris Blackwell recognized Ranglin's skills, as well. Ranglin was the first artist signed to Blackwell's Island Records. A few years later, Blackwell flew Ranglin to England to teach the ska rhythm to a bunch of English session players. That session, for singer Millie Small, became the 1964 hit "My Boy Lollipop," the first the song to bring the riddem of Jamaica to the mainstream. Before he inadvertently helped invent ska, though, Ranglin had made a reputation for himself playing jazz and pop in the bands at the resort hotels. In 1954, he so impressed guest Les Paul that Paul gave him a guitar. Listening to early ska records by groups like the Skatalites, it's easy to hear this jazz influence. Ranglin has honed his craft for going on six decades, better acknowledged among his peers than by reggae fans in general. Bob Marley once asked him to be his live-in guitar teacher. Ranglin only just recently became known in his own right. He reunited with Chris Blackwell while Blackwell still ran Island, releasing Below the Bassline, *a jazzed up bunch of reggae standards like Bob Marley's "Ion Lion Zion." The epochal* Memories of Barber Mack *sounds like Wes Montgomery playing with a hot reggae rhythm section. Not content with this direction,* In Search of the Lost Riddem *took him to Africa where he spent a couple of weeks recording with Senegalese stars like Baaba Maal and Cheikh Lô. His new status as an elder statesman of ska and a current craftsman of something entirely new in his fusions of African music, reggae, and jazz have allowed him some comfort in his late sixties, though he maintains the kind of active schedule he wishes he had in his thirties. However, the sexagenarian gives the impression that his musical explorations have just begun.*

Coxsone Dodd is really on the ska part of it. Chris Blackwell is the ska, too, but we did more with a rhythm and blues thing, while Coxsone was only into one thing. If ska was happening, it was ska, when rock steady was on, it was rock steady. But with Chris it was other things.

It was the things like "Boogie in the Barnyard," the Louis Jordan shuffles, Erskine Hawkins, Bill Doggett, people like those. That's where we get all these things from. There were many people who used to do those things in the rock and roll era. We would take little things from here, little things from there, but it was mainly on a shuffle rhythm. All we did with that shuffle rhythm was cut it down a little bit, make more emphasis on the backbeat. We left off the accent on the first beat, and emphasized the off-beat. That's where we anchored our beat. That's how the ska beat developed. It's a modified shuffle beat. It's the same thing with the emphasis on the second beat. Then, eventually we would really get into that and elaborate on our style.

We were fooling around from the late forties, when bebop was happening. The two great people that I would listen to were Charlie Parker and Dizzy Gillespie. They were the two main people who started me out, by listening to that type of music. Other guys too, because we were exposed to records. We could sometimes get sheet music, too, arrangements that you could play to help you get an understanding of what was going on. That helped us a lot. We were really very interested in the jazz world from that time, trying to put our little thing in.

At the same time, most of these producers didn't want it to go any further. The only guy who really kept that type of thing going was Coxsone Dodd. He was the only guy that would really support what we were doing. And even he would reach a certain point where he would say, "Let's come back a little more commercial."

"My Boy Lollipop." I must remember that. The only person who was Jamaican in that band, aside from myself, was Pete Peterson, who was the first trumpeter. Everyone else on that recording was from England. I don't know if they were all Englishmen, but they had never played that type of music before. That was an adventure. Trying to teach the pianist to hit that little off-beat, it was a little awkward for him at first. When you're first trying to get it, it's a little bit awkward. It's like you're trying to play off-beat, isn't it? So I guess that would be one of my memorable moments.

We had to play mostly in the hotels in the early days. You could get a regular job there. Playing out on the road, not every group can make it. Jamaica is small, also. If you have too many bands on the road, I don't know exactly how they would survive. Maybe that's a good reason why some of us went to the hotels. Some of us went on the road. We would always meet and manage to put things together and keep certain things going musically.

I have a lot of LPs in Jamaica that I've made. Even LPs that I've made that I produced for myself. But I didn't get a decent label to put it out. The other labels that I was with, apart from myself was for the Federal recording company, and people like that. I hear some of those records in America many times, but I didn't hear anything money-wise. I just called it one of those things. I don't know how widely that style was being spread in the mean time. I know right now I'm getting a lot of attention and exposure with it. I'm very happy about it.

I've been around at a lot of recording companies, but nobody was interested in taking my music beyond Jamaica until Trevor Wyatt from Island. He was the man who was responsible for this effort, presenting it to the public. Not keeping it in the corner after years of being in the corner. Nobody really thought about doing something with it.

I'm trying to put two things together and see how it comes out. This is why I'm trying to put this into this new thing I'm doing with African Music to see if it can work. It all depends on how the people look at it, and if they will like it.

When I went to Senegal, I brought just the one guitar. It was an Ibanez. I went straight through the board. It would have been difficult to take an amplifier all that way. I was there maybe about ten days or two weeks.

You leave from Cuba and you go to Haiti and you'll find things that are the same. Anywhere you go. Sometimes it's such a wonder. This sound is all around us. It's nice if you can combine everything and make it into something interesting. I think it's a good effort. That's what I'd like to do eventually, to see if I can do it, combining everything I've every played into one style.

We didn't go to Africa with the intention of "looking for" anybody, so to speak. We had arrangements and we listened to some of the things that they do there. Whatever we were going to do was based on what we were studying from the country. Luckily, Baaba Maal, I'd met him in 1970 when I was there with Jimmy Cliff, and the first day I was there, Baaba Maal was there. I was invited to his home, and we were having a great time. From there on, the magic seemed to be working. That's where it started. Baaba Maal and I were enjoying ourselves that night. There were two separate tunes that came from it, so we had things that we could do together from that night. That was the start of our repertoire for that CD.

The kora player is acting like a piano. It's such a great instrument. It plays like a piano, so he was affecting a piano player. It's a different color.

I guess, if I toured this music, it would have to be a bigger group of people. All of these guys, because they are necessary. If we're going to tour with Baaba Maal's group, he has a big group, too. It has nothing on a Trinidadian pan band. They can get up to 120, and all those big bands. But I generally have just a quartet, you know—bass, drums, guitars, and keyboards. It's easier, more controllable. I guess it's more affordable.

It's nice to try something new, to see if I can put what I have here and they have there, see if I can put the things together. That was one of my main reasons for doing that.

Let's look at it this way. Right now there's crossover jazz. You hear funk and you hear jazz, right? I guess everything can reach the same way. You go to the store today, you can get a papaya and a mango. It's the same thing.

I think when you do things from the heart, you just do it and you don't remember what you do. You just know that you've done something good.

SOCA, CALYPSO, KOMPAS, RARA, AND ZOUK

The rhythms of the French Caribbean are wild, complex, and infectious. Rhythms like kompas direct from Haiti and zouk from Martinique informed much of the contemporary sound of the Caribbean. In turn, it takes much from the rhythms of western and central Africa.

The word "zouk" comes from the Martinique Kreyol patois and literally means "party." It is music that can create a carnival or three just by going over a speaker. As much a musical polyglot as the Kreyol spoken in the islands colonized by the French is a linguistic polyglot, this fusion of culture reflects the area.

The question all of this really demands (avoids?) is what exactly is zouk? The music itself is all over the map. Drawing from music with any kind of a groove, you might hear elements of funk, reggae, and merengue, and the more complex rhythms of cadence and kompas informing the sound, with horn and synth parts that wouldn't sound out of place on an Earth Wind and Fire album.

Needless to say, there is a wide variety of virtuoso dance musics blowing out of where the Atlantic trade winds play.

Some of the oldest recordings from the Antilles, including a piano roll cut in 1922 and a track by Tipical Orchestra of Trinidad in 1914, show this is nothing new. Artists like Roaring Lion, who may have recorded his best album when he was eighty-eight years old, could have been the island equivalent of Cab Calloway judging by the some of his tracks from the 1930s. However, this music remains far from static. Like any other healthy, growing thing, it evolved and took several interesting side trips into the contemporary soca and other sounds of the Caribbean we hear today.

The music of Haiti is rooted in the Voudou culture brought over from western Africa. The music from that half-an-island nation (it shares its bit of Caribbean real estate, Hispaniola, with the Dominican Republic) may be some of the most rhythmically and harmonically complex on the planet. For most of the time this book gestated (about twenty-five years), Haiti was also one of the most dangerous environments for musicians, as during the Duvalier years, anything that even hinted at political content could be hazardous to an artist's health. Political music in Haiti was a flirtation with danger, as even after the downfall of Duvalier, the Tonton Macoutes, the Duvalier secret police, remained very much in evidence and were extremely difficult to uproot. The Macoutes are an undertone of many songs. Musically, this distinction is probably largely lost on uninitiated ears (mine included).

The root kompas and rara grooves offers a tremendous foundation on which Haiti's artists build. A lot happens in Haitian music, with elements of reggae and samba, acoustic, upbeat and infectious grooves, making it some of the most complex dance music on the planet. Indeed, there are very jazzy elements that run through Haitian music (not surprising, considering the common roots), ranging from the various exemplary horn charts to ultramodern keyboard work. The entire francophone Caribbean seems to breed some very heavy players with pretty amazing chops.

AUGUST DARNELL | KID CREOLE & THE COCONUTS

Just a few words from August Darnell, eponymous leader of Kid Creole and the Coconuts. An American group led by Bronx-born Darnell, this band plays a mixture of pop, soca, calypso, and Latin sounds. For sheer calypso-pan-Americanism, nothing else comes close. They make a sexy, swingy mixture of contemporary dance music, soca, reggae, salsa, and any other Caribbean beat Darnell can sneak in there. As such, Darnell has probably done more to help the spread of Caribbean music on a worldwide level than any indigenous artist, with a passel of European hit records using those rhythms. He became so associated with the sound he created, he became the "go-to" guy for that kind of music as a producer and collaborator. The songs are as rewarding lyrically as they are musically, like so much soca and calypso. August "The Kid" Darnell's suave/sly/wry double entendres have a developed sophistication worthy of Cole Porter.

My folks were into music. It's always passed down through the genes, I imagine. Dad was a musician and an actor. He played guitar. So, I guess it just naturally came about that I would get involved in music.

But the other influences came from, apart from the genetic ones, my ex-wife. My ex-wife was a Haitian. She used to play this calypso, reggae music all the time. What this did, I imagine, was regenerate in me my childhood experiences. My dad used to play Harry Belafonte like twenty-four hours around the clock, and that sort of seeped into my brain cells, until I grew older and was influenced by the Beatles, as everyone was, and the whole Motown thing. What living with this woman did was regenerate this early calypso influence. That, coupled with the forties, created another bizarre amalgamation, sort of Ricky

Ricardo–like. So, I imagine, every strain of music, if I looked close enough, I could tell where they all started. Those are the two strongest elements in my music today, would be the island, the Latin calypso feel, which, as I say, came from early childhood and my experience with this Haitian lady, and the forties, which would come from listening to so much Glenn Miller and Cab Calloway.

"No More Casual Sex" was written for the film of the same name. It was an assignment task, like, "We have a movie coming out, *No More Casual Sex*, can you write me a title song?" I called up my brother Stony, of Savannah Band fame, I said, "Yo, I've got an assignment here. You wanna come in on this?" He said, "Fine, whatcha need?" I said, "I need a calypso feel. The song is called 'No More Casual Sex.' Give me a track." He wrote the song, passed it to me, I wrote the lyrics, and we went in together and cut it. It was used in the movie. They used Buster Poindexter and the Banshees of Blue's version of "Hot, Hot, Hot" and "No More Casual Sex" for the movie.

Then they were doing a pilot of a show called *Dr. Paradise*. They called our management, "Kid Creole has been recommended as the guy to write the title track to this *Dr. Paradise* thing." So, again, I called my brother, "Yo, Stony, I've got an assignment here. Do you feel like writing something called 'Dr. Paradise?' It should have an island feel." So we wrote one, and I wasn't happy with it. So, I wrote another one. The second one I wrote is the one that was on the Kid Creole album. I submitted both to the TV company, I said, "Here are your two choices." They picked the first one, the one Stony and I wrote together. The one I didn't like. So, consequently, the one I had written became my own track, I just spruced it up and put it on an album. The TV show had one show, and that was it. It died a miserable death. It had Frank Langella playing the good doctor.

While I tend to blend my influences, I like what my song "When Lucy Does the Boomerang" is saying about assimilation and about how cultures get swallowed up by other cultures. And of course I'm an addict for that soca beat, so that's how it got on an album, even though Tommy Mottola begged me, when they signed me, not to do any of that calypso shit. But don't print that. I might need him some day. After the record comes out, and it's successful, you can print that. Hold that quote. "You're not doing that calypso shit are you?" "No Tommy, man. All funk, brother. All black dance music for you man, all black dance music for you."

I just learned how to swim in the last two years. It's an amazing story, but it's true. I had this fear, this phobia about water for the longest time, until a few years ago, I took a trip down to St. Thomas, and a girlfriend of mine taught me how to swim. It was one of the greatest accomplishments of my life, to be honest with you, because it was a personal conquest. It had nothing to do with gold records or platinum. It was personal. It was overcoming a phobia, which is always the greatest conquest you can imagine.

JOCELYNE BEROARD | KASSAV

For all intents and purposes, Kassav invented zouk. Kassav perform their zouk in Kreyol, but the music itself is all over the map. Kassav draw from music with any kind of a groove, a fertile mixture of the Haitian cadence that dominated the francophone Caribbean, African Soukous, and whatever other music happened to cross paths with this Franco-Caribbean supergroup: on-the-one American funk, on-the-three Jamaican reggae, and kompas inform their sound. At their height, leader Pierre Edourd Decimus was the music-of-developing-nations version of George Clinton, pumping out a dozen different albums a year for a dozen different labels under a dozen different names, but all with essentially the same band. Jocelyne Beroard became the group's spokes-person outside of the Kreyol and French world, as ranking member with the best English.

There was this thing, "world music," that was very big. I hate that word, "world music." For me, it's like a big basket where you put everything that's not English or American or French. They could just add the word "third" to it, call it "third world music." That would be less hypocritical. More honest. That's the problem with world music. The Polyphony of Budapest has nothing to do with Caribbean music.

You know about the story of Kassav? We're starting to be very popular outside France. Before that, we didn't have the chance. They wouldn't believe in our music in the French business. It was only after doing eight big concerts at the Zenith with up to eight thousand people each night that the French companies started to be interested in the group. From that time, our sales have tripled.

"Zouk Is the Only Medicine" started to make us really big and recognized by everyone in the West Indies. I'm talking about

Martinique and Guadeloupe, Haiti, Guyana, in African and then in Europe. In Europe it was only in the Africa and West Indian communities. French people really didn't know about Kassav. We didn't have any promotion. I'm talking about the newspapers, radio, and stuff like that. It's little by little. We were doing such big concerts in Paris without promotion, they just couldn't keep on ignoring us. At the time, about three years after we really started the group, the record companies wanted to sign us.

They didn't know about us, the music from the Caribbean. With Kassav, they got with it, so there are, little by little, groups getting to sign with the big companies here and getting on TV and everything. But they still don't know how to . . . not sell it, but present it. When you come in with Kassav, you don't have the argument for it.

Now they cannot really tell us what we have to do because we made it before they really got us. So, we feel free to say we always made it like that so we are going to keep on doing it the way we feel like doing it. But they do come to us from time to time asking us to do something more commercial or French songs. From time to time.

Not all French people can understand Kreyol, for example. So that's why now we're trying to get a translation of the songs or a literal explanation of the meaning of the words.

Kassav is like sixteen people with five singers. I was called by Pierre Edouard Decimus and Jacob Desvarieux, who were the two that created Kassav, to do background vocals on their second album. I was working with big French stars as a background vocalist at the time, so I had to wait to join them on tour. All the singers had different lives before they joined Kassav. So, with Kassav, Pierre Edouard Decimus and Jacob Desvarieux made all those come together and work together. This became the strength of Kassav, because we could all write songs and sing and everything. That was one of the ways of Kassav, to get people who were very popular. People would look for Kassav, because it was a new sound, a new type of music, new arrangements. They started calling it "zouk." Before that it was called cadence, which is a mixture of Haitian, Dominican, Guadaloupe, and Martinique.

I couldn't tell you what makes zouk different, because it always draws from something else, some other type of music. If I were to say happiness, I would be drawing from African music. If I were to say the arrangements, I might go close to raggamuffin reggae or funk. The difference may be the Kreyol, the language.

I was in Paris, and those of us who were not in Paris, like Jean Philipe Marthely, he used to come often with a group, so they had the chance to hear Jean Philipe and call him. Little by little, everyone was settled in Paris. For the recording, it's easier, for the studios. And also for travel. If you have to go anywhere, for example to Africa from the West Indies, you have to go through Paris or New York. If you have to go to the Far East, you have to go through Paris or New York. So, the best place for us was to stay in Paris.

I am from Martinique. There are six other band members from Martinique, four from Guadeloupe, and there's one African, one from Algeria, and five from France.

For African musicians, living, performing and staying only in Africa won't give them a lot of money, because of the piracy in selling records. It's better for them to come here, because they have a chance to have their records out here and get some money. For us, it's just because our islands are small, so we go back there often. We go and get the vibe of the country so that we don't forget our roots and everything, but we cannot do more than one or two concerts a year there.

Here in Paris we can go and see a lot of different concerts, lots of different people coming from everywhere in the world. You get to see more live performance compared to the West Indies. Everything can influence us, being here. We can hear all kinds of music. But it's more when we go to the countries, like we've been traveling a lot to Africa, Zaire, Congo, Cameroon, and so on, so we were really into it. We were really with the people. We were really feeling the beat of the country. That period, we had more African-style songs. In Paris, it's mostly the technical part that interests us.

But Martiniquan music is not to far from that. There was a time when we had the Rocofil Jazz sound that was from Congo. That came to Martinique. From the time we were kids, we used to listen to all kinds of music from Martinique. I'm talking about Caribbean music, reggae, calypso, salsa music, and American music, and European music, and African music, too. We grew up with all those musics; all those musics were part of us. We had all this inside of us. It wasn't something we were discovering at a certain time because it was some kind of fashion in music. That was the music that we liked, that we loved to listen to when we were kids, that we were dancing to, and we're still dancing to all those musics.

Martiniquan and Guadeloupean people are very mixed too, due to the colonialist times. We have African people coming from different countries, we have French, we have English, we have Spanish, we have Chinese, we have Indian. So we have all these cultures mixed up. We are accustomed to being mixed up talking about the people themselves, the bodies, the culture, and the music, too. It was easy to take all the music coming to us if we had a feeling for it, so that's why in the zouk, you can find all kinds of things. It's not something that we are programming, saying like, "Okay, we're going to do a reggae now, because reggae is hot." It's not like a fashion for us, it's a fact. It's music that we're accustomed to, that we like. We feel that this song should be more calypso or more funk of more this or that.

Every time we have a single we go on TV. They invite us regularly, so, we feel like we are more into the French business, though we're not completely in it. Some people are asking me if zouk was a fashion at one time. I always answer that zouk is not a fashion for me. It's my life. That's like asking James Brown is funk a fashion. It's not. It's a style.

When we played Africa, they were not really organized to produce concerts. Most of the time, you had someone decide to have Kassav perform in Africa, in this country, just because they knew the popularity of the group, they knew they could have a full stadium they could make a lot of money out of it. The problem is, most of the time they had never made such a concert or never made any concerts. When we would come, there would be a lack of organization. They wouldn't have paid for the hotel, or they would have a deal with the airline that gave him the tickets that he would pay after, so we'd have a return ticket, but it wasn't paid at all. So, we'd travel in the first part and when it came time for us to return, they would not have the money. They would tell us that we'd have to pay. Or they just disappeared. Even if we told the manager of the hotel that we're not responsible for paying the thing, if the guy disappeared, as we slept in the hotel, we had to pay for it.

We had lots and lots of problems there. A band went to some countries before us and acted as if they were Kassav themselves. They would pay with checks and there would be no money at the end, so when we arrived, they would ask us to pay for the thing. We were always victims of people that were not honest. But we always had good concerts with big crowds and people who were really happy to see us.

It's still the same thing. If you have to go to certain parts of Africa, you have to have many guarantees. If they give you a ticket, you should ask the airline if the return ticket is paid and have them sign a paper for you and everything. Also have any kind of protection, like from your consulate or embassy, to make sure that you are there and not responsible for the lacks of the organizer. But it's such a pleasure to go there. Everyone is so hot. There's so much love doing those concerts there.

We hope that people are going to come to discover all the musics that are going to be there. They're all happy musics, and with the sunshine, we're all going to have a great time.

FRED PAUL

Fred Paul continues as a linchpin of the Haitian music business around the world. A remarkably talented man, he plays, produces, and arranges, but mostly he sells Haitian music out of the Miami area. In all of these capacities, he has earned the respect of the Haitian musical community, and of others like director Jonathan Demme, who had Paul help in on both his documentary Haiti Dreams of Democracy *and the documentary album* Konbit *that introduced many Haitian artists to America. Beyond all that, he leads the Mini All-Stars, a remarkable group that plays in traditional kompas forms and even went so far as to modernize and record the compositions of early Haitian star Nemours Jean-Baptiste. He kept the fire of Kompas Direct burning bright from the fifties through the nineties.*

I've always taken this business and this art that music is very seriously. I've always wanted to open up the market. But to do that, you need the machine and you need the money. You need to be able to hire the right people and have the right people interested in what you're doing.

In the last twenty years, we haven't seen that many American tourists in Haiti because of the political situation. The tourists who went to Haiti before then are used to our kind of sound. When these people now have the opportunity to go back and listen, it's another market that we didn't expect that we will get. They will have interest in that because it will be like the good old days for them, when they used to take the little prop plane and go there and have a good time, buy some souvenir paintings and so on. We haven't seen that in some time. Take the flight going to Haiti, and you'll see that it's all black people. It's all Haitians. But before, it's a lot of tourists going there.

Zouk is more like Haitian music. Zouk has been on since the mid-eighties. We dominated the French Carribbean market for over twenty years. These guys playing zouk nowadays, they used to come to Haiti and make records with Haitian musicians. What made zouk really better sounding is that these guys are West Indian and French at the same time, so they are using the same technology that the French pop artists are using. The Haitian doesn't have this chance. If they don't have enough money, they can't go to a good studio. The other part of that, it's very difficult, when the music is not selling, to make a good deal with the musician. We don't have any places like BMI or ASCAP, no publishing. The first market is the Haitian market, and the Haitian radio are not giving the artists one penny. Not getting any royalties like that makes the whole process so difficult. When I have to deal with these guys, I have to pay them a lot of money.

There is a difference between zouk and Haitian music. When the basics of Haitian music are done well, all the guitars are in tune, it's a good recording and you have the right musicians, you can feel that jazziness. There's more chords going through it than the zouk that's going boom, boom, boom.

That's the way I see it. It's not that I don't like zouk. I'm very close to the guys who play zouk. Everybody I've worked with in this business, and I've worked in great studios, Power Station, I know guys who have recorded all the big artists. They're friends. And I know what these guys feel. James Farber has a kompas song that I'll be putting on my next record. The music James really likes is jazz, but he wrote a kompas song, and I'm going to put it on my record. James is a good piano player.

My main market has always been the Kreyol community. It is a very limited market, and you don't have that much income.

So far, I can say I went past that market, that community, not really in America, but in Europe. I've had hits in Europe that were in the pop charts with Barry White at one time. I had a song called

"New York City" that was a big hit with Tabou Combo. That was a big hit in France, in Italy, in Germany. That was on Barclay.

After this interview, I have to go to my lawyer and bring the whole file and try to recoup all of that money from Barclay. I stopped the payment to the other guy who I licensed the record to, because I wasn't getting money, but Barclay never paid the money that he kept to anybody. So since I have a judgment, I have to take the judgment and find time to go to France and take care of this myself. Sometimes it's late, but you can always find a way to get to these people.

It gets to a point where legally they might tell you the company doesn't exist any more, but you can touch them as human beings, so they say. You tell them, "Here, we had a deal, we expected both to make money. Now you're doing good and I'm doing shitty. What do you think of the integrity of a man who has succeeded and is not paying his bills?" Sometimes it works. It worked last week on somebody very famous, but I have to do it to Barclay, too.

Not too many groups do good at the same time. When Tabou is not doing good, it's Ska Shah. When Kassav is doing good, Tabou is not doing good at all in the community. That's the way it's been going. When you're not doing good, and you don't have money coming in, it's very difficult to make things happen.

Mini All-Stars has always been me. There was a time when I made the mistake of keeping them steady. It is a mistake. It's better to have them working, and put them together whenever you have to. When you have to work every time, especially in this market, it's no good. It's a waste of time and energy. At this time, they were playing steady every weekend. But now, it's anytime when the tracks are there and the musicians are there.

Tabou Combo has been doing good for a while. They've been investing the money in equipment, and so on. They are the most professional Haitian group there could be. Things are happening, and they have the opportunity to do different things. They are better organized than the other Haitian groups, and that's why you are going to see more Tabou for a longer time. But that doesn't mean that in the Haitian market, they're always the most demanded.

They haven't gotten the break that they need yet. They've got the foothold. What's going good for them is they have had more exposure than some. For this, they are the best equipped, the best known, and the best prepared.

Ska Shah is one of the top Haitian bands. They are in dire competition with Tabou Combo, and Tabou Combo is in dire competition with Ska Shah. I always work very closely with these groups.

Coupe Cloue is a very well known artist. When I used to sell records in Haiti, most tourists, they would come and have me try different artists for them. When they came to the Coupe Cloue, that's the one they would always buy, before Tabou Combo, before Ska Shah, before anyone. Coupe Cloue is a very popular guy in Haiti.

Magnum Band was put together by Dadou Pasquet. He's a very talented, if not the best, Haitian guitarist. He used to play in the seventies with Tabou Combo. When they had their big European hit, "New York City," he was the lead guitar player. He's a very, very good guitar player. After some time, like anything else they had a break-up and he left Tabou Combo. He joined his brother, who was playing in front of a very well known Haitian band, the Gypsies. He's a very talented drummer. They put together Magnum. They always play differently from all the other groups. They have their own type of music. They play very clean and very tight. They are very well known, especially in zouk countries, like Guadeloupe, Martinique, and France. They really like their playing.

DT Express is a band from Haiti that had its best days a while ago. It was done by a very well known—but unfortunately he passed away—artist named Timanou. Timanou was like the Haitian Bob Marley. He sang a lot about injustice to dance music. He did a lot. Unfortunately, he didn't last too long. He was so well known that it was difficult to kick him out. They couldn't hurt him. See, when an artist is a celebrity in our country, you might put him in jail for a while, but you can't kill him. He really had said things and denounced things that could put him in a lot of trouble. Unfortunately, when Duvalier fell from power, he wasn't around to say more. This was a great and talented musician.

Sakad is a different type of music that probably doesn't have that big a market in the Haitian community. It's very different. It's done by a Nicole Levy, who is himself a keyboard player and arranger. He does arrangements sometimes for other Haitian groups, but what he arranges has nothing to do with what he plays. He's very political. He's been talking about injustice, singing about injustice for a long time. He's had good songs on albums that didn't work. He could have had trouble with the Macoutes, but he went into exile, especially after he recorded an album called *When the Sun Had Risen*. It was all about injustice and the Tonton Macoutes and so on. The whole thing was very political. He's still living in America.

I got involved with Samba Yo when Jonathan Demme asked me to go to Haiti to produce them. Jonathan and Ed Saxon were the first ones to send me a copy of their music. This is not the popular music in Haiti, the kind of music I've been selling, but this is the music of the people. This is the real African roots. After I listened to the music, I really fell in love with them, and would like to do an entire album of them, a good project with a mixture of good American musicians.

JONATHAN DEMME

So what is Academy Award–winning director Jonathan Demme doing in a book about artists of developing nations in their own words? Well, Demme has probably done more to hammer these artists into our collective psyches than any other person on the planet. If you've seen the films Married to the Mob *or* Something Wild, *you've heard artists like Nigerian Sonny Okosuns, dancehall reggae diva Sister Carol (who also has a supporting role in* Married*), and Les Frères Parents, blind Haitian musicians. His infatuation with Haiti led him to produce and direct the documentary* Haiti Dreams of Democracy *and a parallel audio documentary called* Konbit, *released by A&M largely on the strength of Demme's name and reputation.*

There's something that I should be the first to acknowledge: I am not an expert on music. I am an enthusiast, but I am painfully uneducated in so many areas of music that I would like to be, especially the kind of music that we share a fondness for.

I don't know if this is a function of my age or the state of white American popular music, but at the moment I find it just exceptionally boring. But long before that, I became interested in the excitement of music from other shores or what have you.

I have probably had a fairly typical avenue into music from other countries. I started getting into reggae in a big way twenty years ago. As it's come here, I've been opened up to it. Nigerian music, that was a body of work that I learned the magic of when King Sunny Ade and Chief Commander Ebenezer Obey and Fela were starting to become available to a certain extent. Sonny Okosuns, who we even have a song by on our soundtrack for *Something*

Wild, and on the album, too. *Petit à petit avoir fanish*, little by little the bird builds his nest. The interesting thing for me is that I can't believe that I didn't find myself learning about Haitian music sooner. But, again, Haitian music, for whatever reason, is ghettoized a little more than other kinds.

The idea of *Haiti Dreams of Democracy* was to provide a forum for Haitians to speak about what's happening, through spoken word and through music. As soon as you go down and you tell people what you're doing, everyone says, "Then you've got to find Mano, then you've got to find Frères Parents." And in Haiti, everybody knows somebody who knows somebody else. It's impossible, if in America, you don't know Bob Dylan, you know someone who knows Bob Dylan. If we were in Haiti and paralleling like that. Nobody's difficult to find if your motivation seems to be pretty good.

A lot of Haitians, especially in the capital, can help you out on the English level. Not only that, but Kreyol is such a tantalizing language that if you're there and you're hearing people speak it, you want to get in on that. I immediately started picking up on it. I don't speak French, and I think that was a benefit to me, because I haven't tried to bring French rules to my attempt to learn Kreyol.

For the vocabulary, the more Kreyol I learned, when I see it some French written down, the more words I can get. That's a little bonus. In Haiti they say, "*Parlez Fracais pa ne esprit*," which means, "Just because you know French, doesn't mean you're smart." It's a good lesson for a lot of people to learn.

There are some great independent stations down there, and you know something? I hate to admit, but even the government station, Radio Nacional, is *great* for music. Man, I'll give you a tape, ninety minutes right off the radio, that will kill you. Radio in Haiti is key to everything. There is not a lot of written word stuff, because a lot of the people haven't learned how to read by benefit of schooling. So radio is the big communicator. It is a culture that still cherishes the spoken word, unlike ours. I mean, it's going away. The Garison Keillors, the Spaulding Grays become rarer and rarer.

One of the reasons I favor, on film soundtracks, the music of artists like Frères Parents—I used two songs by them in *Married to the Mob*—Sonny Okosuns, Celia Cruz, is because these artists have in common the ability to move you through their music, to move you in a very positive fashion. So, on a very manipulative kind of level, I want to capitalize on that ability to move the audience and bring out feelings of warmth in the audience. So that's why I have this ongoing desire to incorporate music like that in my films.

I wanted very much to get David Byrne to write a song to start *Something Wild* off. I knew whatever he came up with would be great, because he's a fantastic composer and recording artist, plus, he's a filmmaker, so I knew that if he could get him to do a song, it would get us off on such a great first foot. We're friends, so we hang around together, and I sort of know what he's interested in, because we talk about that kind of thing. His interest in Latin music was really growing at that point. I figured the best way to pull David in here would be to suggest something specifically, like "David would you please consider doing a song to open our movie, and hey, maybe it would be an opportunity for you to team up with Celia Cruz," who he turned me on to, and we were both nuts about. I spit that out and David came back with "Loco De Amor." So I'm claiming credit for that, even if my memory is wrong on that.

I went to see Judy Mowatt perform at SOB's and halfway through the show, she brought out for one song a guest artist, and it was Sister Carol, who I had never heard of and never seen. I had rarely been so devastated by a live performance as I was by Sister Carol during that one song, which I think was "Screwface." I just had to meet her, which I forced my way downstairs afterwards and met her and told her I wished that I could work with her in some fashion. So we sort of agreed. She was very patient and generous with me. We agreed we would try to do something.

This is a person of extraordinary personal positive impact. I wanted to end *Something Wild* on a very positive note, with a tremendously humanistic kind of feeling, and I felt that Sister Carol would bring a lot of that, just by virtue of who she is, to the party, if I could cast her at the end of the picture. So, without thinking musically, I cast Sister Carol, she agreed to play the waitress at the restaurant. Then we're shooting the movie, and I'm thinking how absurd it is to have Sister Carol in the film, but she doesn't get to sing. And somewhere in there was the idea that Sister Carol doing her interpretation of the song "Wild Thing" would be the greatest possible way to end the movie. It all worked out.

Music is such a big part of my life as a citizen. I depend on music do make me happy and keep me connected with certain values that I hold important. So I listen to a lot of music, and inevitably, I want to bring this feeling that this music evokes in me, I want to bring that now to the films that I make in the hopes of passing it along to the viewer.

CLIFFORD SYLVAIN | RARA MACHINE

Former Skah Sha percussionist (he was on their hit "Men Nimewo A") Clifford Sylvain has straddled the expatriate experience with deep Haitian extraction—his father both served in the government and was arrested by it. His music fuses rara and Voudou ritual music with contemporary pop sounds and equipment, bringing a modern touch to very ancient musical roots.

Any time you write something in Haiti, you have to be political. You have to be if you are going to tell the truth. I remember when I was eight years old, the Army and the Tontons Macoutes, they got together and went to my father's place. They actually brought my father to us, blood all over him, almost dying. They beat my father with the butt of the rifle all over his body, his head. My father was bleeding when he came back. Because he would stand up against the Duvalier regime. They told him to leave the country and he said no. He was in hiding. When he came out, they tried to kill him. He had to be smuggled out of the country. We went to Miami together and then to New York. Since then, they've tried to kill all of us. My mother was in hiding, we, the sons and daughters, were divided. Some of us were at my aunts' house, my mother's sisters, my father's brothers. We grew up that way when we were young. My father had ten sons and daughters.

Haiti was not a country that was born in the island. We are a people that have been imported. We were imported from Africa. Before that, all Haitians did not come from one place. You have Haitians that come from all slavery. They come from Senegal, Gore. Everyone knows Gore, because that is where every slave passed by to go to the West. Gore is an island near Senegal. Until now, you find some old chain, some old guns, you see where the slaves passed by to leave Africa. That was a safe haven. So, a lot of Haitians passed by Gore. Mainly, you have Haitians who came from Benin, Nigeria. Some of them come from Mozambique and you have them from Ethiopia. If you look at Ethiopia, Ethiopia and Benin have the most old-fashioned Voudou spirit, Voudou folklore. Ethiopia is a very strong country as far as Voudou is concerned.

Haile Selassie was a Voudou priest. He came to baptize Papa Doc in Haiti. After Haile Selassie went to Haiti, Papa Doc became a very strong man. Haile Selassie was a very, very powerful Voudou Priest. I think that's why all the Rastafarians adore him. I think that's why they see him as their master somehow. He was very powerful in that aspect. Haile Selassie was very strong.

Any guy who steps in and tries to do a revolution, he cannot be simple. You have Haile Selassie, who is a strong Voudou priest and a strong man, a fighter. You have Nelson Mandela. Those guys can't be alone. They have what we call the black magic spirit. They have that. You have Aristides now, in Haiti. You can't kill them just like that. No, no. Sometimes they die, you don't know how they die. You don't see them.

People don't know how Duvalier died. I was in Haiti, I was a kid when Duvalier died. There was a big wind, it was like a cyclone. The country turned upside down. There was dirt all over. What you hear is a "wooooooooo" and then you see this big wind turn the country all over. That's when people knew that Duvalier was gone. He was so powerful. And guys like Father Aristide. Father Aristide, how come they couldn't kill him the other day? Nobody knows. Do you know how many times they tried to kill him? Three or four times already. They shoot at him, but he's still alive. Every ten years you have a guy like those guys.

I started playing with Skah Shah. I made one of the biggest hits for Skah Sha, "Men Nimewo A." That was my song. That was a hit. But they didn't give me credit after the album was out. So I said, "If that's what they do, they're going to regret it." I stepped out.

They said, "How can you leave Skah Sha, such a big band?" I said, "It's not the band that's big, it's me and the other guys."

Every band that's big, it's because they have some good musicians. If there's no good musicians, the band is not going to be big. If a country is big, it's because it has good people. When a country is falling apart it's because the leaders, the people who organize the country, are no good. That's why a country falls apart.

So I didn't play with Skah Sha again. I went and studied some music at home. Then I met with some guys from a rock and roll band called The Big Brigade. They had some songs like Paul Simon. They have music like Kid Creole. So I played with them for about six months. We traveled to North Carolina, South Carolina.

What I was trying to do was mix the Haitian rhythms with rock. When I started doing that, it fit so nice and we really had fun. The band was doing fine, but when I started doing that, putting some good folklore rhythm in the rock, and I started singing for the band in Kreyol, not in English. It was like a few lines, like sixteen bars of one song that I was singing. The song started in English, and then in the middle of the song, when the song got hot, I had some nice solo drums, like three congas, two timbales, bongos. I made some good tension for them, and the guitar played some good rock fusion. So, I took my microphone and sang something in Kreyol. Everyone was singing along, and then I did some African leads on top of it. People enjoyed it. It was something different.

Take folklore music from Haiti, like my music, Rara Machine music. There's a song called *"Kase Chenn,"* "Break the Chain." The rhythm comes from Haiti. In Benin, they have another name for it, but it's the same rhythm. Where did that come from? It didn't come from Haiti. It came from Benin. It couldn't have come from Haiti. We have a rhythm that's like the Santeria in Cuba, that they play with the bata drums. We have that in Haiti, they have that in Benin. Most of the Haitian rhythms, I found out that they come from Benin. Benin has a lot to do with Haitian music. That's why I want to travel to Benin.

Where does zouk come from? Why do you have the zouk? Zouk, in Kreyol, it's part of the kompas music of Haiti and the soukous of Africa. That's what zouk is. The real Martiniquan and Guadelupean music, the real rhythm, is an old beat they used to play that doesn't have to do with soukous or nothing. They have their own rhythm. They don't play it anymore, but you can go outside of the country and you'll hear that rhythm. People play it, bands like Company Kreyol, they play that rhythm. It's called the *contredanse* of Haiti.

In Haiti, we have fifty-two rhythms. There may be more than that, but I know there are fifty-two rhythms in Haiti. Fifty-two rhythms that can make people dance all night, sing, rhythms that are so much better than the kompas that people say is the real Haitian music. For me, kompas is a good music. It's a music that came out in the 1950s going into the sixties. The other rhythms, these are the rhythms we came from Africa with.

We Haitians modernized these rhythms a lot. The way they were in Africa is not the way they are now, we modernized them a lot and changed their name, too. They are not called the same thing in Africa that they are in Haiti. That's the kind of music we used to play before the time of slavery, our folklore music. We didn't have kompas. This is the type of music we used to have. That is the real Haitian music. From Benin, from Nigeria, from Côte d'Ivoire, and from Mozambique and Zimbabwe. We have roots from those countries. Zaire, too.

There are a lot of Haitians that live there, in those countries, a lot of the teachers that left Haiti at the time of the Duvaliers. That was a hard time for everything, and that's when the kompas really took hold. You had bands like Nemours Jean-Baptiste and Weber Sicot. Those two guys were the big ravers. They used to fight against each other in music. Baptiste was called kompas direct, Sicot was called cadence rhumba. Those two guys used to play in the same band, two saxophone players. One used to play tenor, the other used to play alto. When the band dissolved, they each formed their own band, and that's when they really created kompas and cadence.

Cadence is a rhythm and kompas is a different rhythm, one played with two congas, one played with three congas. That's when we started having problems with our folklore, when those two guys started. Kompas and cadence were very popular musics, but we paid a big price for that in our culture.

I'm trying to bring back what we had a long time ago, our folklore, our rhythm and our culture in a different way. I live in the U.S. right now. I had a chance to go to school here, to modernize that music. That's what I do.

I have all this music at home. I have computers, I have software, new equipment. I'm trying to study these rhythms and modernize them, put some rock on top, some R&B, and stuff. Make it very modern, so people can dance to it and see some change. When you hear the music, you know what kind of rhythm it is, but the way it's going to be modernized, it's going to be very well advanced.

It's going to take me time, but someone has to do it. Boukman Eksperyance started it. But what happened to them, after they had their tour of the United States, the band went back to Haiti, most of the members of the band left. They started their own bands.

A band like Boukman is a band that needs to be around. To do what I'm doing now, I need bands like Boukman around, bands like Samba Yo, Sakad. What I really want to do is go beyond the line.

With the international community, like the Americans and Europeans, if it was up to them, our music will go far. There used to be a time when the international market really didn't care about what we were playing. Right now, they do care more, and they do give us more coverage, they do give us more everything. They understand that this is good music, this is music that's going somewhere. If you listen to Kid Creole, the type of music he's playing, it's very close to us. Kid Creole is from Haiti. What he's playing is Haitian. If he would go back to Haiti and do some research, his band and what he is doing would be better.

Haiti was beautiful when Aristide was there seven months ago. You had to see that. You had fifty different bands from Martinique, from Guadalupe, from New York, from Paris, from all over, they came to play. We had a big, big festival in Haiti. That was joy for everybody.

ACADIAN AND ZYDECO

Two of the elements that seem to contribute to great music and hard core tradition are tragedy and diaspora. Combine that with the isolation that allows music to develop on its own terms, and you have the conditions that gave birth to much of the roots music of Louisiana.

About as isolated as any part of the United States is from the rest of the country, there are several reasons why many of the indigenous musics of Louisiana often find themselves in the "world music" bins. The cradle of jazz, the foundation of funk, the inspiration for reggae, New Orleans was a central port of the Caribbean while the French still held the territory. This led to a lot of fundamental differences about how slaves were treated—they were allowed to congregate and continue to practice their own religions and play their own music.

However, the main sound of the state comes from an even more isolated area north of the port. The roots of the sound date back to Acadie, the original French Canadian settlements, circa 1604. When the British took over, they expelled these settlers. The Acadians went down the Mississippi and found a place in the bayous, so remote they figured no one would bother them again. Here, in swamps that were isolated until just before World War II, the Acadian refugees settled. For centuries, the only way to get to these areas of Louisiana was by boat. Few outsiders had the need or even the yen to explore this remote area. Little wonder the music that grew up there sounds like nothing else. In this cultural seclusion, the refugees' music had the opportunity to develop away from the mainstream. They even continued to speak—and sing in—French.

This would make Acadian music the oldest indigenous to North America, save for music of the Native Americans.

Acadian music, sometimes called Cajun, developed out of the folk two-steps that the Acadians brought over from France and down the Mississippi. With button accordions and fiddles, tub basses and washboards, this is folk music at its most elemental.

Even with the mass communication revolution that began the twentieth century, Cajun music remained a very local phenomenon. Early in the twentieth century, few outside of the Acadian community had heard it. Over the course of the last quarter century, however, Cajun music has gone (relatively) mainstream. Madison Avenue used it to sell heartburn medicine and cars.

Same with its good neighbor, zydeco. For a hot minute in the 1980s, zydeco went worldwide. Artists like Clifton Chenier and Alton Jay "Rockin' Dopsie" Rubin started the ball rolling as early as the fifties, fusing R&B with the more traditional music. However, it took a record cut on a four-track studio in the garage of the late Rockin' Sidney Simien, the infectious dance tune "My Toot Toot," to burst zydeco into mainstream consciousness. Covered by a host of artists, including John Fogerty and Denise LaSalle, it became a hit on both sides of the Atlantic and earned Sidney a Grammy and two W. C. Handy Awards.

Zydeco is the African-American French music nurtured in the bayou. The slaves that escaped into the bayous adapted this music as well, and fused it with their own rhythms. It diverged into a whole other genre.

Traditional Cajun and zydeco have very little to do with anything else that comes out of Louisiana (or anywhere else) musically, though. They have strong shared roots, bred in the bayou for centuries, relatively unmarked by the changes that went on outside of that culture.

MICHAEL DOUCET | BEAUSOLIEL

Beausoliel has topped the world music charts, an ironic thing for a band from the United States playing music that's been indigenous to America since before the Revolutionary War. But that's one of the shining ironies of Louisiana. Doucet's odyssey has taken him from rock to folk to Celtic and French folk-rock back to where it all began, the bayous of Louisiana. Here, with a who's who of the Acadian (a.k.a. Cajun) music scene, he brought the roots to the people, which has been his mission ever since.

Let's deal with Acadian for one thing, the French music from southwest Louisiana. There's also the zydeco, which is sort of the Afro-American French music nurtured here. Of course you have jazz. Not dixieland, jazz. New Orleans–style music. You have the blues from the delta, Baton Rouge, up. You have country and western, that are closer to the borders of Texas, because you have swing kind of taking over there.

To most people, this is not vanilla music or pop music out of L.A. or New York. Look at New Orleans. If that's not a world port . . . It always has been the center of the Caribbean. It's one of the oldest ports there are. It was the port for the Caribbean, Mexico, Africa, the whole bit. New Orleans has gone through so many changes. When people went down the Mississippi, they went one way. That's down to New Orleans. After they got to New Orleans, they'd dismantle their boats and build homes. It's always been kind of an open town.

I think the music has led to that, as early as the early 1700s. There was a whole black orchestra, they had black operas there. They had different strata of what the word "creole" meant. A

Creole was originally a Spanish or French plantation owner. But then it became a language and a name for free men of color. It became a whole lot of different genres. And of course jazz happened there. With this music, because it's the tropics, we have tropical weather, the fact is with French, Spanish, and Americans, it's really the melting pot of people who were pioneers in the colonial world. Not that there weren't pioneers other places, but if you went down to Louisiana, you knew that was it.

The Acadians chose to move to a part of Louisiana that was more isolated than even New Orleans. It was accessible only by water. At the same time, it was inaccessible if you could not ford the rivers. Of course, the first bridge over the Mississippi was built in the 1920s. So, they were pretty much isolated for about 150 years. That's how the music matured.

The same thing happened in the Caribbean. We share more in common with the Seychelles Islands, Mauritius, Reunion Islands as far as the traditional music that was done years back, with the accordion and fiddles. They play these old-world French quadrilles. In Haiti it's almost the same thing, but it's almost a purer sound. That's new world.

I think the language presented some difficulties. In Louisiana, you have people singing not only French songs, but Acadian songs. They were like a nation of people. They had their own place in the world that they were moved out of. The deportation is pretty heavy on these people. Just the fact that it is treated as a social function, the music and the people and the people who play the music. I don't think I know an Acadian family that doesn't have any musicians in the family. It's just so much a part of our culture that the acceptance is always there, and the fact is that we share it. The outside world could look at it but not understand it. It was always that secret, kind of clannish little club that you know you could share, and you know people would understand and people were like you, even though the world was changing around you. It was something to go back to, to hold onto. The values were there. The values have been nurtured since the early 1600s. So they were tried and true.

Yet even though this music is French, it is definitely North American. The foundation of this music was from the 1600s on. I mean they founded Acadie in 1604, and most people started moving there in the 1620s. They weren't deported from there until 1755. So the basis of the songs, the music was there. The changes took place in Louisiana from about 1760 on. That's a long time to build upon a song. It is the whole new world, North American phenomena. I guess it was like Cairo in the early days of the port of New Orleans. They said even slaves would walk down the street singing songs from *La Traviata*. Jelly Roll Morton creating jazz. Music was everywhere. Here, you have people saying they would come down with Virginia reels, very well known for their home style of playing it. Then they would get to New Orleans, and come down to the docks. They didn't know how to describe it, but they would say they were doing something funny. Obviously, they were playing blue notes. They were playing the blues back then and they didn't know what the thing was. It was just a certain place where things happen. Just like Paris was the head of civilization for a long time and made interesting changes. I think in the New World it was, and in some cases still is New Orleans.

It was also the only place in the South where slaves were allowed to congregate and play their music, hence Congo Square, and the different strata. There were free men of color. There were Afro-American French speakers who owned plantations and slaves. Into that whole culture of things, they just fit in a completely different place. It was just totally bizarre. Still is. But it was the sharing of all this. The word gumbo, of course, is African. But the cuisine, what is this? It's shared throughout Louisiana. It's what the products were at the time. Our home-grown tomatoes, we call them creole tomatoes. I think people just tended to enjoy life, and not be so uptight.

My band, Beausoleil, goes through different stages. We change, just like everybody else. We just don't change in the same way. I think it's unique to us. When I started this, the whole thing sort of came backwards, all this recording stuff.

Basically I was a researcher. I had a grant from the National Endowment in the early seventies. The Smithsonian needed to know where to find the older musicians. I did that. I also transcribed a lot of their music and stuff like that. I wrote a book back then that's never been published. I might do it one of these days. I did put out a set of "How To Play Cajun Fiddle." In the six tapes, I go through a lot of the people I studied from.

I was always interested in finding why was this stuff different. What, exactly, makes this stuff different. So, I went on this quest to find this guy named Amedi Ardoin. Basically, he is like Buddy Bolden, a mystery guy. This guy did record. He's a black guy, he plays accordion and recorded in the late twenties, early thirties. Amazingly he recorded as a duo with a white fiddle player, an Acadian by the name of Dennis McGee, who lived to be like ninety-five years old. They sort of incorporated everything. All these different styles that we talked about, New Orleans, Afro-Caribbean, and of course Acadian or Cajun.

I think what we try to do is show these things are still here. In the seventies, that wasn't the case. This music wasn't known throughout the world, and this music wasn't appreciated, even down here, much less outside of Louisiana. It was still a minority, and a minority that was put down because of our language, and people made fun of what we ate, and of course what we played, because they couldn't understand. In those days, I knew there was so much more to music. Throughout all our history, I've always tried to show not just the two-steps and waltzes, the simple songs. The songs that are very popular and everybody says, "Okay, this is good. You've got to learn this." But the stuff that was missing was the ballads, the African American field hollers, the blues, the jazzy parts.

We play ballads and *contredanses* and French stuff. For me, to know this stuff through my research and not extend it or share it with you, then it would not be real. This is how I perceive the music. I don't perceive it as the "okay, let's get drunk" tip of the iceberg part. I try to see the whole iceberg, below and above the surface. To me, that's how you understand the heart and the soul of a culture, by as many sides as you can possibly portray from an honest standpoint.

The very sad part, that people don't hear anymore, is the ballads, because you can't dance to them. That's the side that tells the stories. That's why some of these two-steps sometimes don't make sense, because it's not all there. It's like somebody who knew this long, ten-minute ballad story song and didn't have the time to do it, would just sing like parts of it. It became a few couplets from this ballad would be incorporated into a two-step. So, the people who would know the ballad could understand and respect the song, but the people who never heard the ballad, didn't know the story, might be lost.

I always wanted to do something that sounds like us. I never wanted to be pinned down. I wish it was just music. There were traditional Cajun artists who put rock and roll into their music, even in the late fifties and sixties. That's another element. Louisiana is heavy into early rock and roll. The fact is, that's what we do.

Sometimes, for the young kids, you've got to say this stuff lives. It's not just the old people. When we were growing up, it was just the old people who played this music. I want to say, 'Man, everyone can play this music! You can share this music.' It's hip. Even though it's old, it's hip.

I just don't want to be called a Cajun rock band. I want the music to be hip and spontaneous and now, without having to be categorized into a certain element. I made fun of that at one time. I made an album called *Cajun Groove* where I recorded a lot of songs like "Louie Louie" and "Wolly Bully" in French just to show that you didn't have to say, "This is rock, you put the drums to it, it becomes Cajun rock." It doesn't have to. You have to have the essence of the music, and the music is so strong, Cajun music and the influence, that you can take any genre and Cajunize it. That's what people have always done. That's why the music is so diverse. That's why the musicians are so diverse, and everybody is such an individual. They just took the best of what they liked, and they made it their own.

People always say that there's got to be some kind of gimmick. But it's basically a love for this music. I came through the ranks when this music wasn't accepted, when people couldn't make a buck and there was no such thing as a Cajun restaurant. They were all seafood restaurants. All the big guys in New Orleans burn the fish, and all those seafood restaurants change to Cajun, and Cajun New Orleans and Cajun the world. But before that, it was much simpler. The people who played this music played it because they loved it. As simple as that. They didn't need to be known. These guys were back-porch musicians. They weren't playing publicly. But they were incredibly spiritual guys who had survived a whole lot of changes. I think their tenacity and their integrity saved the music. I was lucky enough to go out there and find these guys and record them and get a little bit of their take of what the world should be.

The accordion is sometimes an obnoxious sounding instrument. So people will say, "Do you play that chanky-chank music, that old style music?" I took that and said, "Yeah, we do that, and we're really proud that we do." We don't mind, like a friend of mine says, "It doesn't matter if you're old and ugly. Just *be* old and ugly and you'll be fine." Don't try and be anything else. So, the chanky-chank, that's what we call our music. That's what we like. It's not for everybody, but it's definitely for us.

TERRANCE SIMIEN

One of the leading light of zydeco, Terrance Simien and his Mallet Playboys might also be the most revolutionary musicians in this ol' music. With intensely soulful vocals and more than a touch of R&B in their sound, they have helped take zydeco to the next level and won praise and plaudits from the likes of Paul Simon, who recorded with them, and actor Dennis Quaid.

I'm not from New Orleans. I'm from Lafayette. Although we're not that far apart from the Crescent City, we have two totally different styles of music. It's two totally different worlds. We're just 120 miles away from the city. But, like around Mallet, in the rural area, southwestern Louisiana, which is where I'm from, that's where the Cajuns and Creoles settled.

Back in the small towns, that's where the Mardi Gras celebration started. It started through the churches. We do a different celebration. We have what they call a Mardi Gras run, where a guy will go out, and there'll be a couple of musicians, accordion, rub board, maybe a guitar, and they'll go from house to house with a bunch of guys dressed up in costume. It's like an adult sort of trick or treat. You go from house to house and you ask them to contribute something to this big gumbo that they make and they invite the whole neighborhood to come and eat at Mardi Gras, right before Lent. Most of these people are Catholic, and they try and blow it out during Mardi Gras time, so they can give up something for Lent. That's how we celebrate it, just go from house to house. There's not no parade or nothing like that. It's sort of traditional. They go from house to house either collecting money or whatever they'll give 'em. To try and get some donations and stuff like that, they'll play a little music, and if you give 'em something, they'll play a little music and dance. If they don't give 'em something, a lot of the people have livestock, they'll probably open up the gate of the hen house, or something. Loose their chickens. Do something, kind of get back at them. But everyone usually participates, so there's not much of that going on.

My parents grew up singing in the church choir, stuff like that. They didn't play zydeco or nothing like that. I picked that up on my own. A lot of the music is just handed down from generation to generation. I grew up listening to a lot of different things, a lot of different styles and been influenced by a lot of different styles. Zydeco was my first love, but I took a lot of things from a lot of different styles of music and tried to put it together. Percussion was one of the things that we've been wanting to do for a long time and it all worked. It all worked hand in hand because zydeco is a rhythmic dance music that is really up-beat, up-tempo sort of stuff. This percussion, a lot of it, works hand in hand with the music to add to the dance feel.

But, my music is just pretty much myself. That's pretty much what we're known for. We play a lot of different styles of music. A lot of the stuff I write is not just traditional sounding stuff. I write a variety of things, and I just wanted to give a bigger variety of what we're capable of doing.

We did a Chevrolet commercial a couple of years ago. The accordion is just another instrument. It can fit with just about anything. Everything is not going to sound like zydeco, but the accordion is an instrument that pretty much fits in with just about everything. I play a button accordion. It's all in one key, the same principle as the single row harmonica. I have G, C, F, B flat, E flat, A, and I also have a D.

We spend a lot of time on the road. Being able to play music and make a living at it, to me, it don't get better than that. Being a musician and knowing that what you have to offer can turn people on, and you're stuck in a situation where you can't get it out. That's more frustrating than anything.

For a long time, people have lived in these small towns and worked and pretty much provided for themselves. You didn't have to go off into the city to make a living. They kind of stay away from that, stay away from the big city.

New Orleans got their thing and we've got ours. It's totally different stuff. Not to say it's that different that you can't get off from doing it, but it's a different world.

LATIN AMERICA/SALSA

While rooted in the Spanish Caribbean and Central America, salsa is another one of those musics that developed in the diaspora, particularly in the melting pot of New York City. Growing predominantly out of the pre-Castro sounds of goodtime Havana, the traditional salsa sound blends a big band type horn section with Afro-Cuban percussion. That paradigm changed very little from the forties to the sixties, when young players raised on rock started to bring their contemporary cultural take into the mix. Players like Willie Colón, Eddie Palmieri and the Fania Allstars began bringing electric guitars, pianos, and basses to shows and sessions, while some musicians opted to eschew the trombones altogether.

A few artists tried to retain some *folklorica* to what they did while still fitting into the general swing of the music. They superimposed jazz and pop and rock into the mix while maintaining the roots of the tradition. Some did it by staying with the old forms in new packages. Some, like Yomo Toro, maintained their connection with their instrument, playing it at such a virtuoso level that it didn't much matter what they played.

Meanwhile, in another hotbed of expatriate Latin music, Miami's heavy-duty Cuban population has created some of the most popular music on the planet, from the pop of the Miami Sound Machine to the high-tech noise of the world perpetrated by Joe Galdo with artists like Angélique Kidjo. Even at it's most pop and Western, this music retains enough of its roots to make it stand out. The roots make it the extraordinary pop that it is, break it away from the bland, add the whiff of exotica that pushes it beyond the run of the mill.

The irony is how this music spread back to countries like Panama, where artists like Ruben Blades had to come to the U.S. to actually make a living playing it. As much as Cajun and zydeco, this is one of America's major contributions to the noise of the world. They're not the only ones by a long-shot.

EMILIO ESTEFAN | MIAMI SOUND MACHINE

Emilio and Gloria Estefan have been the brains and voice of the Miami Sound Machine since the seventies. Their rise and residence on the pop charts parallels a growth and awareness of the Hispanic American community. The most rapidly growing ethnicity in the U.S., with a population growing five times faster than non-Hispanics—30 percent vs. 6 percent—it has already changed the sound of music in the U.S. One of the first pop groups to bring it to the Anglos was the MSM.

Gloria came from Cuba when she was one year old. She was brought up in South Carolina and Texas. At the same time, we are Cuban Americans. We grew up with the two cultures, so for us, it's a lot easier to have that flavor of the Anglo market.

The first album we recorded was bilingual. The first single was in Spanish, and it did real well and we started touring all of Central and South America. I told them, "I think we have a unique sound." They said, "I don't know if people will like it." You get that insecurity from a lot of people. They wanted to play it real safe.

Seven years later, we did "Dr. Beat," again on a Spanish album with two songs in English. That was the B-side of a Spanish release and became #1 in South Korea, and six weeks later was at the top of the dance charts in England, and then went to the top five in England, Germany, France, Poland, and Japan. So we went to promote "Dr. Beat" all over Europe.

We were in a big discotheque and we played "Dr. Beat" and people wanted more, more, more. We didn't have any English material ready, so we played a conga, a real, authentic conga from Cuba. The people just started jumping up and down, they went real crazy.

So Gloria told our keyboard player and music director Tiki, "Why don't we write as song with a conga beat and English lyrics?"

Between Poland and England, Tiki wrote a song. When we got to Miami, we went into the studio. We used a lot of American drums, but we used all the technology and all the guitars and the acoustic piano, all the flavor of the salsa. That's how we got into the whole thing with salsa.

That's what happened to "Conga." I think "Conga" is breakthough music. You feel that in the United States, you feel that in a lot of commercials, in a lot of productions now. You hear a lot of percussion, a lot of timbales, a lot of things that never were used before. All that rhythm from Africa. I think it's great, to incorporate that to the music that's happening now. You have to go with something that's a little bit different.

I think the next wave of great Latin pop probably will come from one of the islands, like the Bahamas. It will be easier coming from one of the islands because it will be more authentic.

What is happening, I don't know what anybody's doing now in terms of production, but I hope that they're doing something unique, that will impress the competition in the States. And you know what the competition is in the States. I hope they do something unique and quality-wise, will be the best quality they can do on the record. If they don't come with the quality and they don't come with a unique sound, it will be hard to do. It could happen. It happens every day. I wish all of them a lot of luck. They have a chance.

That's the reason we live in America, because it's the land of opportunity. Someone asked me, "If they told you twelve years ago that you'd be nominated for a Grammy, would you have believed it?" I said, "I'll tell you the truth, living in America, I believe anything, because your dreams can come true in this country. It's true."

Latin and salsa are great music. I was talking to Celia and it told her one of my biggest dreams would be to produce at least two tracks for her next album. I told her it would be an honor to do it. Because she's great. To me, she's one of the best performers I've ever seen live. She's a great performer and she's a great human being, and that counts for me, too. I think she will sing in Spanish and make it with an American audience, and she will be one of the few who could do a Spanish track and be on Anglo radio, because she is a great performer.

The European market is very open. You listen to the top forty in England, and you listen to maybe a salsa, and you listen to an Indian thing and you listen to jazz. I think that's what is going to be happening in the States. I think it's going to take a long time, but I think it's going to happen, bit by bit.

Radio was very open to us. That's one thing. I have to thank a lot of the radio people. This was the first time we recorded in English. I mean, we did it on our first album, years ago, but the quality was very low budget. We did our own album. It was sort of a demo album. It only cost us two thousand dollars to produce that album. CBS International put it out for us, and they opened the doors for us and they were very open to play new music.

The first production I did by myself was "Dr. Beat." I used to be the co-producer with Pepe Luis Soto. He was the guy who did Celi Bee. He was one of the guys who did our first Spanish albums. Except for the first album. That was done by me and this guy from Miami, his name is Carlo Oliva. He has a group there, the Gorgeous Nephews. And they're great. I saw him last week. He still has the group. I did that album with him. The second album was done by me. I produced the second album. Then the third album we signed with CBS International and they used the producer who used to do Celi Bee and did a song called "Superman Man" years ago.

That's when I went with this big thing to the company: "I think we have a unique sound. Let me just do the album. Let me do at least two tracks on the album." One of them was "Dr. Beat." "Dr. Beat" was so well received that it ended with them saying, "Okay, produce your next album." He wanted to do more ballads type thing. He didn't want to, especially what I was looking to do. I was looking for a lot of percussion, a lot of African instruments, a lot of horns. I had already in my mind, I knew what I wanted at the time. I am a percussionist. But he said, "I don't know if the company is going to like it." So we went with the line. The ballads were very successful. We had four or five number ones in the Spanish market at that time.

Years later, when I produced Matt Bianco, we spent about a quarter of a million. That's very good money. But I love what I did for him. It's one of the songs that I love. It's a combination between Latin music, Brazilian, and jazz. It's very danceable and he did a great delivery on the vocals. It's not real Latin, but it has that influence. It's very danceable.

On "Rhythm Is Going To Get You" we're using a lot of instruments . . . a bata, all the instruments we're using are a lot of African instruments. As opposed to that or "Conga," "Bad Boy" has nothing to do with Latin.

The ballads we record have the highest chart positions. "Can't Stay Away From You" was #1 adult contemporary. So it's a lot of songs that doesn't have to have the flavor of Latin music. Still, I don't know if you know, but on "Can't Stay Away From You" I use a tabla. We did that, and we sampled it in a way that made it sound like a bata.

Living in Miami, you hear everything! You get reggae, black, Latin, salsa, rock and roll, you name it. Music is music. Whether you sing in French, German, it all depends on the acquired taste of people to like it or not like it. I think it's great that everyone will try it to see what happens. It all depends on the production, how they do it, how they focus on the songs. I think the songs are most important.

GLORIA ESTEFAN | MIAMI SOUND MACHINE

One of the world's most beautiful and charming people and performers, Gloria Estefan also has a good sense of her history and heritage. While she will be the first to admit that she made her beginnings singing pop en Español, the massive hit "Conga" gave her the leverage she needed to put more Latin in her music.

Whenever anyone has any success of any kind, or a breakthrough like that—for Hispanics, this is a big breakthrough because before us, nothing's happened since Santana really, that qualifies as a Latin music hit in the United States. Jose Felicano who was before then. It gives everybody a boost, it gives them some hope. Before that, it was like—I remember when we first tried to put out the records, everyone would say, "It's impossible! It's impossible! You'll never do it! There's too much competition in the American market. They'll never take you seriously." We battled that all the way.

Actually, the most Latin song we did was "Conga." Musically, we were pop music in Spanish before. We've grown more Latin in the American market than we have in the Spanish market. Language doesn't make it Latin or not. We were recording pop songs in Spanish before. Emilio always wanted to sound more Latin. At the beginning, when they gave us producers, he always wanted to put more percussion in and do that style, but it always got watered down, because we didn't have complete creative control. When he took creative control in 1984, with "Dr. Beat," that is when our sound really started to come.

Africa is where all the Cuban music comes from, ultimately. "Conga" is an Afro-Cuban beat. And the rhythms are very African, too. We are using rhythms from Santeria, which is an Afro-Cuban religion. It's very religious music, almost like possession. People get possessed by spirits and they dance to this kind of rhythm.

The conga itself, it comes from the Congo River. That's why they call those drums conga drums. They used to tighten them with actual heat in the streets in Cuba. It wasn't like the ones you buy here that are pre-made and stuff. They used frying pans, and anything that would make the sounds.

JOE GALDO, RAFAEL VIGIL, AND LARRY DERMER | THE JERKS

After making their bones as the machine behind the Miami Sound Machine, Joe Galdo, Larry Dermer, and Rafael Vigil went off on their own. While never a solo act, per se, they were the power behind so many Latinate productions and other noise of the world through yesterday, including—individually and collectively—Burning Flames, Angélique Kidjo, Baaba Maal, and Barry Manilow. The name came around as a joke: "We're not important, we're just a bunch of jerks."

JOE GALDO: The reason we call ourselves the Jerks is that everybody in this business thinks they're somebody, everybody walks around with this air of heaviness to them. A lot of it is hype.

RAFAEL VIGIL: Especially in production.

LARRY DERMER: It started off as a joke and we threw it against the wall and it stuck. Then we got nominated for a Grammy Award under the name, and we decided we might as well stick with it now.

GALDO: Rafael and I are Cubans. We have been in rock bands that had Latin material. I've been making records in Miami since the early seventies. I was on a lot of the TK stuff. I was in a band called Foxy, which Larry was part of. But we also worked on all kinds of people, whether it was Betty Wright, Timmy Thomas, KC and the Sunshine Band, the whole stable of the Miami sound, going way back to Bobby Caldwell, all kinds of people.

I was never really close to the really silly disco. Some of the disco stuff that came out of Miami, the real prefab sounding stuff, we didn't do. I think if you look at the music that we do, it has a lot more substance than the stuff that is going out right now. It has a bit of a Latin tinge, but it lacks any kind of oomph. Listen to the Miami Sound Machine, listen between the grooves, and you'll hear something beyond the dance market out there right now. Songwriting, as well as performing and arranging.

Foxy used to do a lot of Latin material on our albums. We had Tito Puente's son, Richie Puente as our percussionist. Rafael was up here [in New York] in a rock band who did a lot of Latin, too.

VIGIL: It was a rock and roll band, but every now and again, we'd write a Latin thing and throw it in.

GALDO: We realized that Latin music, the rhythm of it, is something that gets people up, whether it puts a smile on their face, puts them on the dance floor. It's just like reggae music, or Brazilian; you just hear a sort of music, and all of a sudden, you're in a different place.

VIGIL: The first thing we did together was "Mucho Money" and we discussed how we should write songs. Our idea at the time was very primitive drums—see we weren't thinking per se Latin, thought that came out because of the blood, I guess—we were thinking very primitive drums, a lot of percussion, with very high tech sounds. At the time, there was nothing like that.

GALDO: Primitive and future. Now, it's a big thing to do. We were doing it way back.

VIGIL: We weren't thinking Latin, but with the Miami Sound Machine stuff, the Latin flavor fit it all of a sudden. Here was the band known for the Latin thing. Actually, it was very good chemistry. What they were looking for, we had, and what we were looking for, they had.

GALDO: They had a record deal, we had music. Great marriage.

When we decided we wanted to look for things on our own, and we walked up to the presidents of record labels and we told them the same thing we're telling you now. Some of these people would say, "These guys have to be bullshitting me. I don't know who these people are. And they're telling me they did all this playing and production and arranging. Yet, on the record, I don't really see their names as doing such." Sometimes they would call the Sound Machine office and double check. That really bothered the shit out of me.

DERMER: Basically, I think the documentation on that speaks for itself. If you look at the previous albums, before our services were enlisted, you could be able to tell the difference from that point to *Primitive Love* and *Let It Loose*, which are the records we did.

GALDO: We did "Dr. Beat," too. That was our first involvement. Then, when it came time to do the next record, Emilio came over to my house to hear a jingle we were going to do for them. We had some songs we were writing for an exercise record. *Salsasize*. It was going to be called. "Mucho Money" came from the *Salsasize* record. "Movies," too. We did "Bad Boys" for a black artist locally. None of it had been out yet, so Emilio made a deal with the people. "Bad Boys" was supposed to go to *Salsasize*, it was our music, our publishing, everything, so we gave it to him. The Miami Sound came from that project.

You know what really did it for us? Computers. A lot of musicians—and I don't blame them for saying what they do—really come down on computers, usually for two reasons: because they've never caught on to the technology, and it's intimidating to them, because a lot of them have lost work because of it.

Had it not been for technology, I would have been a studio drummer for the rest of my life. What people used to hire me for was not just to play drums. I would go in there and arrange the rhythm section. The producer would say, come in here and play drums for me. Then they'd go back home, or take their kid to school, or work on their boats, then they'd come back, and I'd have the whole kit and caboodle ready for them, they'd pat me on the back, say, "Good job. Here's a couple of hundred dollars for playing on the track." And that was it.

Then computers started coming along, and there was no doubt as to who did the actual creative work. It was all done in my house, in my living room, in the garage. It helped us get our feet in the door, because now we weren't just sidemen, we were arrangers, and from arrangers we went to writing, but no writing until we met Rafael, because until you can make it into a song, no one wants to hear a music track. So we love computers. We hate computer sounding music . . .

DERMER: All computers did was gave us the ability to record our ideas before we walked into the studio, where someone else would grab all the credit.

GALDO: That's a real sore point with me. I'm so tired of the wrong people getting the credit. If we hire you to do a background vocal, we will put your name there. There are so many people who don't do that, including our ex-employers. They want to scam the world.

VIGIL: Another thing that sets us off, and there's a big Miami thing about this, it's the "producers" who own the project, lock, stock, and barrel. And they make all the money, and the artist doesn't make any money. That pisses us off too. We're not in that boat. Although we're from Miami, we're not in that. There are a lot of track acts. I think that's totally wrong. We're producers, but we're producers who were musicians, so we've been stuck in many ways throughout the years. So we don't want to stick the musicians.

We would like the people to know that we have done a lot of work. But at the same time, we don't want to take it away from Emilio and his rap, and we certainly don't want to take it away from Gloria, who deserves . . .

DERMER: Everything!

VIGIL: As producers, we don't want to take too much from the musicians. That's why we're the Jerks. Yet arrangement-wise, playing-wise, creative-wise, you're looking at them.

JON SECADA

As Cuban Americans go, Jon Secada is unusual to say the least. He arrived from Cuba in the early seventies, no mean feat. He has a master's degree in music from the University of Miami and spent five years teaching in the public schools before two of his college buddies brought him into the Miami Sound Machine sphere of influence. After several years of paying his dues as a backing vocalist, both live and on record, he wrote the Gloria Estefan hit "Out of the Dark", and has since written well over a dozen award-winning songs, won two Grammy Awards, and helped the careers of a new generation of Latino stars including Jennifer Lopez and Ricky Martin. We spoke in 1992, before the rise of Mandela and the fall of apartheid, just one of the issues we dealt with in a wide-ranging talk.

My family left Cuba in the early seventies. It was kind of difficult to leave, but my parents somehow did it. You had to go through this big political agenda and bureaucratic process, but eventually, through the paperwork and the money and the things you had to go through, they let us go, but it was a pain to do it.

They just wanted to raise me in a different environment. I'm an only child, and they just weren't happy with the way things were there. That's the reason we left. That's the reason they wanted to take me out of Cuba. Coming into a new state and making a new start is tough.

My music doesn't really have a Cuban feel to it at all, actually. It's more the underlying percussion aspect that's in there that gives it a little bit of that Latin taste, but it's definitely hidden in the arrangement and very, very understated. It's just a little bit of the percussion in some of the tracks that gives it that Latin flair, but that's about it.

Now that I have a career in both languages, sometimes I want to keep it separate. Some songs work well in either language, but some songs you have to start from scratch in one language or the other. They're good adaptations. They're not really translations, but they're good adaptations. They kind of keep the feel and vibe of the song. But they're different songs altogether. That's what you're after. Otherwise, it's not fair to the song, not fair to the language.

Crossing over to as many formats as you can is incredible, and for me to now have a career in both English and Spanish is great. You can really see it when you tour and do gigs. You really get a good crossover audience during shows.

I think it's the responsibility of any Latin artist to really promote and allow the culture, to allow the Latin community to have the respect that it always should have. As a member of a Latin community who has crossed over to the pop American market, it's great to be able to be an example in that way, a positive example and a form of encouragement and respect for other Latin people.

One way is just by example. The fact that we can talk about it, and the fact that my music has crossed over to the Latin market and I can talk and do interviews and reach the Latin people. Them seeing me in that kind of light, being in both markets and making it in both markets, it's a credit to what the American dream is all about for the Latin community. It's a great opportunity.

Having hits in Singapore, Indonesia, Malaysia, I never expected to cross over to so many territories. Man, I'm excited about it. It's great. In fact, we're going to Japan and Southeast Asia. I'm very happy with the way my career has taken over so many different countries.

I'm going to go to South Africa, which I'm really, really excited about. I'm going to be not only crossing over all these territories as a black Latino man, but also speaking my mind and saying how I feel and being an example and working and trying to succeed and bring my music across to all these people. It's really special, and it's the responsibility of every Latin artist.

The record company left it up to me. They told me, "The record is doing well there, do you want to go to South Africa and promote?"

I didn't have to go, but I jumped on the opportunity immediately. I really wanted to go there and express myself there. If I'm asked questions about how I feel, politically or otherwise, I'll talk about it.

It's my responsibility as an artist to do stuff like that, to try and reach out to people and talk to people and say how you feel. Especially being black, Latin, and in my situation being from Cuba. That kind of puts the whole thing into a different perspective, coming from an oppressed country and going to a place that also has that form of oppression, in this case apartheid. It's a good angle for me. I really want to do this, and when they told me about it, I jumped on it immediately. If approached with questions about apartheid and things, I will speak my mind and express how I feel and my concerns about the situation. Also my concerns about the world, humanity, how I feel about Castro, how I feel about oppression. I probably never will write anything that's political, but given the opportunity to talk about how I feel, I definitely jump on it.

I still have a lot of family in Cuba. Apart from sending them stuff, and hoping that it gets there, that's all I can do. That's all anyone can do. You're really limited. You can't really reach family down there.

I lucked out. I completely lucked out. I got my record contract in English. The record company didn't know I could do anything in Spanish at all. It was an experiment to do those two songs in Spanish, just to see how well they would do. As a result, I have a career in both English and Spanish, so I can't complain. I'm doing all right. In this business, you're here today, gone tomorrow, and if you don't invest your money wisely while you have it . . . that's dangerous.

EMMANUEL

This Mexican pop star would have rather been a bullfighter. Hugely popular in his native country since the mid-seventies, his music is informed by soul, R&B, and gospel as much as his Mexican roots. He tried to bring his talents to a wider, English speaking audience, but it was one of the few things that just didn't work out.

Trying to break into the English market is a challenge. When I started to sing, I decided on my goals, and I decided to sing in all the world and all the countries, and one of my goals, my most important goal, was the American market.

A lot of people ask me why, if you've got your gold in the Latin market, why try to get into other places and other worlds, and it's because you want it. That's all. You want to sing in Germany and Italy and Japan and China and the United States.

You must work. You have to work a lot and there's a lot of challenge and there's a lot of things that you must do. But if you can make it in the United States, you can make it in all the world. It is the most important challenge, the United States. So I'm going to have to sing in English.

I don't think I'm going to have problems singing in English. I think there's no problem between the artist and the audience. These are minor problems, the contact you have with your audience. The big problems are in the media that have to believe in you to launch you. The record companies. Those are the people you have to convince. Once you convince them, their job is to convince the radio. Your job is to convince everybody. But if you don't have the people who can launch you, you cannot work.

I started to be a bullfighter when I was fifteen years old. It's in my heritage. My father was a bullfighter. My voice is also my heritage, also. My mother was a singer. So the art comes from both my father and my mother. My grandfather was a dancer. One of the greatest dancers in the history of Spain. So the art came from the family.

I wanted to be a bullfighter when I was thirteen years old. I started when I was fifteen. I was fighting for about three years, then a bull broke my two knees. I had two operations and the doctor said I had to stop. It took three years in the hospitals trying to fix the kneecap and the ligaments. The bull gored me. A year after the first operation, when I settled down, the operation didn't work right and one knee failed and a bull broke the other knee. It was horrible. I started fighting the doctors.

When the doctor said I cannot fight, I started to sing. It wasn't a problem to me, becoming a singer. I used to play at being a singer when I was little. I'd play at being a singer; I'd play at being a bullfighter.

The world of the bullfighter is a very passionate life. You have a very, very passionate life. You play with your life; you play with danger. You have to do the art with the bull, the danger, and yourself. You must create the art. It's very heavy, it's difficult, but it's beautiful. It's very, very beautiful.

The thing I want to do is American music. If we can introduce something really original, our things from the Latin market, if we could put some of that into the music, it would be good. This is my chance. Not because the time of the Latin market is working now. This is my time as a singer.

It's good that now everybody is open for this market. I came at the right moment. But I didn't try to find the right moment. I tried to find *my* moment.

YOMO TORO

The master of the Puerto Rican folk instrument the cuatro, Yomo Toro has had his own TV show, preformed on countless Latin records, and still lives in the South Bronx. One of the true virtuosos, he remains little known, but to see him play is to be amazed by the speed and fire of a master.

Jíbaro is a music from the mountains of Puerto Rico. Because I'm a Jíbaro, I put some flavor there, too. I don't want to lose the feeling. Everybody who was born in a country, that music belongs to that person. This person wants to put the flavor of his music in everything he does. That's what happened to me. Sometime, I put a little feeling of my beginnings and life into my music and recordings. Because music is music. Music is beauty, and everybody in the whole world likes music. No matter where you come from, there's music. So I got to put a little bit of that, too.

When I learned to play, it was not my guitar, because I was very poor. I was a poor kid in a poor town. I learned with somebody else's cuatro. But I'm lefty, and all those other guys were righty, so I learned like this, with the thing upside down. I remember one time, I was playing a show here in New York, and this big guy, the leader of the Los Panchos Trio from Mexico, he played cuatro too, and he was righty. First time he saw me in the back stage, I picked up his guitar and started playing it from the left side. He told me, "What happened to you, you are a lefty and you play the righty guitar. That's no good. Don't do that." But then he heard what I was doing with the guitar, he told me, "Forget about it. Stay like that. Don't change it."

I play opposite, but I don't think people notice it. I don't think they care about the difference. They hear the music. I'm a lefty and I play with a righty guitar. The chords are against me. This means I have half the facility that a righty playing would have. But I still play it. This means I have to be one and a half guitar players good! Or just half! If I'd learned with a lefty guitar, I probably would be much better. Then the talent that I have in my mind and in my hands and me would be double guitar good.

I'm the only person around who plays the cuatro professionally. There was never a cuatro in any other band, any sort of music, just Yomo Toro playing. I came with the idea, and I entered the bands as a kid, playing the cuatro, and all those bands started making it with that cuatro sound. Like Willie Colón. One of the biggest LPs that he made, he made with me playing the cuatro. I didn't get that much credit, but I grew a big name. People know. That's a standard record, forever. People break it, they go out and get a new one. *Asalto Navideño*, that's the name of the record. I worked with Celia Cruz; I did four volumes with Willie Colón; I made very big hits. Fania All Stars gave me a gold record.

All the Spanish people, they know me. I have a big name here in Spanish. There's no doubt about that. But this is a small market. This is a market of a hundred and fifty thousand people. From those a hundred and fifty thousand people, two hundred thousand people, there is just a little amount that buys records. There are a lot of groups around, a lot of competition around. To make a hit, is very hard. You sell twenty thousand LPs around here in New York, and you've made a hit! Which is a small amount. It's nothing!

I was recording a lot, as a side musician, with all those groups in Spanish, you know? And then I recorded with Edie Gorme and Los Panchos Trio, but that was as a side musician, too.

I've played in the same group with Mongo Santamaria. I played with Tito Puente a lot. I even did a commercial with Tito. One for Crest toothpaste. I've done commercials for café Goya. A lot of things.

I did some albums as a leader before, but that was on very small companies. There was one label called Panoramic. I think I did around four albums with them. I did one for ABC/Paramount. That was a big one, but that was in like 1960, around there. *The Spanish World of Yomo Toro*, something like that. I did one before that with Cameo records, called *What a Guitar*. But that was a long time ago.

With small companies, like Panoramic, Ansonia, BMC records, all these companies I did some stuff, but these companies don't go too far. Those companies don't distribute to American stores. They stay with the Spanish markets, always. With the small stores. Those records that I do, they never travel too much. I did one with Fania records. That was salsa. Just salsa. I did that with a band, there were thirteen, fourteen musicians with me. But that was salsa. At the time that I did that record, Fania quit. They couldn't work the album because they went down, the whole company went down the drain.

When you go to that monster market which is America, and Europe and things like that, that's a giant. Everybody's dream is there.

The Island records are going to be in the hands of everybody. Everybody is going to have the opportunity to hear the records and hear about the record. Maybe the people will hear the record and start to like it. That is the worst trouble, to try and jump to this giant market, and I feel very happy.

The other day I did a jam with Kevin Eubank. We were supposed to do Salsa Meets Jazz. But that was no Salsa Meets Jazz, that was a jam. We start the music, everybody stopped playing, just him and me alone. He did one solo, I did the other solo, I did one, he did four. I was looking for trouble. I almost had it. He's good, man! I was looking for trouble with him. He got very hot, and when he got very hot, I was scared. He's great. He's a very good musician, and a young kid, which is very important.

The records that I did with Island Records is my dream. With this album, I can go very far. I can show audiences that there's one Yomo Toro around.

I've been playing around for a long time. All my life, I've been very disappointed. Not disappointed with the music, disappointed with the life. Sometimes I feel depressed. I know I have the talent, but I don't know how to get to the big audiences. I'm struggling.

Photograph: Chuck Pulin

WILLIE COLÓN

El primero salsero. Willie Colón has been at least partly instrumental in many of the musical innovations in salsa. His band was a breeding ground of talent in next generation salsa, salsa that moved from the strict big-band horn sound that informed Cuban music in the forties to more modern music. Ironically, many of his former sidemen talk about their erstwhile boss as if he were the dinosaur. Willie, however, remains a maverick.

Salsa is an American music. First of all, you can't forget that the United States and Canada are not alone in this hemisphere. You're just surrounded. And they're going to keep coming. Florida was founded, there are old colonies of Latinos there since before there was the United States. All the way up to Montana was part of Mexico for some time. We've been here for a long time, the Latin culture.

Of all the "foreign" cultures, the one the U.S. knows the best and is the most comfortable with is the Hispanic culture. It's just osmosis. You listen to any commercial on the TV, it's got conga drums and little shakers. It's accepted to be Latin. It's been here for a long time. We're the minority they know the best.

Salsa was only a New York music at one time. This is where it was born. There was tropical music, they used to call it Afro-Cuban music and mambo and stuff like that, but salsa came from New York. It was different. It was me, Ricardo Rey, Eddie Palmieri, the first guys to really give it that twist and mix these different kinds of genres.

Somewhere along the line, when they closed Cuba off, they were in the middle of this big band thing, Jimmy Dorsey, that sort of thing. When that got cut off, it got frozen in time like something out of the bible, a ritual that everyone would perform; "Oh, we're starting a salsa band, you need four trumpets, blah, blah, blah." Like something from *I Love Lucy*. But I think, if the geopolitical things that did occur hadn't occurred, the music would have progressed parallel. Cuban music would have progressed. And since everyone gauged what this music is supposed to be by its Cuban predecessor, they stayed hung up on the big band concept. But if [the embargos] hadn't happened, it would have had a rock group. It would have been exactly parallel, but it wasn't able to happen.

I don't think there was much of a possibility, when I was growing up, of going into rock or anything. The world wasn't ready for me yet. Salsa was the path of least resistance for me.

But to me there was no conflict, no contradiction with mixing some bamba and plana with Cuban, or copying a line from the Beatles. I just lived all of it. It was integral in my makeup, my musical programming. So early on, I found experimenting would work for me, being raised biculturally and bilingually. In New York, it works for me. There's so much to draw from.

When we started doing the experiments, they kind of stopped and said, "Now wait a minute, you're messing with our shit." So that was good for us.

I first used a synthesizer in 1976, on *Angelitos Negros*. That was when they had those first kind of Moog things that looked like an operator's switchboard and made a little dinky sound, like a Casio does now. My last album had some synths on it. I've had my own little electronics studio and worked with synths since 1984. It's weird. As soon as I stopped being the main trombone player, it gave me more flexibility. It changed my instrumentation. The more singing I did, the less dependent the sound was on my trombone playing. I think that my putting in the synths and the funky sax kind of tied me into mainstream music, because that's not there. The kind of crew that I was looking for had to do with the change in the sound. I was looking for kids with an Hispanic background, but that were playing other genres, like funk and jazz. The only real *salseros* I had was the rhythm section. So that kind of explains it.

My track record can become a detriment, excess baggage, because I found that going with RCA and Sonotone and A&M, multinationals—I'm so independent, I'm used to saying when do you want the record by, and that's it. I'm not used to people going over budgets with me and sitting down and picking out my material, "Let me hear what you're doing," or coming into the studio. This kind of derails me a little. What I do is instinctive. So I found that it was not a good environment for me as an artist. If I was signed just as an artist, I kind of suffered under another producer, because that's what I am. I was not happy, and it led to a rebellious attitude. I was not able to survive at RCA or A&M. At Fania, they never even ask what the record is going to be about. There's no discussion, it's "When can you have it?" and that's it. That's how I do my best work.

I maintain my independence; I maintain my international licenses. A veteran with so many years in the business, it's kind of scary for a record company, because they can't get me that cheap. I may not be as profitable as some of the youngbloods. Where I could be the most use to a record company like that is as an executive producer, in artist development, in that kind of capacity. I don't think there's anybody out there that has a feeling for both cultures like I do.

When you make a mistake in the record business, it's usually very costly. That's why I wound up with Fania. With them, there is no doubt that I can hit a home run. At least as far as what they need.

The market is always changing. It's not a stable thing. Whenever I think, "Whoa, that was a big hit, let me do that again," it never works. It's like surfing. You have to be on the right part of the wave to ride it.

I never wanted to cross over, just for the sake of crossing over. I just wanted to make a certain kind of music. I've always been a very music-oriented person. That's why I take so long with the production and the arrangements. The music has to be right. I'm selling music. I have to reconcile doing a really professional recording, straddle the line between something that will do well commercially and something I can be proud of musically. I think that being third generation, I'm totally bicultural. I have no problem with either of the cultures, and that kind of makes the music I create something that is bicultural.

If I were to just alter everything I'm doing, and just change course for a crossover, even if I were to make it there, there's no real foundation to support it. I think that it has to be a precedent of events, something to base it on so you can continue what you are doing. The music I am doing is nothing that is not spontaneous. I've got a good feeling for it. I know what works.

There's a little contradiction in trying to do salsa music and heading for the crossover. I think that maybe there's a junction up ahead, but we can't head straight towards a crossover, because people are not ready.

Some of the things that make salsa what it is are not going to allow it to be a mainstream pop kind of bubble-gum music. First, we have the language thing, and we're going to have to address that. Are you going to do salsa in English? Anything can work, but it has to be done organically. It has to be worked out slowly. I've heard a lot of those monstrous experiments, and they lack any kind of coherence or spark.

The crossover I was looking for was I wanted to make salsa a pan-American music.

I've used reggae feelings. When I started mixing all these musics together the veterans started saying, "You can't do this. It's not right. It's got to have a clave, it's this it's that." But I found it worked real good for me. I started writing a kind of bass line that would tie all the rhythms together that would run through the rhythm changes. That kind of helped to give me a different sound, a different concept. It was good. I was able to make some kind of music that anybody could dance to.

I said, why not? I got into the Brazilian thing because Brazil, they speak Portuguese and not Spanish, they live a segregated life. There is not a flow culturally. And it's a tremendous country. It's so big, and it has excellent music and lyrics, but it doesn't seep through. It doesn't get through to our stuff. So I started translating a lot of Brazilian songs, and bringing in these different chordal modes and stuff.

I felt it was really necessary for the music to evolve and to continue, and I really got tired of these I, IV, V changes. I found that so limiting that I had to change it. It's just part of salsa. Salsa differs from the other things. There are different chord progressions, different rhythms together and the lyrics are not about grass shacks and cows and cutting sugar cane.

So the II, Vs, and the cycle of fifths and stuff. Just breaking up the structure of the music and using the components of it. Using a little chorus and a long verse using the cycle of fifths. It would really knock the people out. And the musicians. I started having jazz guys coming over to see the group, because they thought it was some genius group. We didn't even know what the hell we were doing. A couple of my first records were Latin jazz instrumentals.

I've done stuff about Napoleonic generals, I've done stuff about the nuclear age that got Arabs and Republicans mad at me. With Ruben. Ruben was one of the most political writers that I ever worked with. There were times when Ruben had to wear a bulletproof vest.

In order for kids to relate to the music, it has to be put into a mainstream format, without losing the honesty or the swing or the purpose of the music. The cavemen used the rock and a stick for a hammer, but we have more specialized tools to do the same job better. Times change, and the music has to be brought up to the twentieth century. That's why I made a small, nine-piece group. It's very electronic. I have some funk and jazz players in it, a good musical cross-section.

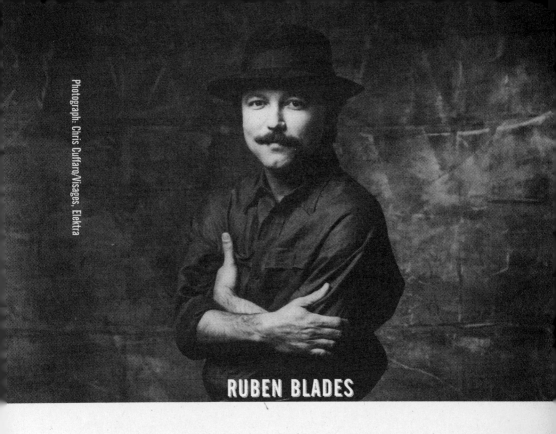

Photograph: Chris Cuffaro/Visages, Elektra

RUBEN BLADES

A remarkably intelligent, well-educated, and talented man, with law degrees from both his native Panama and Harvard University, Ruben Blades chooses show business over the other pursuits, even though he could become president of Panama by acclaim. As a musician, he moved out of Colon's band and brought salsa, and Hispanic music in general, to a level of mainstream critical acceptance few have enjoyed.

My grandfather came to Panama from the West Indies. He came from St. Lucie. He was an Englishman, citizenshipwise. I don't know how he got to St. Lucie, but a lot of people from the West Indies went to Panama during the construction of the canal, and during the period preceding the opening of the canal, and during the period of the canal itself, because in terms of that particular area, it was the place that provided jobs. That's why you have a lot of Panamanians who have their first names in Spanish and last names in English, like Mauricio Smith, is a very good sax player and flute player. You get names like Rod Carew, who's also from Panama, Ben Ogilvie, Orlando Woolridge, who plays basketball.

For many years, before I got to visit the countries, lot of Latin American DJs called me Blah-days [the correct Spanish pronunciation for the way he spells his name]. It's okay. It doesn't bother me because I sometimes say Blah-days. I always wait to see how the other person pronounces it. Then I follow suit. I don't have any problem with that. But for people who want to know, who ask me, it's Blades, and that's the reason why.

The salsa field is so full of guys who like to play jazz and like to play all types of music, and yet the format is very limited to the repetition of the sound structure that came from Cuba, and/or the formats of the big band that was modeled still following the Cuban format or structure of melodies, etc., with an opening, singing, a break, a *coro* [refrain, chorus], a *soneja*, which is the inspiration of the singer, followed by a mambo, the followed by a coro, more sonejo, and a coda.

I couldn't really write down all the sonejas in my songs and type them in English, because then we would run out of space. We wouldn't be able to write everything, at least not in a legible or readable format. So, what I do, basically, is present the gist of the song, meaning all the lyrics in the front of the song, and leave the rest. Some people ask, but I take the position that people who do not speak Spanish will listen to the melodic turns of the sonejas. And will get a feel for what it is. I wish, someday, I'd be able to write the whole thing down, because you do miss part of the intent of the song.

What happened to me was something that happens to everybody in every field. We're working, we play music, but we also have to deal with the commercial aspect of what we do. After I worked with Willie Colón and I went into the experimental phase, I was using synthesizers. When you break from the brass and you go into synthesizers or vibes or whatever, it throws a lot of people off. They are so accustomed to the dynamics of the brass sections, in that particular style of arranging, that whenever they hear something else they are put into the position where they have to hear it a lot in order to become more comfortable with it.

It's really a matter of information in my opinion. Everything is a matter of information. It has to do with information, and you can fall into a discussion, an argument, which was first, the chicken or the egg? What is more necessary? Information? Do you need the company to push the record? Do you need the DJ to play it? They say that people don't like it. Well, is it that people don't like it or that they haven't had an opportunity to listen to it?

If any radio station in the United States, that has a powerful signal and has a public that tunes into this particular radio station, if in the format, whatever they play, whether it's country, rock, or jazz, if they, for instance, were to play an opera cut, if they were to play *Madame Butterfly* and they put it on rotation, chances are it's going to become a hit. People are going to hear it; they're going to be listening to it. Play something twenty times a day, and you're going to find a public for it. The problem that we've had, and I find that it's a general problem, as an example, I give you Kid Creole and the Coconuts. They record, and because they don't fit a format, they're not played. Now that can be the format of the company, and it can also a kind of mental format they have, in the sense that whatever is alien is also considered to be alien to others. The decision's being made by the record programmer and the DJ or both.

If people are not allowed to listen, then that also contributes to the anonymity of the music, not necessarily from a lack of response from the general audience. Latin music has been around forever. How can you make out that, in New York, for instance, you don't have an FM salsa radio station? Or that people who play rock music, or whatever, totally ignore the 2.5 million Latins that are here? And everything then, all of a sudden, becomes ghettoized. That's why I once said, next thing you know, you're going to have colored dials. You want black music, go to the black dial on the radio. That's absurd. Music should not have that problem.

Panama has access to the ocean on both sides, meaning we have ports on both sides. We constantly receive music from all over the whole world. The DJs in Panama played whatever the hell they wanted to play. There wasn't a guy telling them you can't play Chinese music, and you cannot play rock and roll, and you can only play Panamanian music or within the Panamanian structure of music, you can only play salsa music. Nobody told them that, so you would listen to all kinds of things. You would listen to Nat "King" Cole, then, depending on the DJ, you could listen to Duke Ellington, then you could listen to Tito Puente and then you listen to the Beatles. And that's the way I grew up, so I didn't have that hang-up, as to like I can only listen to this and I've only been born to play this. I never had that problem.

Politically, there is no perfect country in Latin America, but that doesn't have any effect on the music that's played on the radio, at least not in Panama. In Cuba, it was a bit different at one point, because of the particular ideology of the country's leadership. Some felt at some point in Cuba that jazz and rock were representative of certain type of society, and they tried to prevent that music from becoming popular to the point that it could obscure or defeat the Cuban music in itself, or place Cuban music in a degree of subordination, but that line of thought disappeared after a while, because it proved impossible to prevent Cubans from listening to the transmissions that were coming from Miami, and in general from being aware of what was going on all around them. As a result, music in Cuba has continued to grow. Whereas in other areas in Latin America, it is simply derivative or stagnant in terms of progress, in Cuba you have a lot of different groups. You've got Irakere, for instance. They really went all the way, in terms of jazz and Latin, even further than I would have thought to be necessary.

But in Panama, in terms of music, people continue to listen to whatever they want. You would not be surprised if you listened to Panamanian radio, and first you hear a jazz tune, then you hear a salsa tune, then you hear a cumbia. Pretty much the same freedom, musicwise.

What I wanted to demonstrate is that it's a choice that one makes. It does not mean that one has forgotten, or rejected that background or considers that background to be beneath our interest or whatnot. It's just our way of going back and saying these have been choices I've been making musically, but we can still go back to the 'bone and play like anybody else plays.

A lot of times we don't necessarily go for what we need, but rather what we want, and what we want does not necessarily respond to any practical need. I was just trying to present objects that would seem to be so out of place in the context of a jungle or what people that live in that kind of surroundings would actually need. I mean who would need French panties in the middle of the Amazon. But it's just that little wild side of the entrepreneur, the native there, that picks up what he thinks is going to do well, and then you have this incredibly contradictory situation, of stuff people bring. You'd think that people in the jungle have no need for a *Playboy*. It's just the way it goes. It's part of that surreal atmosphere that kind of exists all over Latin America.

You live in the midst of the absurd. You can have five presidents in two years. You can wake up one day and find out that somebody has declared that only people whose last names begin with D are going to be citizens. Nothing can surprise you in Latin America. You've seen a lot of stuff. What would create a short circuit in the mind of a Norwegian would perhaps not even provoke a raised eyebrow in Latin America, because it's part of what happens every day. You never know what's going to happen.

We *react* to the unusual. We don't ignore it, but it also doesn't scare us to the point of attributing it to some sort of supernatural value. It's just that this is the way it is. And the solutions to these problems are very much dictated by that kind of grasp on the ridiculous. It would seem to be a society that is very unusual, but I find that it's very normal. When there are certain things you know can happen, you grow up not being stunned by certain things that would, in a Western civilization concept, provoke a lot of thought, and a lot of analysis. Over there it's, "So it rains for forty-four days in a row. So the guy that was building this ark stopped after the fortieth day, and now that's where he's going to live." So you've got a guy who lives in an ark, and nobody gives a shit about it. Here, it would probably make the cover of *Time*.

I moved to America from Panama in 1974. I came here and stayed. It was a mixture of things. I had been working in a bank in Panama as an attorney. I didn't like my job. I liked music, always did. I figured, in my life, I've always asked myself what is it that I'd be happy doing, and music was the thing that I wanted to try. And that's why I came over. After a while I decided that I would stay. My family was living in Miami at the time, so I figured, I'd be in New York and they'd be in Miami. If my family had been in Panama, I don't know how things would have worked.

My band's original name was Seis De Solar, Six from the Tenement. Now there are nine, and you get a lot of people asking why is it six when there are nine? (Wasn't that a Jimi Hendrix song?) So I hope I realized that problem by calling it Son De Solar, which is a word play as well. *Son* means they are from, but *Son* is a word that also means sound. Sound from the tenement. And that resolved the predicament of how many people I was going to have in the band. Originally there were six, then there were seven, and now, with the two 'bones added, there are nine, and with me, ten. So it's like, let's call it that and save ourselves the constant explanation.

What I personally wanted to do was to present the possibility of a work by a salsa musician in English where I wasn't trying to create some watered down project that could then be accessible to Anglos. I just wanted to demonstrate that I could sing and/or play any kind of rhythm, or any kind of direction within pop structures or the rock structures. That's why you have a reggae, a kind of Latin jazz piece, a doo-wop, you piece with a Brazilian rhythm percussion section. You have different elements in it. Next I'm going to try to blend in more of the Afro-Cuban background, and the reason I'm going to do that is that it's easier for me to play with my own band than it is to have two different groups formed if I am to tour.

I have a good sense of humor, but many people don't even know that because they are not real close to me, or close enough to know the differences between the performer and the person. But when I write songs, I choose to tackle themes that are usually not addressed, nor sung, nor presented by singers, particularly in salsa. That brought with it a certain weight, in that many people see me and think of me as sort of a singer/politician, and they tend to judge me very rigidly because of that. I project a certain rigidity, which has to do with the themes that I choose. So on every record, especially albums that come on alternates, I try to make it a bit lighter. But I always try to include a song or two that would maintain that direction of analysis, of confrontation, in the work.

There are comments there about my neighborhood, about my family, memories of women I've been involved with, break-ups, etc. It's all pretty much a Panamanian part of reality, the difficulty of the man and the woman in terms of the relationship, not knowing what is expected of one, not knowing what one is supposed to do. I have a lot of affection for those things I write about. Even the things that bother me. For instance, one of the most difficult songs I've ever written was "*Disaperones*," "Disappearances," which was on the *Buscando America* album. But even in there, there is something about the subject matter that at the same time it hurts, it also gives me a nice feeling in that I think of all of these people as people. I don't think of them as numbers or statistics, and in the empathy that I feel I find that there is hope because I think others will also make that connection and feel for the characters in that song. By creating that feeling, or not creating, but creating the conditions that allow that feeling to be expressed, or accepted, identified, right there, in my opinion, lies a hope for re-addressing the situation and the prevention of the situation in the future. Or at least take the wind out of those who use violence as a way of shaping emotions or intelligences.

I find problems, very obvious problems, here when you are a musician, particularly in this country. In Latin America we have them, but they're different. Here, the problem is, to what degree are you going to be controlled by the media, that has been led also by the record company, to what degree are they going to have control over what you do, and how are you going to reconcile the trappings of fame, of money, or attention that are bestowed upon you because of your success. You'd find yourself in a very difficult position if what you were doing was unfocused politically, or you didn't really understand, or you had a very naive perception of the problems, or you really just wanted to make a certain mention of them, but not really get into it or whatnot, because you're stuck with a label, and then you're also stuck with the repercussions of what you've done.

I know I'm going to return to Panama eventually. I'm going to work in Panama, and there's going to be a point in my life when I'm not going to be involved in music, and I'm not going to be involved in movies, I'm going to be involved working on Panama. In what capacity, we'll see. But it is very clear to me that I'm not doing all this to make the cover of *People* or to make the cover of *Rolling Stone*. That is not what I want.

I will do everything in my power to, at the same time, take advantage of the platform that I have, to express points of view responsibly, and points of view that are really connected to my lifestyle and over which I have total control. There's no publicist that is going to start saying what I should say and what I shouldn't say, and what picture is approved and what picture is not approved, and what I should wear and who's going to do the lights in my show. I don't have those problems. I still walk the streets. I am very popular with most Latins, but they don't bother me in that sense because I never let it go to the point where, all of a sudden, I'm this star. I never played that.

Other people, for instance, who have been singing about the everyday man, and the working class and this and that, all of a sudden find themselves with twenty million fucking dollars! And the question is what are they going to do now? Because you can only talk and sing for so long. There is only so much you can do, and you've got to be aware of that. And then at some point you've got to *do* something. Someone is going to come up to you try and define you and say, "What are you, a socialist?" or "Are you a communist?" or whatever. Or they're going to attack you. That's what's going to end up happening at some point. You've got to define yourself in some way. That doesn't mean that. I've been accused many times of being a communist and the other person accuses you of being this, you're always going to find that, because of what I write about. I can sit down and have arguments with everybody, with the communists, with the fascists, with whomever. But I know who I am, and I know what I'm going to do, and I stand behind that.

I don't depend on a label, I don't depend on a publicist, and I don't depend on the mind of someone who created me. Nobody created me in that sense. So I don't have that problem. But I see others who are going to have that problem, because all of a sudden they reach that place where it's a very tough contradiction.

I find it very difficult for people with nowhere else to go, or people who only do one thing. I have absolutely no qualms about becoming a writer at some point and working for a newspaper. I can try to write a script or a play. I have a lot of different interests.

What happens is we all tend to think in absolutes. We all tend to make images of people according to what we hear and like or dislike of them. It's a little like, who can imagine their parents making love, you know? It's that kind of thing. You ascribe to your parents this authority; they become these figures of authority. I'm not saying that people see me as their parent, but we all do that. Sometimes you hear somebody talking very seriously, or somebody that assumes or is given a certain responsibility, and all of a sudden we tend to look at them from this perspective of seriousness, and we think the person doesn't laugh, or the person doesn't have any other things that they're interested in. Then we're very surprised to find out that they collect comic books or something that we don't consider to be that serious.

It's like some people think that doing film is not that serious. Like, why am I doing movies? And my answer to that is, it's a challenge. It's an area where there's very little Latin participation, and it's an area, within the context of this country, that provides me with a platform for interviews or attention that I can use to present points of view that hopefully will help dispel the negative stereotypes that exist about Latins in this country. A lot of people don't think that a Latin can express himself in ways that would touch common points with those of the Anglos here. That's a mistake.

Three of the members of my band live in the Bronx. They are three of the smartest men I ever met. But the perception is, "Hispanic? Lives in the Bronx? Oh, thief!" or "Not sophisticated enough. They wouldn't catch this, they wouldn't grab this joke.

This is too esoteric." That's a lot of crap! So if you get this platform, you can explain these things away.

On the other hand, it's a lot of fun! I grew up watching movies, I was always curious about the process. I've had a lot of fun working with Richard Pryor, who I've always admired as a comedian, and all of a sudden I have the opportunity to work side by side with him. It's been very rewarding. It's a lot of fun, too.

In terms of income, of course I'm not making a lot of money from it, but sometimes it's better than doing a month of touring. Just running around in a bus with people you alternatively love and hate, it's very hard. I see myself also spending more time in my house. I just got married two years ago. I love my wife. I'm getting along very well with her, I'm having a nice time at home, and I'd like to be more at home.

The thing with films, you do five weeks and that's pretty much it. And it's at the same location, more or less. There's not so much running around. When I tour, the gig I love, the two hours on stage, I love. What I don't like are the other twenty-two. It's just the daily thing, like where is the equipment? Did it get here? Where's the drummer? What happened to the mic here? The promoter, you can't find him? It's only half of the dough? Oh, god. The guy forgot to put gas in the thing? You're talking to a guy who ran out of gas, the bus ran out of gas in the Lincoln Tunnel.

I've been through hell and high water. I go through all kinds of shit. That's the way it goes. Now they're nice anecdotes. I laugh at them. But you have to go through a lot of aggravation. I love the gig and I love the people, it's just the before and the after. Plus living in hotels. You do this for ten years! Give me a break, man. I finally got a house, got a wife, got a dog. I like to be there. I like to plant my flowers and watch them grow. I haven't seen my plants in two and a half months. I can't wait to go back.

Which is another reason I moved to California. People in New York kept telling me, you move to California, you'll become an avocado. You're going to stop thinking. That's bullshit. You can turn into an avocado here in New York, too. We've got assholes here, too. But the thing is, what I don't get here, is I don't get a garden for what I'm paying over there.

I'm in L.A., but I don't drive, I don't go to the parties. Nobody invites me and I probably wouldn't go if they did invite me. We have a home outside of that area. And we get along there. We're very happy, just the three of us, my wife, myself, and my dog, a mutt that I found in Santa Fe doing *The Milagro Beanfield Wars*. That's what I like.

When I do an album, I do an album myself. And I'm very, very organized. The other guy I have known who was so organized when recording, from a firsthand experience, was Joe Jackson, who's a friend of mine. I'm very organized when I work. The thing I find incredible about movies is the hurry up and wait. You spend a lot of time waiting around. But the two genres are so different in terms of the execution that leads to the final product.

I'd like to try directing at some time. At least once. You get a taste, again, you have control of things. You're accustomed to making things happen on your own. Then, all of a sudden, you're elsewhere, and you're doing what someone else is telling you to do. Which I think is great, and it's a very humbling experience as well. And you learn and stuff, but you also become aware of how you would do things if you were in charge. And I like that. One of the things I like about working in a band is just that, working *in* a band. Granted, people tend to focus on the singer, in this case because I'm the alleged band leader, but I never encouraged that in the sense that I always gave my musicians the distinction and the praise that they deserve.

Success comes from a combination of elements. One of them is discipline. I'll say that a very large part of the success that I have is because I'm very disciplined. I never did drugs, so I never had the problem of not knowing where half my life went. I'm also very loyal to my idea, my notion of integrity. So, I don't cry over things that could have advanced my career if I had chosen to compromise myself. I think that it's almost like, if you don't look desperately for these things, they'll come, provided you surround yourself with good people, and that you're comfortable with the direction and the decisions that you take. Everything happened, not because somebody came over to me and said [he does a very bad W. C. Fields], "Kid, I'm going to make you a star." I never had that. And everything worked okay. I got to meet this guy, the guy liked me, so he hired me, and on with this. Then we did the record, and they told me it's going to fail, but we did it anyway and it worked. That's the way it went. So now, I have a smile, and I hope others will follow suit, because I don't want to be the only one. That's not the purpose of anything I've ever done.

OSCAR HERNANDEZ | CARABALI/SON DE SOLAR

When they started working together in the Bronx, they called themselves Carabali. They became one of the most progressive bands in Latin music, especially for eschewing horns. This attracted Ruben Blades. As his backing group, they became known first as Seis De Solar ("Six from the Sun" or "the Ghetto," depending on how you wanted to translate Solar*) and then Son De Solar ("Son" meaning either "coming from" or "song").*

Raul Alomar, who had put the group together originally, had started using a few other people. Then we met, and he spoke to me about getting involved. They didn't have anything steady, and he needed some guidance and direction, really. And he needed some arrangements. So I got involved with him and I wound up producing the album and playing on it and getting totally involved in the project.

Playing Latin music without horns is different but it's not something that hasn't been done before. It was very popular in the sixties with Joe Cuba. He made it really popular with the sextet. Then it was very popular on the West Coast with Cal Tjader, although that wasn't salsa, per se. That was more like Latin jazz. But in terms of what the norm is today, yes, we are not traditional at all.

Just the fact that we have progressive players and progressive arrangements, you can say that the Latin jazz element and influences are there. I come from a jazz background myself, sort of. I'm more of a Latin pianist, but I do play jazz, and I have listened to a lot. I was brought up listening to that type of music. So the influence is there, without a doubt. Same goes with some of the other musicians in the group. I've always had a progressive head in terms of Latin, salsa music, in terms of harmonies and melodies. I've always incorporated that in my style. I think that's what makes my style.

The English tune on our first album was played quite frequently on WBLS and on a few other stations. Of course they weren't mainstream commercial stations. We speak English also, so why not record in English? We didn't do it with airplay in mind. I had certain reservations about the tunes we chose to record in English, but we did them. I just feel that there's absolutely nothing wrong with us recording tunes in English. That's part of our culture also. I mean, I'm born and raised here, in the United States. I speak English just as well as anybody else. So why not incorporate English tunes? It may not be the same with the other members of the group. Maybe with a few of them, with Valerie, who speaks good English, with Mark. One or two of the other guys are Spanish dominant. Raul speaks more Spanish than English. Ray Martinez is another one. But even they have been influenced, and they understand that this is part of our culture also. We're second generation—third generation sometimes—Latinos here. It's not like we're just off the boat.

In terms of tradition, I feel I have a really firm grasp of both elements. I really feel it's important to understand and be able to play the traditional-type music. I like to make the comparison with jazz: it's like trying to play jazz without ever having heard Charlie Parker. It gives you a whole new perspective on how music has progressed from that time. The same thing with Latin. Having absorbed the tradition of the music, and listening to the masters, the roots of the music, and then bringing it up to today, with the influences of jazz artists and other musicians.

I can't say that there is anything that I've taken directly from jazz and transferred it to this. It's been an accumulation of studying and listening. What's come out is all the subconscious elements that were there from listening to a lot of jazz people, listening to the Cal Tjaders. There's a lot of people I can mention, a lot of great jazz pianists who have been an influence on me personally, but I can't say you can make a direct link to what you hear.

Going with a mainstream company like Mango Records is an opportunity for us, as it is an opportunity for Mango records. I produced an album for them, Daniel Ponce's album. We started a relationship with that. They were really, really happy with that. I think I exceeded their expectations as a producer with that. So, I spoke to them about the Carabali project, which we had in the can, sort of. We hadn't finished it, but there were no funds to finish it, and we didn't have any backers. We told them that there was some track record. We did have a record that was out there three years ago that got some response, strictly by word of mouth. The album did well without any distribution. It was something we released on Primo records [one of the Tenth Avenue record companies].

There are five percussionists in the band. The piano and the vibes are both percussion instruments.

I met Valerie, the vibraphone player, when I came into this situation. I was pleasantly surprised, because she is originally a marimba player. She plays four-mallet marimba. She is really great on that instrument. We got her to play vibes. She had never really played vibes. They're different. One is electric, one is acoustic. The vibe is really acoustic, but now they have pickups and you can midi them with synthesizers and all of that. She is very much into African music. She plays music of Ghana, she plays four-mallet classical music. She used to play in the street as a matter of fact, and make a lot of noise, make a lot of money doing that. When she came into the group, people said, "Oh, yeah! I saw her playing on Fifty-seventh Street." She used to get really good response from people. She has her own group. If you ever see her play in person, she's got a lot of fire, a lot of energy, and she can play. She doesn't come as much as I do from the jazz side, and she wasn't really a Latin player, per se, but being that she can play the instrument, and she's very much into ethnic kinds of music, she just really blended in. It took her a minute to grasp the music before she got it down, but she is a great player.

Everything she does is in the arrangements, except for the solos. She of course has more recently gotten into absorbing the jazz tradition, and that's been an influence, but she hasn't been known as a jazz player. She has been more known in the ethnic circles as having a group with a lot of African influences.

Ray Martinez is a bass player, originally from the Dominican Republic. He has been living here for about fifteen, twenty years. We played together with Ray Barretto, and then he did a stint with Mongo Santamaria. Very capable bassist. He had his own group for a while, that got some recognition. A group called Conjunto Tipico Criollo, which was a salsa group. He did well with that. When he got tired of doing that, he started playing with Mongo's group, and we got him involved with Carabali. He's a friend of mine and a good musician.

Mark Quinones is playing on just about everybody's session nowadays. He's like the young supermonster of percussion. He's playing with Spyro-Gyra right now. He's one of the most talented percussion players that I've ever met in all my musical years. And he's really young. He's a super professional. He goes into the studio, knocks it out. No mistakes, no nothing, reads from the chart, and plays his ass off. He's firmly established a reputation in the last few years as being the top percussionist in New York City. I think I would go out on a limb and say that, in terms of Latin music.

Ray Colon also established himself as one of the top bongo players, if not the top, one of the top two or three, in this city. As a session player, as a guy with drive, as a guy with a great sound.

The only person we haven't talked about is Raul, who is the leader. He originally had the concept of this group. It is his concept he put it together before I got involved, actually. He's played in some bands. He didn't have that much experience as the rest of the group, but he can play also. It was his concept, and he put it together with our help, with my help.

Carabali was a tribe of African descendants in Cuba. It was kind of like a secret society with religious influences, directly connected with the African influence in Cuba.

We all are heavily influenced by Cuban music. The roots of this music is Cuban, mostly. He's a Santero, which is the Cuban religion, so that probably had an influence on him.

I think of Afro-Cuban music as the music that was really popular in the forties and the fifties. It sounded different from the sound of today. It was an influence that we have, being born and raised in New York City.

Then there's salsa, which is more of a New York and Puerto Rican sound. That's where the term originated. Up to the time it became popular in the late sixties and early seventies, it wasn't known as salsa. That's when it became known as salsa, and it caught on everywhere else. But I would say that would be an apt description.

Of course, now you have salsa groups being popular from Colombia, from Venezuela, from Panama, and most recently from Japan. They've become very popular. A group called Orchestra La Luz. They're all Japanese, from Japan, and they play salsa. They don't speak it, which is amazing, but they play it well. They sing it in Spanish. They were a big hit. They were a big phenomenon around here. Everyone from all around would go, "Hey, did you see this?" They were at the Village Gate. They did a few of the clubs. They toured Puerto Rico. It was a unique thing to see this group up there playing salsa, and they're all Japanese guys from Japan, not from here.

Now there are good players from all over. You could say the same thing about these South American groups playing salsa. Ten years ago we used to laugh at them, but now you've got to say wait a minute. They've polished their act. They're listening. They're studying. I can name a couple of jazz pianists, Makoto, I love him. He's bad, man. And there's a few of the guys who can play. They've got the feeling. They've studied the right stuff, without a doubt.

Basically, everything has been done for the group through me, but I'm not a businessman. I've told the people I detest it. I'm a musician. I'll sit home and I'll write and I'll do anything that has to do with music, but to go out there and have to deal with club owners, it's just not me. The sporadic work that we've gotten is because people have heard the album and happened to call me.

It's all business, but in the salsa scene, per se, you've got to go out there and kiss ass. You've got to play politics and go out there to all the clubs. That's not me. I refuse to do that. So, as a result, we don't work as the band should. When we have worked, people come out and say, "Man, you guys sound great." But it's tough. To really get it happening, you need a band that's working consistently, to get those creative juices flowing on a high level.

I think that, nowadays, because the world is moving forward and people are a lot more open-minded about things, people are just listening to new things, just like people are tasting new foods they've never tasted before, being exposed to all kinds of cultures and living next door to all kinds of cultures and being very open-minded about that. I think that's the positive influence on different types of music, which ours is. It is not mainstream pop music. I don't think it will ever be received on that level, but I definitely feel that things are opening up for it. I don't think it will obtain that status, though, achieve mainstream AM airplay.

We feel very positive in terms of what we're doing on a musical level. It's some good music. It's not the run of the mill something that we just slapped together. Like I said, all the musicians have been with the top groups. We take great pride in our level of musicianship. Anything we do. Any production I'm involved in.

DANILO PEREZ

Born in Panama, Danilo Perez is most often regarded as a jazz musician. However, early on, he realized that jazz is an outgrowth of the African music that also informs the music of Panama. An audacious improviser, his gift is the skillful merging of all these sensibilities, along with the ability to communicate this merger first to the musicians he works with and, through them and his own playing, to his audience.

I've been working on this kind of mixture, the African is always involved, the Latin jazz, the cross rhythm, the odd meter, that sort of stuff. The roots of our music are from Africa, and I was just trying to make a connection. We have the same roots.

It's not in Africa, it's not in Panama, it's not in Cuba. The whole first part of *The Journey* is a vision, a dream about what I see from here. It's actually not traditionally African, but it has the elements that you would call the African elements, which is the blues, a little bit, the rhythm the percussion players use, the instruments that my percussion players play from Africa, mixed with the vision that we are here, the swing. That's something that developed with African roots, Afro-American music. That's actually linking everything together that comes from something else, but with the cultural traces of each one. You can definitely hear it in the percussion. What he's playing behind me, the percussion, is completely African.

In my dreams it started with them being captured. It was like a connection, a common point. It wasn't going to be an African record, or even a Latin record. I don't know what it was, actually. As far as music goes, I think it's just a perspective. I don't think that I was trying to do African music, just show the connection. I didn't think, "I'm going to do an African record" or anything like that. The story came first.

My goal is, at one point I want the music to meld, so that you can't say this is Latin music, this is jazz, and this is classical. It's just music. Even though we're playing Latin rhythms, we're using those rhythms to play the music. That's another thing. Even though we're playing Latin music, I don't want it to be Latin jazz, people playing jazz over a Latin beat. I want everybody to play. There's one part where we're playing in a quartet, and we're all improvising. We take a motif. To me, this is taking the music a step forward using the rhythms that are available. It doesn't matter that the rhythm is coming down from the south or from the north. Sometimes, you can hear us playing Latin in 6/8 and we go into swing. It changes the image that we have, but it works perfectly.

SOUTH AMERICA

BRAZIL AND ARGENTINA

South American music is another thing altogether. While it and some North and Central American musics use similar parts, like multiple percussion found in salsa, much of it feels more pastoral, even the sounds of Rio. Samba has become synonymous with "chill out" among the lounge culture.

The irony of this is most of the South American music that flies over the radar of the noise of the world is both urban and urbane. Even samba and bossa nova grew up in the clubs of Rio, taming the Afro-percussion of Bahia with the suave sounds of the southern city.

On the Pacific coast, tango grew up like jazz, in the whorehouses of Buenos Aires, but rather than a pastime, the dance was more like foreplay. A favorite of the more daring set of Americans and Europeans when it busted out of South America at the turn of the twentieth century, both Queen Victoria and Kaiser Wilhelm agreed that it was nasty. The Vatican proclaimed it a path to damnation.

Little wonder it survived and grew. In the hands of Carlos Gardél, it became art, and when he went down in a plane wreck, it fell to Astor Piazzolla to pick up the pieces. It took Piazzolla nearly four decades to do it, but he has left in his wake a healthy school of new tango enthusiasts, both at home and abroad.

NANA VASCONCELOS

Brazilian percussionist Nana Vasconcelos has been one of the major purveyors of Bahian music for several decades. Born in Recife, on the northeast coast of Brazil, by the time he was twelve, Vasconcelos was playing percussion in the city's marching band and working with his father, a guitarist. Through the sixties, he learned all the Brazilian percussion instruments, concentrating on the berimbau, a bow with a wire and a resonating gourd on the bottom. He is now the acknowledged master of this instrument. After playing in nearly every musical organization in Recife, from the orchestra to street bands, Vasconcelos moved to Rio de Janeiro and worked with Milton Naciemento. Since then, he has played with artists ranging from Gato Barbieri to Paul Simon's band. As such, he has straddled the worlds of non-Western music and jazz in both his solo work and his contributions to other artist's projects. Before his career in music took off, he worked with disturbed children in a psychiatric hospital in Paris. This remains important in his life.

I work with children a lot. Every tour I do a special program for children. I go to hospitals for handicapped children. Just recently I did the United Nations School and I did a school in Harlem, myself and Don Cherry. We show them instruments and tell them where they come from.

    I come from Brazil and I play the berimbau. We use ethnic instruments. Most of them come from Africa or Brazil or India. We just show that to the kids and play for them. This is something that is part of my organic work.

I try to mix my ethnic roots with the technological heritage of today. The mixture of my ethnic instruments, my organic work, with electronic instruments like synthesizers and drum machines.

Some albums I do mostly by myself and invite some musicians in to work on the album. Some result from a band experience. Then we compose together. It is much more live, because a band that has played for two years before going into the studio plays together. That is one of my elements, my collaboration with Don Cherry in Codona, my involvement in world music with Jan Gabarek. It's really a collaboration. The fact that we played together gives more of a balance between the electric and acoustic.

We composed a song for a film with the name *Bird Boy*. The song has the same title. Each song has its own story and its own history. A lot of my work always relates to nature. The reason I called one album *Rain Dance* is because I always liked the sound of the rain in the river in the rain forests. They have a certain sound. I try and look for the simplicity. How we can make the musical sounds simple, so everyone can enjoy it. We play for young people, old people, for a jazz audience. You have to use your imagination.

AL DI MEOLA

While best known as a jazz guitarist from his seminal work with the groundbreaking fusion group Return To Forever, Al Di Meola has dedicated a large portion of the last few decades of his career to promoting various noises of the world, particularly roots Latin musics and especially tango. His acoustic oriented World Sinfonia *covered various genres, often blurring the lines between them, and always touching on that area of the music that encouraged improvisation. However, this was also always an important subtext of his electric albums as well.*

I grew up listening to Latin music. I always had that element, from the first album. The third-world influence on my music was evident from album one. The branching out and exploring different areas of the world and different folk musics, that's been happening all along, but slowly. More so on the last bunch of albums, four of five albums. It's become easier to have access to ethnic sounds due to the availability of these instruments that are on the market. Songs like "Purple Orchids" have sounds that conjure up the Orient. Each song has sounds that hopefully will immediately bring you to a different area of the world.

The tune "Global Safari," for example starts off with bata drums, which is an Afro-Cuban drum. I've always wanted to use them on my album, any one of my albums, and I got to use two of them on the beginning of the tune and on the end.

When I was a teenager—even before that—when I was a kid, I used to listen to a lot of Latin music on the radio. And then, when I was in my mid-teens, I used to go into New York and hang out at the Latin clubs, like the Corso. A lot of times, I went by myself because none of my friends liked that stuff, but I really had a special connection with this music. Understanding, feeling, and playing Latin rhythm is a special thing. You are either born with the ability to feel the up-beat syncopation against the clave or you're not. You can't learn how to play Latin music. You can learn a certain aspect of understanding how rhythms are played, but you can't learn how to feel to play Latin music. That is something that is God-sent.

The *World Sinfonia* is something that's radically different from most of the other projects I've been involved with. I find that element extremely intriguing. Combined with the other elements, we've created something new.

I became friends and was introduced to the music of Astor Piazzolla, who was the leading contemporary tango composer out of Argentina. We met back in 1985 in Japan. We were both on the same festival over there. I had heard of him before, and I had heard about his music, but it wasn't until then that I got to experience what I found to be some of the most passionate, intriguing music that I'd heard in years in years. Nothing has inspired me that much since hearing Chick's music originally.

Before I got a chance to record with him, Astor suffered an extremely severe, just about fatal stroke. I was with him two weeks before this happened and we had planned on doing something together. When I was in Buenos Aires before he passed on, I went to see him. He was lying in a hospital, barely sixty-five pounds, kept alive by the machinery. It wasn't a good thing to go and see.

What I find appealing about Piazzolla's music is his awareness and inclusion of jazz harmony mixed in so well. It creates a new kind of music. Now, I just approach playing through harmony in an improvisational way, just thinking about the chord structures, basically. The same way I would approach playing on a jazz standard, I also do it on this kind of music. The harmony, even though it is a contemporary classical piece of music, the rhythms are not typical of what you might expect from classical music, because we deal so much with a tango passion in the rhythm that it's very unique. There are other forms of Latin rhythms that have also been included.

His spirit and his music will live on. He's regarded very highly in the classical field and the contemporary music field, except in the United States. Maybe, through my recording his music and the underground following that exists here, he'll become more widely known. Certainly with guitar players. They'll learn about his music through my records, I'm sure.

Calling Piazzola's own instrument obscure would be putting it lightly. Nobody knows what a bandoneon is. Not here. There's a lot of world music that's not known here. But how could it be? The only music we hear on a large scale is what Paul Simon has done on the African vibe, and maybe some stuff Peter Gabriel has done. It's the same old story. We just don't have the support that rap music and heavy metal music gets nonstop.

I rearranged the "Tango Suite," an amazing piece by Piazzolla, to suit the instrumentation of the *World Sinfonia*. There is a form of music that the *World Sinfonia* plays that works well in an acoustic ensemble setting but might not work as well in an electric group.

My electric work is different from the *World Sinfonia* albums in that, with the *World Sinfonia*, I'm mainly playing a nylon string flamenco-style guitar. It's not traditional flamenco, but variations on Latin rhythms over the course of many years. With the electric guitar, the whole mood of pieces like "Morocco" is very different from *World Sinfonia*. It has Northern African elements, as well, and it definitely works when you think of those images. But that piece, in particular, is one of the more complex pieces in terms of harmony. The harmonic movement in the solo section is a good example of what I was talking about, in terms of the emphasis on unconventional harmonic movement, with almost every bar having a different time signature. Without it being disturbing. Some odd time signature stuff can be disturbing. I don't want to disturb. I think it has a real good flow, and it swings. You don't have to have an educated ear to know that this is something different, something perhaps unique.

DINO SALUZZI

The new Tango King, Dino Saluzzi filled in for Astor Piazzola on Dimeola's World Sinfonia *projects. Many saw Saluzzi as the heir apparent to Piazolla. On record throughout his solo career, his music got filtered through the audiophile, atmospheric ears of producer Manfred Eicher, but he could still churn out some of the high-class, low-down Argentine hot dance music.*

I think we have many things in common between jazz and tango. I like this idea very much. They were born together and they come together on the blue world. They took this parallel way.

Tango has a strong rhythm. It's the same as jazz. It depends on the musician. Sometimes the tango goes really like chamber music. For example Piazzolla.

Every young musician in Argentina is influenced by Piazzolla in one way or another. He made a strong personal imprint on the art of tango. Maybe less in my case. I think of my music as a little different. I got influenced by the capacity of the work, the capacity to go ahead with his culture. In a certain way, I got influenced by Piazzolla. So did every young musician in Argentina.

Jazz has the same process as tango. Jazz comes from the poor people and tango, too, comes from the poor people. It helps with the betterment of the non-classical musician, the non-academic musician.

The development is not by academic musicians. After, when the music matured, both the tango and jazz became academic music. Everything is systematized. That means academe.

I've been playing the bandoneon since I was seven years old. My father gave me my first instrument in my hometown, and my first connection with the music was the folk music of my hometown.

Later, I made the connection with the tango, old tangos like those by Augustín Bardi and Francisco Canaro.

I don't know if I really play jazz on the bandoneon. I hear jazz artists, and it changes our inflection of the playing of the tango. I'm very near the jazz musician, but I don't know. I don't know the category of my music. Maybe it is jazz, because it's really open. If the tango is open, then my music is tango. It's so difficult for me to pick the exact category of my music.

Both jazz and tango have very strong sentimental feeling, too. The phrasing of the tango is nearer to Italian music, but the tango takes one way in it's development and jazz another.

In my family, we are musicians. Celso and Felix are my brothers and Jose is my son. He's studying composition now. He's a bass player, piano player, studying composition. He's sixteen years old.

Tango has a similar family orientation to flamenco, with one major difference. Tango is more open than flamenco. Tango means more than just the form of the tango, it means the world of the tango, another rhythm from Buenos Aires. Like waltz or milonga, are combined with the rhythm of that.

I studied in Buenos Aires with Lorca and Fischer and my father first. I studied composition with my father.

He was very influenced by Gershwin, I think. Both took the music of the cities. They reflected strong impact from the life of the cities, like New York and Buenos Aires.

I write, too. I wrote a concerto for symphony and bandoneon. I performed it with an orchestra from Hanover, Germany. It went over the German National Radio Network [Sudwestfunk], too. At this moment, I'm writing a string quartet with bandoneon. I may record this in London, for ECM. I've written many pieces for small groups and strings. For classics, I grew up in Argentina.

I think my record in Buenos Aires gets a different feeling outside of Buenos Aires from musicians in Buenos Aires. This is very interesting for our culture.

This is, for our life a very good sign, this coming together. All cultures need cultivation, not confrontation. All cultures need to go ahead together. That's the best thing in the world.

NORTH AFRICA

Louie: What in heaven's name brought you to Casablanca?
Rick: My health. I came to Casablanca for the waters.
Louie: The waters? What waters? We're in the desert.
Rick: I was misinformed.

If you've seen *Casablanca*, you can understand—even through the filter of Hollywood—why people describe landing in the Magreb (Francophone North Africa) as arriving in a time warp. While the modern world is evident everywhere, in many things the old ways remain *the* ways. The souk is still a place where people bargain for prices—to take the price on the item is an insult to the vender.

Sharing common culture with many of the Arabic countries of the Middle East and Mediterranean, the music of Morocco, Algeria, and Tunisia is a pretty diverse despite itself. There is music based on slave culture imported from West Africa centuries ago, music based on strings that date back to the beginning of recorded time, rebel music that started acoustic and became the last word in dance music for a great portion of the world. There are traditional musics that developed into classical forms and classical musics that nomadic tribes adapted into folk. Just when you feel you've got a grip on it, the wind blows and it shifts, just like the sands of the Sahara.

ANOUAR BRAHEM

Tunisian oud virtuoso Anouar Brahem recognizes the essential balance between the old and the new in maintaining a living tradition. Brahem records for a decidedly Western company, ECM, but his instrument comes out of the depths of Islamic antiquity. His music has deep roots in tradition, but Brahem refuses to be isolated within that tradition. So, while the oudist directs the Music Ensemble of Tunis, he has also lived in France, been exposed to jazz, and worked with musicians as diverse as Manu Dibango, Fareed Haque, Jan Garbarek, and Manu Katche. The oud is an ancestor of the European lute, a sire of the guitar. The fretless instrument has six sets of double strings tuned in fourths. The body is made of fifteen alternating strips of walnut and pecan wood, the face is white palissandre. It has been made essentially the same way for centuries.

The best ouds come from Egypt, Iraq, and Turkey. Traditionally, a pick is used to play the oud. I always use one. Through the ages, the preferred pick has been made of the feather of a vulture, soaked in olive oil and worked until soft. These picks are difficult to find these days. I use a pick made from the horn of a bull. Plastic picks are also used.

My training is traditional, but the music I play is very personal. It is influenced by traditional stylists, but what I do comes from inside me. Of course, the traditional influences are all there, but my music is not strictly traditional.

After my training, I began to look at all the musical styles that were related to Arabic music. Everything in the Middle East, Persian music, Turkish music, and also the influences of the colonizers who came in, the musical influences that they had, not just in North Africa but in all of Africa and throughout the Middle East.

Intensity and sincerity are the most important aspects of my performance. I seek to be good *inside* the music. Audiences do not react well to an exhibition of technique. Sincerity is what's attractive.

HASSAN HAKMOUN

A fully trained Moroccan Gnawa (musical healer), Hassan Hakmoun plays in both the traditional way and using his instrument, the sintir, in a pop/rock/world context with his band Zahar.

The sintir is the oldest stringed bass in the world. The face is camel skin. The string is catgut, from the stomach. Before, they couldn't make strings, there's no nylon, no nothing. This is the first string they could come up with. This is camel skin from the neck particularly. The back is from a tree. They have a few different kinds. The neck is just regular wood. In 1988, I was playing at Yale University. I finished my first set, went upstairs, and I broke my original neck. I had like fifteen minutes to come back and play. They have a factory in the school, so I went downstairs and I made it. I just used regular wood. The first string is A, then this (the center string) is high E, and (the last string), low E.

This particular instrument originated in West Africa and came to North Africa, where I lived, in Morocco, and the rest of North Africa, five hundred years ago. This instrument comes by slavery.

The Gnawa people come five hundred years ago to Morocco. They came with this instrument and with other instruments, castanets, metal castanets, which the Mussulman use to call for the prayer. This music, as we know it, comes from West Africa.

The joujouka is not very popular in Morocco. The Rolling Stones might go there and try to use their music, but I mean, when you say the Gnawa to any Moroccan, they'll say "Yeah!" But when you say the Joujouka, I don't think anybody knows it. They might see it in the folklore, where every year they bring the musicians to perform.

But the Gnawa, it's something used. It's like medicine. This music is used for healing, for trance, for spiritual stuff. That's the difference. It has a history, a very strong history of how it comes and how you are allowed to play. A lot of things happened.

A long time ago, this music was not allowed to be played, because the slavery brought it. When they finished working, they'd get together and trance and speak of their feelings and everything, and they'd sing this kind of music and they'd heal themselves. They'd do miracles, like they'd cut themselves with knives and no blood comes. They would do a lot of things. The miracles they'd be doing with this music, playing this music and getting into a trance and healing people that have something wrong.

For a long time, people were against it. They didn't want to see it. So they'd prove to them that they could do something. They would go to a wall that's very old, and they'd take a bit of the wall and throw it into the fire and it would become incense. A lot of things like that, so the king said they were allowed to do this thing because they had a lot of miracles caused by with it.

They use Gnawa music as medicine. A lot of people, they would go to doctors and the doctors can't do nothing. They come to the Gnawa. The Gnawa trances all night long, does some spirit trance and when they do that, they cover the man or woman or child with different pieces of material, different colors. Each color means something, has a spiritual direction. Each time they play a song, they use the color that is related to this song. When they use that and they finish a song, then they change the color. They keep going until they pass through all of the seven colors. Then the person becomes healed. If the person is sick, then everything will be cool.

When I was five years old, my mom, she used to be the one who got the music, she brought this to the family. My father and his background, his father brought other things related to these miracles and other stuff. My sister, she's younger than me. I was five and she was one or two, and she got touched with a genie. If you believe there are other people who live under us in the ground, in Africa people believe things like this. So, she peed in the drain behind the house. When she peed, it was very hot and it burned some child of the people who live under the ground, so they burned her back. All her body turned to become marked with cigarette marks, all over her body. Then a friend of my mother told her she should bring the Gnawa to the spirits. That's the only way, because we couldn't bring her to the doctor. So she did.

The Gnawa, they came and they performed the spirit chants and ceremonies all night and they played the music. In the middle of the night, they said, "Bring the goat." So, they brought the goat, and they killed it and let the blood go down the drain. That means making peace with these people who hurt my sister. After the blood comes, they took the body and the skin of the goat, and they stick my sister, naked, inside the skin of the goat. They played for a while, and they took her out and everything was gone.

That's when I fell in love with the music and I became very strong and close to the music. I wanted to know more. I wanted to be a musician. I wanted to be a master.

It took me a long time. I had to travel all over the country to learn from other people. I played in the streets, played for money. The only thing I wanted to do was learn the music. I quit school for a while. I went to the streets to support myself with the music. At the same time I was making money for myself and learning with other people.

At the age of fourteen, I became a master, dancing, singing, drumming, and playing this instrument. Doing some acrobatic stuff.

You might see an American Indian do something like that and you might say they're crazy. But they have reason to do that. They saw something, or something happened to make them believe. It's not just one time or two. Maybe many lives had been saved, and that's what makes them strong to do that. Sometimes, if you think it's going to happen, God will prove it to you. Even if somebody tried to fool you, and they take your money and stuff, and then you got healed because of your believing. That's part of it, to take the spirit from other people. So, you just have to try and see. It's worth a try. I've been doing this for a long time. I've seen a lot of things happen. A lot of miracles happen.

This is the month when they perform this miracle I told you about. It's this month that it happens in Africa, in Morocco. I'm going this month, and I'm going to videotape some of it. It will not be people acting. It will be real. The real thing happening.

This is before Ramadan. When Ramadan comes, the musicians don't touch their instruments. They don't perform that. So they have a big long month where they do that. They have a whole month when people don't sleep. They party everywhere. It's not just parties for fun, it's for spirit and healing. Musicians gathering, especially the women, supporting the music. They give them what they need. A lot of things happen.

They play for a month, and then they put down the instruments. You can't play the instruments for the spirit. You can play what the people dance to, but not what the musicians trance to.

One reason I'm playing my music with a rock band stuff is the music we play is not very popular around the world. Nobody knows who the Gnawa are. Even us, you hear a lot of music in rock, funk, and jazz. To me, it comes from that music. I've played with jazz musicians, classical musicians, like the Kronos Quartet. I wrote a song for them, for *Pieces of Africa*. Anything I do with other musicians, the music fits. I never have a problem with anybody telling me can you play with this or that. Anything I try, it works. That's because I'm using the traditional technique into the modern technique, and it fits. Especially if you come with a new idea, everybody wants to hear.

I'm doing it because I want a lot a lot of people to know about the Gnawa, and I want the Gnawa to reach some high level, to be respected, for people to know them, for their music to become big.

When I play, I go somewhere. It's not like people these days, rock people or hip-hop singing, "I love you baby." Sometimes, when I play, I'm out. I don't look at the audience. I'm just with the music and the feeling and the trance.

I'm not losing the magic. I'm doing the same thing, it's just a little bit sped up. Instead of doing it the traditional way, it's just a little bit sped up and some different style, but it's still the same feeling to me. The singing has changed. There's still the same words, but there have been some changes in the vocal stuff.

Nobody is doing the style I do. This is the first album that's going to reach Morocco to make it very, very big, but the Gnawa music is known. It's known more than the rai because of the history and stuff. Everybody knows rai, but everybody knows the Gnawa.

People in Morocco know about me because there is a channel like MTV there. They play my stuff. The kind of rai that they're using is different from the Gnawa. In the style I'm using, it's stronger musically, also. The rai is good, but it's commercial.

I like some of the raï, but I don't like others. Most of them are doing the same thing. A lot of songs Algerians sing, they're Moroccan songs. They're stealing things, like Dissidenten. They steal things from Morocco. I don't like that. Many songs I've heard, even in the rai music, relate to the Gnawa musicians.

There are not many words in rai music. If they translated to English, the lyrics wouldn't make sense, because the words are not very strong. We do have musicians from Morocco, that I like better than all the rai musicians. They're very political. They use strong words and they're very powerful. They're big, very big in Europe. They use the traditional instruments, but they go they travel around the world. They've been around for a long time, since the sixties.

I'm not political, but I have music with some words that are very strong. Where I'm coming from, I don't think you're allowed to say political things. But even if you did, you have to explain what you're saying and who you're talking about. I have songs, the politics doesn't have anything to do with where I'm coming from, but people might still think I'm talking about that. When you don't mention exactly what you're talking about, you can be talking about a lot of different things in one song. Maybe people think you're talking about love, but you're talking about something else. Maybe people think you're talking about government, but that's not what you're singing about. I like to sing songs that are political but have a lot of different meanings so everyone can understand it differently.

In Marrakech, I was playing a lot in clubs and hotels. This dancer came from Madrid, was asking for a musician who could do everything. Instead of taking five musicians or six to play different instruments, she wanted two musicians or three who could do all that, one who could play oud and guitar and drums and all that and dance and sing. So she came looking for me in this big place where people play all day and all night. They found me, we went to coffee, and we talked. She said, "I want to audition you." We went to her house and we just did a little nothing and she said, "That's what I'm looking for." So we worked in Morocco, and then we got work in Lincoln Center, so we came here and played Lincoln Center and other places. I have a friend who said, "You have a visa, you should stay here and make some money before you go to Africa." So, I stayed.

I saw what I would like and what I would do and I saw it here, the possibility of making what you want. This country is the dream country. If you have something nobody else has, something you can come with and you feel strong about in any way, you will make it. Since I've been here, I've made several albums, one with Don Cherry is playing on it. That one, *Gift of the Gnawa*, was number one in France. It's kind of a jazz African.

In 1989, I was on David Sanborn's show with my band, Zahar. Miles Davis was playing there, so we met, me and Miles Davis and Marcus Miller and many, many musicians. Daniel Lanois was there. After the gig, he came over to me and said, "Hassan, do you need a record deal?" and I said, "No." He said, "Why?" I said, "Because the musicians who are with me, I'm not happy with them to do an album. They play, but are not ready." He said, "Okay. Give me a call when you're ready." Three years later, they gave me a call. Peter Gabriel called and asked if we wanted to do it now. I said, "Yeah!" So we did a bunch of different ideas. Peter, he's a very nice guy. He was around and he treated me very well. All the people there were very nice.

Right now, I'm tired of American music. I'm tired of seeing a lot of videos with violence. I don't watch MTV. I have it, but I don't watch that. I listen to good music. I like Stevie Wonder. I like Ray Charles. I don't like a lot of rap. I understand freedom of speech, but at the same time, that's not the way you do it. What I listen to now is traditional African music. When I came here I was listening to American music a lot. Before I came here, also. When I came here, I didn't find any interest in it, except some of the vocal stuff that I love. I love a lot of different musicians here, but not a lot of rappers. I mean people who are just jumping on stage and making sex on stage, selling their own body naked. You don't have to show half of your body naked just to make the people come and see that. That's not making people interested in your music, that's making people interested in your body. That's crazy.

I grew up in a country where it's very hard to make it. What the rappers are doing is crazy. I'd like to hear from them about this, because I'm willing to face them. They're crazy, what they're doing. Even the record companies that accept them, that's terrible. The people are just doing this to make money. I don't think they're giving a message.

One thing about living in America, you can die anytime. When I come out from my house, I'm in a war. That's what it's like to live in America. I was mugged once. Crime happens. You can be killed by an accident, no problem. Even if you don't talk to the people, the people will say, "What are you talking about, what are you looking at?" Then if you get into a conversation, you're in trouble. I don't feel safe, no matter how many police officers they have here. You can get beaten by a police officer and you can go to jail for no reason.

Where I'm coming from is very safe. No guns. There are guns in South Africa, but no guns in Morocco. Even the police don't carry guns. So, if you see a fight, it's by hand. And if there is a fight, it's just two people. No one else gets involved. Your friends won't help you until you're done. Then they'll say, "Are you finished? Are you okay?" Or people will get involved to separate the fight. Here, man, I don't think people care. I don't see a life living here. I'm not going to spend the rest of my life in this country. I might have ten years to go here, maybe less. Then I'll go back to my country. I'm just doing business here.

I'm looking forward to going back there. I miss Morocco. I miss my family. I have a brother here with me, and I have a son, but I miss my father and mother. My father is an old man. And I have older brothers and my sister. It's been four years since I've been back.

It's very peaceful there. When I come here, I looked at it and I found myself, I was happy there. Here, I'm happy with the music, but the way I'm living is crazy. When I go home to Morocco, there are no papers. Now, the whole house is papers and bills. In this country it's built in, whatever you make you give. You don't save. There's no saving here. When I've done my work, I think I'll go back home. I can come back here to work and go back home. In ten years, I think I'll go back to Morocco. I want my son to grow up. I have to have him here for his education and stuff. When he turns eighteen, I'm done.

Zahar has had Americans and Jamaica people and sometimes they don't even want to ask for money, they just want to play. Many musicians want to play with me in America, especially in New York. They say, "If you ever need a drummer, I would love to play your music." It's like studying a new style and becoming comfortable doing something they're not able to play when they play jazz or rock. There's a lot of freedom in this music. It's not like just holding on to one thing. You can go a lot of different ways.

Music is medicine to the people. It is to heal people to make them feel good.

WEST AND CENTRAL AFRICA

West and Central Africa—one of the most volatile places on earth.Tthe first memories most people of my generation have of seeing starving children came out of the Nigerian civil war of the late sixties, pitting the predominantly Yoruba western/coastal part of the country with the seceding Ibo eastern part of the country, calling itself Biafra. Millions died. The country remained under martial rule until the late seventies and returned in 1983 when a coup ousted the elected government. The temptation brought on by the vast amounts of oil and other mineral wealth in the country proved too attractive for those in power and those who wanted to be. Nigeria may be one of the world's most corrupt countries in terms of government.

Yet as rich as the area is in mineral resources, it might be even richer in music. From highlife to juju to fuji to Afrobeat and all the sounds in between, Lagos is a hotbed of music.

Much of West and Central Africa became incredibly turbulent in the sixties as the colonial powers that had "settled" the areas withdrew and the countries tried to come into the modern age of self-government. These growing pains were felt in Senegal, as treaties with Gambia, new alliances, and new borders came and went on what seemed like a weekly basis. Add to this the encroaching desert and you had a massive exodus to the capitals of those colonial powers that had withdrawn. This drew artists like Cameroon's Manu Dibango and the Toure Brothers of Senegal. But some artists, like Youssou N'Dour decided to endure and create an artistic center in Dakar.

Out of this volatility came some of the most amazing music of the past forty years.

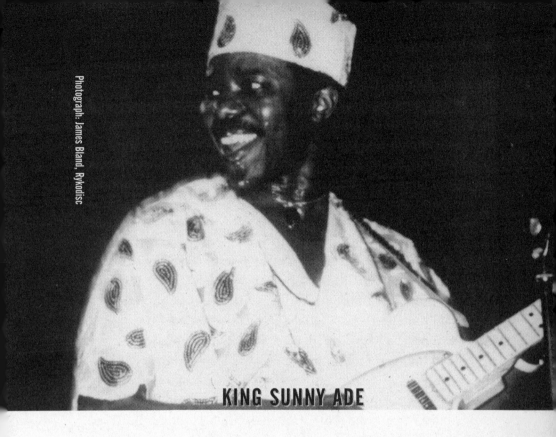

Photograph: James Bland, Rykodisc

KING SUNNY ADE

King Sunny Ade is one of the most popular African musicians in the world. A prince of Nigeria's Yoruba tribe, Ade renovates one facet of his tribal music, playing an updated, electrified version of juju music. At times, Ade will cut out all the electric instruments in his eighteen (or so) piece band, which includes synthesizers and a pedal steel guitar, leaving just the talking drums and other traditional instruments playing alone. That, he says, is the genuine article, as real as it gets, Yoruba music is as it has sounded for centuries. Ade first came to the attention of many Americans with an album he made for Island records in 1982. Riding the wave of African rhythms being used by the likes of Talking Heads and Adam and the Ants, juju music became the critics' touchstone for that year, which thrilled Island. They were hoping against hope that Ade might be the successor to Bob Marley as popular musical champion of the developing nations. In a way, they were right. Fans of African music embraced the Nigerian star on his own terms. His shows featured over ten separate drummers, four guitars, bass, and a pedal steel, over twenty people on stage all told. The music they made was quirky and rhythmic, but just not as accessible to the mainstream audience as reggae. Forgetting the years that it took to develop reggae into a major cultural force, Ade and Island severed their relations after distributing three albums over four years.

I am not supposed to play music, but I do because I just love to play music. Nobody else in my family plays music, except my father. Sometimes plays the organ at church when the organist doesn't come. He is a prince by birth. We are princes, so we can't play music for people, people are supposed to play for us. But as I looked into the Christian way of life, I often look at the songs of David, the psalms. David is a king, and he sings to God. He's a king, I'm a prince, let me try all the things that go along with it.

I started hanging around music because I love to dance, I love to hear music. I've been hanging around musicians since the age of seven.

There are some groups in Africa that are very good, but they don't like to go out. There are some, they don't know the right person to get them out. There are some that can't go out simply because they are under some kind of sponsorship or record contract. There are some that the government doesn't even want to go because they are good. There are groups that are government backed, sponsored. They mainly play within the country. If they want to go out, it has to be between government and government.

That's what we've been doing since 1975. We came to this country in 1975 for the first time. All we've done is cultural exchange. A group will go from Nigeria to America, and a group will go from America to Nigeria. And that's cultural exchange. We have to select the places to go, and when we finish that, whoosh, straight home, you don't need to stop, because your passport and your ticket and everything is with them.

We have thousands of musicians in Africa. There are some that are very good, but if you asked them to go to another city, they would tell you they do not want to go out. There are some who are under some kind of pressure, probably by their sponsors, or their contract or by the government or by the group's organization. It might also be from within the group themselves. There are some groups that are very, very good, but they are working. They consider music a hobby. And the people would tell them, "You'll make a hell of a lot of money with this music if you send it out." And these artists say "no, no, no." They are not like that.

People like Fela, he goes out when he likes. He doesn't look into what kind of money, or how big, or what kind of programs they want him to do, he goes out when he likes. Me too. Our music is different, so we want to play it around the whole world and at home. It's good to bring your music around the world.

Music in Africa is almost unlimited, because we have serious music almost everywhere. Almost every community has their own kind of music. Some of the languages have their own kind of music, too. And the cultures of different areas have their own kind of music. Then there are some religions that have their own kind of music. Then there are some groups that they don't even believe in anything but playing purely music. There are some that combine Western or African or Asian or Latin together to make one music. It depends on what area but those who are known have the chance to expose their music, they have the privilege to record at a better studio, they have the privilege to go to a show with other big acts where they can be exposed, they have a privilege to be backed by a good recording company or management.

You like to take from one kind of music. For instance, we have light jazz, we have acoustic jazz, we have funk jazz, we have rock jazz, we have blues jazz, and we have rhythm and blues combined with jazz. So it depends on what kind of sound we are producing, but under one name—jazz. Those are the things that people like to relate to when they want to differentiate their music or when they want to find their own kind of identity.

I was listening to Kenny G. He was talking about his saxophone, and how he put his saxophone through some kind of effects, and now he has differentiated his own kind of music. Quickly, you can recognize when you are playing his music. You say, "Is that not Kenny G.?" and they say, "Yes."

When you listen to my pedal steel player, you know that it's a pedal steel, but it doesn't sound like country music, because you expect a pedal steel to be country music, and it's not that. Actually, we didn't use pedal steel until we came over to America. That's the first time we saw the pedal steel. When we saw the pedal steel, we picked it up and bought it. Before, we used a guitar with a slide. And the way we slide, we do it in an African way. We don't actually want to go along with any other music in the world. We want to differentiate our own kind of music. That's why the pedal steel player has a normal time to come in, and he plays a danceable sound. Not really to back the song. Not really to take a solo. He has to play his own kind of solo on a danceable step.

I always wanted to introduce the pedal steel into my music. Then I introduced the keyboard. But I didn't introduce the keyboard for the first time. My ancestors had already introduced the accordion. I just don't like to have an accordion with me, because the people who play the accordion used to stand still at a microphone. With my kind of music you have to dance around, you have to jump up. You can't jump up with an accordion on your chest! That's why I introduced a DX-7 to African music. And with a DX-7 you can find so many sounds, I call it the African tones of the instrument that you can find. If you want to play flute, it's good if you can play flute direct, but inasmuch you can play it on the keyboard, it's more or less the same. The man playing the flute would be playing keyboard any way. So this is the difference where those groups that are trying to fuse African music with Western instruments, but play it in an African way.

Everything in the whole world now goes hand to hand. Everything goes side by side with technology. Even the music itself. Nowadays, it is easier, because you have multitrack, that's part of the technology. With multitracks, taking about twenty-four at the same time, we can go in and if we go in as thirty, and the multitrack is twenty-four, thirty people can go at the same time. You get four people on one track, three on another, and the rest will go on their own track. Then those three or four can go in again. Sometimes the studio can only fit fifteen people at the same time.

So we take all the other microphones out of the studio, and they'll be playing as if they were with us. They have their song to play, and they don't see us, but we feel as if we are on the stage. Later on, we can redub it if we need to.

I put out three albums a year in Nigeria. If I released two, I would be so pressurized. All fans would be sending letters saying "what's going on?" They take their idols to be everything to them. They are expecting that every four months I must produce some different songs that will make them move.

That's the difference between there and here. The distribution network is different. Like, you allow one record that people love to be in so many markets for long before you do another one. At home, the song you played me last night, if you repeat yourself today, and we come to your show tomorrow, and you repeat yourself again, you have to create. It has to be new. These people play music all the time, even in the back yard. They play new music every day. You can't go in there repeating yourself every time. Your fans would be breaking off.

Each time we make a record, and the record goes out, we feel that's unheard music. We feel we have to back it up with something that's better than what we played. In the studio, you have to be very careful to touch your strings. You can't let them touch each other. But when you're on the stage, you have the ability to move, you see a lot of people dancing, you see a lot of hands up there waving at you, a lot of people shouting at you, eventually it makes you play better than what you played. And that is why some people are breaking their strings on the stage. They are so happy, they don't even know. If you don't call them quick, instead of playing eight bars, they'll play twenty-four if you don't call them back. So, eventually, that's why the drummer has to cue them when they play. They have to be called back.

I try my possible best, in every one of my songs, to preach love and unity. I don't like to push politics or try to evolve into a kind of political songs or programs for politics. I try my best to deviate myself from politics. When it's time for election, to vote, I'll look into who has the program and then I'll vote for whomever I feel.

But I don't like to point it out to people and I don't like to preach with songs, because the way we play politics, the little I saw from my teen age until now, is really bitter for my liking.

When I started singing songs, I decided to tell people not to take everything with bitterness. Not only politics. Everything a man is supposed to do, supposed to be, friendly, with love. Unity can never come without inserting the program to combine love together. If you are friends you can study what one another wants, their dos and their don'ts. That is difficult, but gradually it can be done.

I don't see anything in the areas where I can comment on politics, simply because the way they do it is always to bitter for me. Anywhere in the world you can play at a rally, and after that, the campaigner or the aspirant can come to the rostrum and deliver his message. Either they clap for him or they boo him and that's the end of it. But on the occasion, they start throwing stones, and throwing many things, and eventually, you will lose your instruments, even lives are lost, so it's like, I always avoid that. It doesn't appeal to me. I think now, the whole mission now is becoming awareness that it is not good to be bitter.

ISMAIL TOURE | TOURE KUNDA

Toure Kunda, part of the modern West African diaspora that has made its home in Paris, rooted their sound in the spiritual music of everyday life in Senegal, as filtered through the expatriate experience. Ismail, Sixu, and Ousmane Toure (Ismail and Sixu are literally twin sons of different mothers, born only hours apart) are partial to native instruments, particularly hand drum and marimba variations, yet that doesn't stop them from employing bands that can create the massive reggae groove of "Emma" or their more Afropop sounds. Now, both the Toure brothers and their children are part of this Senegalese band, creating an Afropop limited in worldwide appeal only by the French dialect in which they perform.

In Senegal every year they have training for young boys and girls. They take them to the sacred forest. They teach them how to get through life, how to make a song, how to live with one another. During this time you hear music everywhere. That's our first influence.

Toure Kunda's music is based in reality, African reality. That's what we know. We leave the guitar to the guitar player, piano to the piano player. I'm sure that somewhere Fela and Ade, when they play piano think about some kind of African essence.

People don't use their knowledge to fight the desert. That's why it's basically a permanent drought in Africa . . . They have engineers they send to school to learn to try to fight the desert, and they wind up in an office rather than doing what needs to be done to make the situation better.

We come to America . . . We are doing a tour around the world and we think we cannot do all the world if we don't come here. To us, black American music comes somewhere from Africa. The jazz, the blues, black American music is like cousins, related.

PACO YE | FARAFINA

Originally formed as a folkloric percussion ensemble and musical ambassadors from Burkina Faso, this octet brought their tuned percussion to records by artists like the Rolling Stones, Ruichi Sakamoto, and Jon Hassell.

We are very odd in Burkina Faso, because everyone else is playing electric guitars. We were the only ones to play that form, with balaphones and drums to make it so far. We have done many concerts. But the other kind of attitude to seeing that kind of setting on the stage, we get a feeling of inferiority, because it is like going back to colonization. It is a very visceral thing inside the African. That's a very crucial point.

In Burkina Faso, in the traditional form, you have people who come and play together, and whenever somebody wants to join in the music, they just come and whenever dancers want to jump up, they just do it. With Farafina, things are much more precisely done. Instruments intervene or go out at precise moments. It's orchestrated and arranged like modern ensembles of rock or jazz or pop music. Intellectually, in the concept, we have the same way of working as any pop or jazz ensemble.

Of course there are others performing with traditional instruments. It depends on in which spirit it is done. For us, it is a very clear idea to go ahead with that.

The form of orchestration we have is readable to the ears of American audience. If you were to bring a traditional ensemble from Burkina Faso, it would sound very ethnic, which is not at all our case. People can really appreciate the difference, people into ethnomusicology, who know the traditional music and listen to

Farafina's music. They can feel the difference. Whereas often, people feel like they are dealing with an ethnic group, which is totally not the case.

The traditional music is music that has been carried on for generations. When you go to Burkina Faso and listen to the traditional music, it's like here you have blues and country music. It's always the same music. What we have done is not only composed our own music, but we have also innovated in the way the instruments are working together. Two balaphones are usually played with one bara, a drum. What we have done is added a second bara and three other drums to it. They have introduced the idea of orchestrating.

We have been more entertaining than cultural. If we had been more cultural, we would have gotten help from the government. But now, the government will see how much that works, and they will eventually try to recuperate it.

The basis of the music is West African, but what we play is very contemporary. All the things we play are new compositions. They have very little to do with folklore and traditional songs. We have in our repertoire several traditional songs that we have rearranged, but most of our compositions are new. It has nothing to do with tradition. When people listen to it, they should understand that beneath the traditional sound we get from the instruments, there is the modern concept of the way the music is conceived.

Our instruments are thousands of years old. We are on the right road, and some day we will get through. We travel with five drummers, one flute, and two balaphone. The number of people we travel with is sufficient for us. We work it out perfectly. When you have groups with forty or fifty musicians, that's more traditional or folkloric songs.

The instruments come from West Africa, but then there are instruments from other parts of Africa, with which you get another kind of sound.

When you have the big ensembles, mainly they are national ballet ensembles, or government sponsored ensembles, which people put together, coming from different ethnic groups in the country, which makes a large group of fifteen musicians and twenty dancers.

That is the form that is presented to the West. In Africa, that is not really the case. Usually, when people play together, it's in smaller groups. The day to day creative way of playing music. Of course, you might get a large group of musicians playing now and again, at feasts and special ceremonies.

Just to illustrate how much we have advanced within our music, when we return to Burkino Faso, it is a very new music. People are not accustomed to hearing it. It's very modern for them.

Jon Hassel and Riuichi Sakamoto have realized this by listening to us. We didn't go to music school, like Jon Hassel or Sakamoto, in the Western way, but we are still able to work the same way. Orchestration is a way of working that is not that is not often met in African music.

The idea of putting us together with Jon Hassel was started by a concert promoter in Italy, Ricardo Guardini. He is very fond of jazz. He was listening to Farafina's music on a record player and he heard Jon Hassel's music coming from the radio. It was like sitting in the middle of two rooms. He had two artists coming in. He felt that this could work together. Something could be done there.

He called us up, he wrote us, and that's the way it started. That was in late 1986. In 1987, we started to try to see how we could work this collaboration, and we ended up having five concert schedules. We rehearsed for about five days in a place in France, close to Paris, where we stayed and rehearsed for ten days, trying to merge the two musics.

It was a very interesting experience. On the one side, you had the traditional rooted music, on the other side a very avant garde–oriented sound. The two mixed together.

For Riuichi Sakamoto, two of the other members of the group and myself came to New York for a week and played on three tracks of his album.

We are open to all kinds of music. We are partial to reggae music, like Bob Marley, because it has a good swing, but it's quiet to listen to also. Old jazz, like Miles Davis or Art Blakey. We have a wide range of musical interests.

On the other side, we have been invited to all kinds of stages, jazz festivals, rock festivals. We are not screwed into the African scene, like that's where we're from and that's where we have to fit into. We can fit on any stage. If you listen carefully to the music, it is quite jazzy in the way we do the balaphone. That's why we call it from the roots of Africa to the roots of jazz.

We listen to Salif Keita, Manu Dibango, and Alpha Blondy. We used to listen to music from Zaire, but we are getting kind of tired of it. It's dance music, and they don't seem to put much work behind it.

You can hear it in the what happened to Toure Kunda. They say that they're African, but they want to play rock and roll. African rock and roll. Western fans say, "Well, that's not much rock." The Africans say, "Well, what is that?" Somewhere there is a reason why the success of Toure Kunda collapsed the way it did. Other musicians, also. The same might be going for Mory Kante, for example. He is a very successful musician now, but he must be cautious of things. We are not now in that heavy top business. We didn't choose to be that way. We chose to go our own way with traditional instruments. Of course it's harder, but we're very comfortable with how it's going. We feel like we're on the right path.

The feeling I get about Toure Kunda is that they wanted to conquer the Western world. With all its tough business, there is a tendency to forget the source of their inspiration, which is their own continent. They say they're African, but all of a sudden, there is a cut. That's when break with your public. That seems to happen with musicians, like Santana. When he started with disco music, that made a kind of bizarre situation for his fans. He could get it back now, but for a while . . .

It's a form of respect for us to respect ourselves, with what we wanted to research in our own music. We feel that that is respect to the public, because you get your own audience who believe in you and listen to you and follow you. Those musicians come to Europe and the Western world try to get on to the larger music scene.

I live in Switzerland now. It was written in his stars that we go to live in Switzerland. I went to Europe to visit, and got a job offer as a dance teacher in Geneva. That's the way it happened.

I teach dancing from different ethnic groups. There isn't just one form of dance that I teach. I'm bringing several forms of dance. We're also creating new dances, in the sense when I teach, I start with an idea, like going to the fields to work. You go to your fields to work, then you take a break, then you go back to work, then you go home. You have different scenes like the going to work scenes. In the traditional form, they will just dance the idea of working in the field. They choreograph and create and tell stories through the dance.

It's an open workshop course. I work together with an organization that works with traditional music research. It's called the Workshops for Musicology Research. They invite people from all over the world to teach. They have workshops in music.

I teach bankers and professional dancers. Ever since I have been teaching, I have four or five students who started their own classes.

The situation of being in Europe, while everyone else is in Burkina Faso has been an enormous advantage. I am the link between the Western world and Africa. I am the link between our European management and the band. I understand how both ends work. That has become a very valuable asset. That also helps the group move on. The cross-cultural experiences have helped the band. Touring and living in Switzerland has helped us better understand the way music is perceived in the Western world. The way it is constructed conceptually. The fact that the band is living there, and I often come back to Burkina Faso, we are not loosing our ties.

This doesn't create any problems, in that they perform every day there, and when I bring new ideas, it's just not a problem. In the last few years, we have been on tour in Europe four to six months a year. It's just not a problem.

We are not doing this only for our own personal sake. We don't just want to be known in Europe and America for ourselves. It is connected with an effort towards promoting African culture, as well. The instruments we are working with, they are all traditional instruments. If you look over the African music scene, Farafina must be the only group with that way of working. There are other bands that work with drums, but they don't have the same approach. Taking these instruments, which had been considered as a symbol of their primitive culture and cast aside since colonization. We want to tell our African brothers that there is a richness, we can perform a lot of things with these instruments. We want to show how far we can go with that work. It's a very hard way.

It is going somewhere. We have been able to reach people in so many countries that all these efforts haven't been in vain.

FELA ANIKULAPO KUTI

When Fela Anikulapo Kuti died from AIDS on August 2, 1997, in Lagos, the world lost a remarkable and controversial musician. One of the few African artists to achieve any kind of impact on the rest of the world before the term "worldbeat" found its way onto header cards in record stores, Fela's large ensembles and long, incendiary jams always packed a musical wallop. More importantly, though, his lyrics packed a political punch that often put him at odds with his government. The son of a leading voice for Nigerian nationalism, he hated the series of military dictatorships that ran his country. Early in the eighties, he changed his name from Ransome Kuti to Anikulapo Kuti, "Anikulapo" translating to one who keeps death in his pouch. He married all of the female members of his entourage, becoming as notorious for having nearly thirty wives as he was for his music and his politics. Fela formed his own political party, Movement of the People, and ran for president. In the mid-eighties, on the eve of his first American tour in nearly a decade, the police arrested him for currency smuggling. Amnesty

International took up his cause. The next junta freed Fela just in time for him to play the Amnesty International Conspiracy of Hope concert broadcast worldwide. Fela's son, Femi, continues to perform. Fela's brothers continue to speak out. Death might have escaped Fela's pouch, but his legacy continues.

Survival is my spiritual condition. I am very spiritual, I am very knowledgeable about myself, I know what I accomplished about myself. I know how I can improve my mind. I was using the prison as a treatment, so I was ready for any condition whatsoever. It was very bad, but I used that badness for goodness for my personal self, so coming out of it, I feel younger, stronger.

I am more dangerous. I'm a prisoner, I'm a certified prisoner. A prisoner means you only have pity when you have to. People's conditions don't bother your mind because it sees so much atrocities in prison that people's conditions outside doesn't bother you anymore. So if somebody offends you outside, you go into prison for two years, at the end of two years, it's very dangerous for this guy. Prisoners are quite dangerous people, in a good way, not in a bad way.

As a matter of fact, by the time I went to prison, I couldn't play my sax, my tenor sax, because the beating I got in 1981 destroyed one part of my body, I was almost walking down. I couldn't carry my sax. So, I used the prison to get my body together, and at the same time thinking of music, not composing, just thinking. Then I started to think of some music I would write when I come out. Then when I came out, I started to write, not what I was thinking when I was in prison, but what I was thinking now that I was out of prison. Because my mind's developed, and my spiritual concept of life is . . . different, the music is going to be much more effective.

I would like to say how gratified I am for the support I got while I was in prison. I appreciate the support. It has given me the complete belief that this world is for one people, and the whole different races of this world are one people, just different colors and things. I intend to enhance this concept of human internationalism.

When I was in prison, I wanted to release my record *Army Arrangement.* My younger brother Beko, took the tapes to EMI just for printing. We weren't saying, "EMI to put your label on it, we just don't have a factory, we don't have the machinery to make records." EMI has this machinery so we say, "EMI we have our money. Print these records for us, and we'll pay you, collect our records to distribute ourselves." They still refused to print. EMI is pro-Nigerian atrocities, also Decca, all the multinationals in Nigeria, most of them are pro-African governments, because without being pro-African governments, they cannot make any headway. They have to be, so anything that comes between them and the government . . . pshew, cut down.

My country needs new ideology, new systems. I will run for president if necessary. I say if necessary for two reasons: I seem to see the downfall of democracy in Africa as it is now. And it seems as if in Nigeria, the position is that one day they are just going to come and wake me up and say, "Fela, please come and be president." It may not even be necessary to have an election because my popularity is too extreme. I have a feeling I wouldn't even have to run for it, I might just be invited.

When the Europeans ruled Nigeria, I understood what free speech was about. I understood that you could say anything you wanted to say. My mother, who was political, was able to operate in the European system without much harassment. If anybody wants to do what my mother did in 1947 now, it is a different matter. They wouldn't even allow you to march in the street. The Europeans used to allow us to march in the streets, but now if you march in the streets, they shoot you. The problem now lies within us, and that has to be settled now. What matters now is that our own people are doing this to us, which is worse.

People who are going to rule people should understand about pain, understand human feelings, understand what suffering is all about. Then they can lead. People who don't understand these things should not be leading. That's why I think I can now lead effectively. I can understand suffering. The kinds of pains I have, I wouldn't wish on you.

We want to see an Africa where people can come and go as they like, and just enjoy themselves. We are not saying that pan-

Africanism is going to save the world. We hope that it will open the eyes of the less progressive leaders of the world. What is stopping this from happening is the evil minds of the leaders of the world today. Once we get leaders with good minds, you will see less harassment of the citizens of the world.

Music is supposed to have an effect. If you're playing music and people don't feel something, you're not doing shit. That's what African music is about. When you hear it something must move. I want to move people to dance, but also to think. Music wants to dictate a better life, against a bad life. When you're listening to something that depicts having a better life, and you're not having the better life, it must have an effect on you.

It's the African influence in me, that was exposed to American influence a long time ago that's just manifested itself, although American musicians who play what's called jazz are just playing their roots. I was very influenced by it a lot at the early stages of my work as a musician, but now my influences are very limited. I think my approach to my music is very cultural. The result is what you hear. Of course people hear the influence of jazz. Jazz is not jazz, it's African music.

Playing with Lester Bowie was a beautiful experience. He worked on *No Agreement*, he worked on *Dog Eat Dog*. Ginger Baker was good. Working with Roy Ayers was a very good experience, we went on a big tour of Nigeria.

I play five-hour concerts because music is a thing of joy, man. When I play music I don't want to stop. Just play and play.

Now that many musicians are getting very political, it makes me very happy, because I have maintained a long time that musicians should make political music. I'm very happy now. Musicians will soon have to start to play political music. The idea is spreading, and that makes me happy.

Everybody in Africa from north to south loves my music. Everybody in the government has my records. They don't want to see me, they don't want to hear my voice alive, but they like the records. They'd prefer to hear me dead.

I have changed the name of my music from Afrobeat to something else a long time ago, since 1978, like I changed my name. Ransome is an English name, and I'm not an Englishman. Anikulapo means "one who has death in his pouch" in Yoruba.

I stopped calling my music Afrobeat, because Afrobeat is too commercial for me. My music is not commercial music. My music is African music. What happens with my music is that I hold myself with the entire system of African culture, not just with my country of Nigeria, because Nigeria is an artificial country. It's not a country as far as I'm concerned, and as far as many progressive Africans are concerned. That's why we talk about pan-Africanism.

I use the African culture to dictate the effect of my music. I use the continent as a whole. My music is not Afrobeat, it's just very pure African music, very deep African music. That's why it's such a success in Africa. All Africans can identify, irregardless of different ethnic cultures, with my music. All of Africa. Rhythmically, musically, and possibly the movement of the dancing. African music is so intricate and beautiful, that to understand it, you really have to throw away all colonial thoughts of mind. To get rid of the shit is the basis of African music, and to be able to make effective music. So, my music, since '78, is African music.

I'm not against musicians who have to go out of Africa to play. Not everybody has the same mind to stay. It's very difficult for people to stay, very difficult to make headway there. Being in France and playing African music to Europeans is good. There's nothing wrong about it, although I say it's better for them to stay at home and do it, but if they stay at home, it would be impossible for them to accomplish things they could accomplish out of Africa. One can't condemn that kind of decision, but I wouldn't do that because I'm a different person, I guess.

I don't believe in the institution of marriage anymore, for example. Now I don't have any wives. I have women of my children. There are four mothers of my children, but they don't have any say in my way of life.

After the Kalakuta Republic burned down, I haven't been able to listen to music a lot, because I didn't have a stereo in my place. So I have not been able to listen to music. During my incarceration made it worse. To listen to other peoples' records, I go to discotheques in Lagos.

In this world that we have now, human beings discourse, talk, compare, contrast, that's what makes the world happy. I don't really have to bother myself about comparing with anybody. It's not relevant.

Photograph: Ebel Roberts, Virgin Records

YOUSSOU N'DOUR

Youssou N'Dour embraces his culture fiercely. His take on that culture, a music dubbed mblaxa, brings a very ancient African civilization into very modern times. N'Douris a contemporary artist with a big worldwide following of fans among general music lovers and music makers. Peter Gabriel fell in love with Ndour's voice and used it on several tracks of So, then invited him to tour as his opening act. This garnered N'Dour the kind of exposure very few non-Western acts could even contemplate. In the mid-nineties, he was working on many things. One of them was becoming proficient in English. In America, most of the time, when he met the press, there had to be a translator.

I like the way English sounds. My style of English is different, and I think it works well with the Wolof, interchanged. For me it works well.

For the moment, though, I express myself better in French than in English. Singing a song is different. When you are singing a song in English, you learn it, you study it, and you integrate it with the music. It's different. Giving an interview, it just comes out. In interviews, I want to be as sincere as possible. That's why I prefer to speak in a language that I am comfortable in.

I hope, soon, to be able to speak to journalists directly in English. I'm understanding more and more. I'd like to. It's building.

My travels are a big part of it. I enjoy them very much, and it helps. Also, I have a real desire to make myself understood. That's the main motivation.

My music is modern African music. African music is the mother of all these other musics, and that's the truth. It's really hard to say anything more along those lines. I consider African music the mother of all other modern music.

When I first started, my father did not want me to be a musician, did not want me to sing. Musicians were bad news, off limits. It was not the kind of life my father wanted for me. I stuck up for myself, and I argued with my parents. I really fought for it. I said to my father, "I want to do this, I want to be a musician, and I want to show you that I can make the kind of music that is positive."

In earlier days, musicians were stagnant. I wanted to show my father I could be a musician who would evolve, so in fact, my attitude toward new ideas goes back to my first encounters with my father over this issue of whether I was to be a musician at all. I wanted to enter into realms that Senegalese musicians had never entered before. I wanted to work with people they had never worked with before. This was to prove a point to my father.

I can remember being told by people when we first started playing that our music, mbalax, is not really good music. And yes, we were all terribly influenced by American music, and Latin American music and soul music that we thought was good.

After making *Emigre* in 1983, which is a very traditional album—interpreted with modern instruments, but a very traditional album—I met certain musicians in Dakar, including Pap Quien, the drummer, and Habib Faye, keyboards and bass, who learned music through jazz. I had already reached a level of success before this time, but I wanted to meet these people from a different world, if you will, and do something different. For the first time I decided to work a different way. I decided to rent a house, and lived with these new guys, and we worked on music together. Maybe I would try something and one would say, "No, that's not good," and I'd listen. I'd use their ideas. The first product of this new way of working was the *Nelson Mandela* album.

I had a new audience. My old audience, some of them didn't like it, some of them loved it. But it was controversial. I didn't do it for any other reason but I wanted to and I liked it. That was before Peter Gabriel.

In 1984 in Paris, I was playing songs from the *Emigre* album. Peter Gabriel came to a concert and said he wanted to see me. A few months later, he came to Dakar and invited me to sing on his album, *So*. I sang one day with him. We worked on sounds with my voice that were stranger than ever before. Pop, rock sounds. After, he sent me a cassette, and I like the mixture he had made with my voice. Our interchange was deepened on tour with him, when he invited me to open on his world tour.

I certainly liked a lot of the sounds that Peter brought to my music, but by the same token, I think Peter saw in my music some things that he took with him. I think it was a mutual exchange.

Wolof is a culture as well as a language. It's a very old culture. There's Wolof music, there's Wolof rhythm, there are ways of doing things that are Wolof. We're fighting hard to keep our old culture, so it can stay alive without getting lost. Griots are a part of the tradition.

Two things off the top of my head exemplify Wolof. One would be generosity. Like buying a bag of rice that would last in your house for a month, but instead of keeping it for your household, you distribute it to the neighbors for no reason other than for the spirit of sharing. Another thing I would cite would be going to a show, concert, or event, and dressing up in a high style, dressing up more than the person on stage, just for the sheer pleasure of it.

I think the culture is surviving very well. For example, we modern Wolofs, when we get together on the road or in our travels, if there are a whole bunch of us traveling, we all tend to all end up in one room, drinking tea, eating together, talking together. That's just the way we are.

Sometimes in life, before advancing, you have to try some steps. I'm better in the studio. I have more of a mastery of the recording process. Now I go in there and I know exactly what I want. Before, that wasn't always the case, because before I was, perhaps, fearful of sophisticated machines. Studios are a problem in Africa.

I'm living in Dakar. I just don't like living in Paris. Paris is a city that is historically linked to the French-speaking countries. French is the official language in most of West Africa. The traffic exists. There's also an interconnection of the infrastructure of the music business between Paris and West Africa. In West Africa, artists don't generally have their own infrastructures. Studios, the whole system. You can't make a living, generally, in West Africa.

I think I make a pretty hard effort to survive and succeed. Also, I'm interested in encouraging music in Dakar. That's important to me. I think, if I were to live outside Dakar, I would not be doing my part to assist in developing music in the country.

There are young people who see me on TV in Senegal, then they go outside and see me on the street. That might be an example. I think, if I weren't there, sometimes, a young person thinks it's only a dream. They love an artist and they never see them. They think the artist lives in heaven somewhere. For me, it's very important that people like my music at home, that they see me on television, that they see me in the street, and that they can go out and see me perform regularly.

Our experience should be used for the benefit of Africa. I have a production company in Dakar in which I have invested very heavily. I have a studio that's where we recorded *Eyes Open*. It was the first album recorded there. It's a twenty-four-track studio, analog, in the center of Dakar. I think the sound is state of the art, with respect to what you'll find here or in Europe. We believe that the studio will be important for other artists. African artists and Senegalese artists in particular, who need to record can do so now at home. Since then there have been a number of local Senegalese releases made in the studio.

There is also a label. Our aim for it is to serve as an outlet for the release and distribution of artists, perhaps with the aid of my name, in other markets as well as Africa.

Latin music was our biggest influence, dance rhythms from Africa, and like everyone else, I sang Cuban songs. I was in the soup, and I did the same thing as everyone else. And of course I knew and loved James Brown. His rhythms were fascinating to us. All the other influences that are there, I don't know how to measure them.

My music takes on a character according to where I am at emotionally at a particular time when it's recorded. I think I am getting stronger, and I want to present myself as someone who is concerned, to show people that I care about the issues that I'm singing about, and to give an example for the young people and to express their concerns. I feel their concerns. I see what they see, I live what they live.

There are certain companies in Africa that have financial problems, and American companies and European companies are proposing deals whereby, they will, for a fee, accept toxic waste materials and bury it in their country. It's a problem. People are talking about it. There are plans to go on with further dumping. That's really the most important thing. They are talking about making it a more serious matter. It's a very big problem. The song "Toxique" is trying to inform people, so perhaps the problem can be ended.

I don't work for any particular political program and I don't construct my albums with any particular political agenda in mind. Political colors may evolve in the normal course of creating the album, but I don't really design it that way.

A Japanese journalist asked me if "Useless Weapon" was written in commemoration of the Senegalese soldiers who died in the Gulf. There was a plane that went down with almost a hundred Senegalese soldiers after the hostilities had ceased. It was never in my mind.

I know I feel pan-Africanism, and I think that all of us Africans feel it, that over the last year or so there's a tremendous feeling of African unity building. There's a certain feeling in the air that makes us feel like we're all in this together. Young people have been vocal, in the last year or so, in bringing democracy throughout the continent.

There's a freedom of expression that is in the air. I think that must have had something to do with how all that came up on the record.

I signed with Spike Lee's label in 1992 for a while. I think Spike Lee had known of me and known of my music for a long time. I had a number of possibilities to sign a new record deal and was most interested in his. He came to see me, he came to Senegal, and I think that that was very important for both of us. We've seen each other since many times, here and in Paris.

I was most interested in the assurances, especially the artistic assurances that he gave me with respect to how I make my music and creative issues, creative control if you like. Also, I was interested in the possibilities that he talked about with me, to have my music exposed to black people in the United States. It has always saddened me that black people in America don't get into African music. I never understood. I never had any answer for why that is so.

I'm sure you must have appreciated that all my records have been different. I don't know how much of it is American, and how much of it is from other parts. I chose the song "Rubber Band Man" [on *Nelson Mandela*]. We wanted to play an American song. I listened to a lot, and I said, "That's the one I want to do."

Habib Faye and myself arrange the songs. Normally, my method of working is I like to sit with Habib and sing the songs without rhythm, without accompaniment. Very minimalistically.

Generally speaking, more broadly speaking, traditional African sounds sometimes just were not accessible to young people, to the music that played to the young people during the hours that the young people listened to the radio. The music that was being played in nightclubs and played by young people in their own homes. What we've done is given people an option to recognize a music that's not so far removed from contemporary life in the city and that's another option from the strictly traditional sounds that seemed really so far removed from what young people wanted. Sometimes I can actually think of instances where I heard percussion parts in a song and I would say, "Rhythm guitarists, play that."

None of those instruments are part of the Super Etoile, strictly speaking. But they're there, sonically, and in terms of expression, and that's what's important. These sounds are everywhere in all of our songs. We have balafon sounds in the keyboards, which, for us, are really close to the traditional instruments.

Sometimes we sample the traditional acoustic instruments. The rhythm guitar doesn't sound exactly like the xalam, just played in a certain fashion. It's all a matter of expression. The guitarist can make it sound very very close to a traditional xalam. Expression is more important than anything. You can give a xalam to an American guitar player, and it's not going to do any good. He's not going to know. Or you tell an American guitarist to play like Papa Mangone and he's probably not going to be able to do it.

Music, and lyrics more particularly, make suggestions to people. People can take from a song any inspiration that might be suggested. I'm sure of one thing. Music is the first language of everyone.

Photograph: Adrian Boot, Island Records

WALLY BADAROU

Wally Badarou, the Paris-born son of an African diplomat, started learning his craft in Benin. He has developed a global reputation as a producer, recording artist, citizen of the world and for being able to provide tasteful keyboard work for any occasion bringing his high-tech rhythmic sensibility to everything he touches. The diverse list of past customers for his talents attest to this. Best known for his work at a studio in the Caribbean as part of the Compass Point All-Stars, a loose ensemble of musicians that included Sly Dunbar and Robbie Shakespeare, Badarou rose to prominence, if not fame. His session work includes albums for Western artists like Marianne Faithfull, Grace Jones, M, Robert Palmer, and the Tom Tom Club as well as non-Western musicians including Sly and Robbie's solo albums, Gwen Guthrie, Miriam Makeba, and Manu Dibango,

It's kind of strange, somehow. I never considered myself as a sideman, although I've been doing that for most of my time now. I always considered everything I was doing, even when I was not even working for somebody else, even when I'm just programming something at home, even when I'm demoing at home, when I'm doing anything, I'm working for my own, because somehow, it helps show what I can do.

I'm into writing and programming. Right now, I'm sitting in front of my Macintosh computer, doing some refiling of all my papers and sounds and sequencers. I've always been into synthesizers, and a synthesizer, a real true synthesizer to me is that machine that until you put something into it, until you put in your talent, nothing really comes out. I have one distinction, a good synthesizer player has got to know his machine from top to bottom, and there's no way, with all the things that are happening today, that you can keep up with too many different machines. One guy I really admire is Joseph Zawinul from Weather Report. He still works with his Prophet 5, or his very ancient Oberheim modular system. I think that's great. I think that's a great approach.

I think being able to work with so many different sorts of people with so many different horizons was helping me set up an image as somebody who could work on totally different things. This is what I wanted to do.

I was starting to do a lot of recording sessions here in Paris, and I met with Robin Scott's brother. He was playing bass. He just talked to his brother about me and at that time his brother was working on the fourth version of this song "Pop Music." So one of those days I just got a call from Robin Scott, while he was in Paris, telling me to come down and have a listen. That's the way the whole thing started.

I've been trying to show more of what I could do each time. I was trying to show people this is how you heard me with Mick Jagger, this is how you're going to hear me with Manu Dibango.

The whole thing about Compass Point was that I think Chris Blackwell tried to create a kind of chemistry between Caribbean people and European people. At that time, he was looking for a European keyboard player to play on Grace Jones album. He heard about me because of the "Pop Music" thing and some other tracks I did playing on while I was in England. That was it really. At that time

I was bringing some European feel to the whole thing. But then, fortunately, I could show him more than the European side of myself.

The Tom Tom Club was the best session I played. It's funny. Just because they've always been nice guys, and I'm really sensitive to nice people. I mean, basically the Tom Tom Club as well as the Talking Heads. I've met David Byrne also. When I'm saying nice people, some nice people can make you provide the best without forcing anything. Just by the way they act and talk to you. Not pretending to be more than they actually are, which is great. Treating you as an artist rather than a backing musician.

It always happens a different way each time. I only had one session with Miriam Makeba, and at the beginning of the session, I didn't even know it was her. I mean I didn't even know she was the artist. I was just invited by her producer, telling me to come, and I was just getting there and behind an acoustic piano I was playing, I could see her coming and I said, "This is Miriam Makeba!" It was really exciting. I was impressed.

Those people I met at Compass Point, and especially Chris and Tina of the Talking Heads, were definitely those who really understood what I was trying to do and they took it exactly that way. I know that they love my album as much as I do love their stuff, and it's great.

I was trying to do almost the same thing I was doing when I did all those sessions with my album *Echoes*. I was trying to show myself as a multi-oriented artist, a multi-oriented mind. What I was looking for was to score for movies, to start with. I wanted to show some producers that I could write in totally different ways and totally different directions. I also wanted something that was not aggressive, that you wouldn't have to play very loud to enjoy. When you're saying background music, that's not what it's supposed to be, but it can be that and that's a great thing.

You can't predict having a hit like "Inspector General." Although there is a strong tendency afterwards to analyze it and say, "Oh yes, I know why it worked." It worked because it was good. Although it's very easy to rationalize, it's always a kind of surprise when it works, especially when it's not coming out of a big,

big promotion planning. It was just a normal release and it just did what it had to do. I think every artist should always praise the Lord that those things are happening.

I'm going try to make it different. In the future, I'm going to try to do some soundtracks.

That was definitely the idea behind it. It was kind of an ID card I was presenting. But in the process, I made it more personal somehow. But it was definitely a nice card for me. I had that idea in mind to make something for other people; I just wanted to be my own thing.

It was just what I wanted to produce at that time. If I was to go back to the studio, I would probably do something completely different again. I would maybe do something more jazz or maybe more R&B or maybe more pop oriented. I don't know yet. At that time, that was exactly what I wanted to do. So that was kind of personal at that time.

I have a kind of fusion jazz background when I was growing up here. After I spent those years in Africa, I started to play with a lot of French West Indian musicians here, in a lot of jazz fusion bands. That also led me into the Level 42 venture.

The whole thing started with M doing "Pop Music." I met the future drummer of Level 42, and we decided to do something more jazz somehow, and that's how the whole Level 42 venture started. Although I was not officially part of the band, I was with them all the time. I was writing with them all the time, I was recording with them from the very beginning. It could be something in that vein. When I'm talking about jazz, I'm talking about fusion jazz. I don't pretend to be another Count Basie.

A couple of my soundtracks were showing quite good, and I had a chance to work on some of them, to make some noise around, like *The Kiss of the Spider Woman*, I think it worked very well. I believe the chemistry of the film relies on that, although it wasn't really perceived that much. I mean it's something that is very organic. I believe a movie should be almost like a dream. Sometimes you dream about a situation, and all of a sudden, without any reason, you find yourself in a totally different situation. That is what we were trying to create with the film.

The people who made the film *Good To Go* loved one piece of my album, "Keys," the entry track of my album. They started to use it as a working title when they were editing the film. That way, what they were asking me to do was working in that same kind of direction, trying to provide something in that vein to just make it a bit different each time. So that's really what I did. I didn't try to do anything R&B for that thing, and I think that it's great because I always have the chance to come and do something totally different from the main vein soundtrackwise on the film.

It's always refreshing to hear something completely different. What you'd expect would be just a rap thing happening all the time, and here you are, you hear something different.

The whole classical side of the soundtrack is there to project some kind of real European feel, because those scenes are about what happened in Europe, then the synthetic things are very cold somehow, and are there to depict actual things that are going on in the prison cell itself and are more frightening, more scary. It's a story about that whole thing. I think that worked very well. It's kind of surprising just listening to the soundtrack album itself. I don't know. I kind of like it.

I used to be a bit concerned about, am I making some sort of heavy compromise on my African roots, but I didn't have much of that worry, after all, because anything I'm doing I have to do what I feel is right, and what I feel I like. I can hear people like Ray Lima, people like Manu Dibango, everybody has kind of a different approach. There's still a bit of Africa. There could be more of India or more of America or more Europe, and that's great, that's the way it should be.

The whole African expatriated tribe in France was not the world potential up until a couple of years ago when people started to listen to different things than they used to. I guess, like Bill Laswell producing Toure Kunda and Manu Dibango kind of proved themselves, that their music had some kind of value.

You see, as Africans, we always had a bit of underrating of our own music, and contempt of technology, because it's so rootsy, somehow. When you're talking about African music, you're talking about a fairly basic approach to how to record something, how to mix it, how to make it work. And suddenly we realized that that was the strength of our music. When I'm saying we, I'm saying most of the Africans based in France started to realize, and everything is starting to pick up now.

I can hear a lot of new African artists. On the other hand, I wouldn't like it to be spectacular just to be spectacular, because then it would be just a wave, and then it would just disappear in just a couple of years time. I believe African music has always been part of pop music, and at this stage it could become another phenomenon to be exploited over the next four or five years.

I also believe an African musician, whatever he does, if he's playing something rhythmical, his Africanity is going to show up. So it doesn't really matter how interesting he is from other musicians, or from other stuff that he can hear, it's still going to show up. So when I work a piece like "Countryman" for the *Countryman* film, for Chris Blackwell, it definitely had something African, although it was completely, entirely made with synthesizers. Not even with drum machines.

When you have people like Sting doing what he was doing before he went solo, or when you hear other people doing something totally different, nobody comes and tells them because you're Austrian you should play Mozart, because you're American, you should play Gershwin.

MARIE DAULNE, SABINE KABONGO, SYLVIE NAWASADIO | ZAP MAMA

Inspired by the music of the Congolese "Pygmies," this five woman a cappella group created a remarkable fusion of native harmonies and Western sensibilities.

MARIE DAULNE: My family stayed with the Pygmies because there was a rebellion in Zaire against the colonization of Belgium, then the independence. In '64, there was a lot of fighting. Many white people went into the forest to save themselves. The Pygmies saved people.

My mother married a white man. My mother put my family with the Pygmies. I was very young. I was just born in the middle of this situation.

I wasn't there long, six months. Then, I went back at four. I lived with protection in Europe, with my mother, African mother. I lived in Europe for four years before going back to Africa. I stayed there one year. Then I came back to begin school. I started school and had a European education. I grew up, and she respected and conserved the traditional African songs in Europe. I grew up with the traditional African songs in Europe. I grew up with traditional style and society in my house. That's my education.

I went back alone to central Africa when I was older. I chose to go back to Central Africa because there was the Congo native pygmy tribe in Central Africa. The tribe makes music that I like. I feel this music.

SABINE KABONGO: When we arrived in the group Zap Mama, Marie gave us some cassettes of Pygmy people and of Americans like Sweet Honey in the Rock. She gave us music that she wanted us to listen to. The first song we played on stage, she taught us the principle of her polyphony. After, she would make the song and give us our parts. She teaches us the practical things.

DAULNE: In the beginning, we were eight singers. Now, nobody else here actually was there in the beginning. I prepared the songs with other people. I do the arrangements. I knew one day I'd meet the girls who would be in the group to call the group Zap Mama. First, I met Sylvie. I remember her from when I was younger. I remembered her voice, I remembered its feeling. Then I started looking for her, "Do you remember Sylvie? Do you know where I can find her?" Then I met here in the street, and I proposed to her to sing and she said, "Yeah!" After, we go to the park, and we saw Sabine.

SYLVIE NAWASADIO: She was dancing.

KABONGO: I want to move!

DAULNE: She was expressing herself. We knew it was her. We made contact through her timidity. Naturally we sing together. During that time, we'd go on the streets, we'd do the . . . pri-vites?

KABONGO: Private parties. My god, we played some private parties.

DAULNE: They were crazy, really crazy. They were for some very rich people. They were for birthdays. We would arrive and say, "Well, what do we do?"

KABONGO: "Well, sing!" Yes, but there's no place to concentrate. People were there, and there was a table and we just, "Turn around and sing." It was very weird. But it was good because we made it.

DAULNE: We didn't sing the Pygmy chants at the parties, but African popular sounds, yes. And some of the songs of Sweet Honey in the Rock. We love them. And we have something similar.

KABONGO: But opposite.

DAULNE: It's the only a cappella band that we have something together.

NAWASADIO: It's like, when you make polyphony, you hear your voice, but not that much. You need to hear your voice from far, and you need to hear your voice melting with the other ones. That's when you get out of something you think about singing. That's not the point. You need to sing, but after, you don't think about it anymore. You let your voice out and it comes together with the other ones. And it doesn't disturb you the way that you don't hear yourself more clearly than with the others. And that's it. When you make polyphony, you don't need to hear your voice more than the others. When you hear it more, maybe you sing too loud or you concentrate more on yours. So you don't mix with the other voices. When it comes like that, that makes the polyphony sound, then you can hear other voices above. You can hear the harmonic. You can hear another melody above.

DAULNE: We have to open the individualism. Then it's good for the spirit. When you sing alone, all the time the people in music show us it's you, you, you, and you. It's cool, it's very important to feel ourselves, but with the other. Zap Mama, people love us because we can open our spirit. We can give everywhere inside to others. We can just meet everything. Take all your individualism and stay the same. The queen is the same as the pygmy in the forest. The president of the United States and pygmies are little men who have no rights, but they're the same.

NAWASADIO: They can give each other something.

DAULNE: Everybody was surprised that we did a madrigal, "Din Din" on our debut album. It's good. It's polyphonic. Did it touch you? That's why we chose it. We want to touch everybody, every country, every people. They can find something similar in the recording *Zap Mama*. We propose different kinds of music, because we feel madrigals, too. We grew up in Europe, and we learned European harmonies in school, and we feel that. When we are together, we sing African, we sing Arabic, everything, because we open our spirits to every country, every music, every people.

For Zap Mama, I chose a cappella, and until the end, it's a cappella. Then, if we want to sing with others, as a personal experience, then you do that. Sabine and me, we sing together in a soul group. It's with instruments, but we feel that. Sometimes we want to sing with . . .

KABONGO: One day we sang with a guitar player,

DAULNE: One day we decided to do a concert, a cappella, and one moment, in the middle of the concert, we open the door and there are one hundred musicians.

KABONGO: They get five minutes to give everything they have . . .

DAULNE: Then we continue a cappella.

A lot of musicians want to play with us. Everybody says that we listen to you all the time, we want to take our instruments and play with you. One day, everyone will.

KABONGO: Sometimes some friends of ours will say, "Are you going to put some instruments on your next album?" And you talk about it with them and after that you say, "Maybe they've got an idea."

DAULNE: When I've been in Zaire and in Senegal, I've listened. One day, we'll play with instruments. Maybe one day.

We do Zairian music because I feel Zairian music more than any other. It's my culture. There is Pakastani music, and Arab music, other musics because they influence me. There is Zairian, there is American, there is reggae, salsa, French, old, old European songs. There is one that is polyphonic from the sixteenth century, maybe the seventeenth. I have to ask. I went to the convent school when I grew up. I don't want to say the kind, because when I do a salsa, friends say, "Wow, that's a good reggae!"

NAWASADIO: And when we do a reggae, friends of mine say, "You can call it anything but not a reggae."

DAULNE: "That's not a reggae, Marie." When I say I want to do something, I respect the technique. To hear something as reggae, there is some technique. You have to respect the rhythm and bass and the tempo. I mix every technique. When I was in school, in jazz school, my teacher all the time would ask, "What is happening in your head?" Because I would ask some questions. But you learn, and if you always change the techniques and purposes, it's all the same. Get out of the rules a little bit.

That's the problem. When you learn in school about music, it's very regular and very traditional. It's hard for some people who have a lot of knowledge about music and a lot of technique. They have a lot of difficulties. Sometimes they want to play out of the rules. To get out of everything they learn about music, about times and everything.

NAWASADIO: Yes. I left school because they can change something inside. When they took a Charlie Parker song and they analyzed the solo, when I saw that, I had to leave the school. If I passed, it would have changed something in my technique. I left school then. I stopped. When someone would ask me about Zap Mama, I always say I'm going to jazz school. I learned many things in jazz school. I understand a lot of things from jazz school.

DAULNE: In school, we had to sing a cappella when we practiced. I liked those moments. Then the teacher would start. I enjoyed myself. I would listen all the time. It was a good sound. I didn't follow the practice. I just enjoyed myself to hear all the voices. I was a good student.

We chose to record our second album in New York so the music can feel like New York, the kind of music with the energy of New York.

KABONGO: The same sounds can get another energy from the place where are.

DAULNE: You take the energy of the town and you put it in your music. I can't record traditional songs here. Here it's Whaaah! For traditional songs, I go to the forest, to the nature for the atmosphere to sing. It's not right. We don't have technique like everybody. We have different technique and our technique, we have to have a story and feeling. If you can't understand it, you can feel it. For some songs, I don't want to say something. I just feel a story and I let my head put the songs. I don't prepare the songs.

Sometimes words we learn, when we're singing in another language, I have to think what these words mean, and to stay free I let only my mouth and my spirit put words, and some words come in. Some people come in at the end of the concert and say, "I feel it and understand what you say. I feel that." Some person who needs a story, he wants to hear it.

I put Burundi, Zairian, and Tanzanian together. It's different songs I heard, I don't know where. I put them all together. The three songs have something similar. The first, a young girl wants a baby, the second is she had a baby and she wants to make a lot of babies, the third is we are a family and we enjoy ourselves. I didn't think, before that, that it fit together. I put it together, we sang it, and then I realized, "Yeah! There is a story."

I hope that our music, I hope that the American people, and everybody here in America wants to know what happens in different countries, and nobody knows. They are not versed in other kinds of music. Here they only propose American music and they close their eyes . . .

KABONGO: And ears . . .

DAULNE: And repropose different kinds of music. It's like a little piece. A little piece of this and a little piece of that, and after, you can choose. You can go to a big place and find it.

EAST AFRICA

As heavily redolent of the Middle East as the Maghreb, the turbulent eastern section of Africa has its own share of the kind of postcolonial strife that informs so much of life in West Africa. From military strongmen to "civil" wars, tribal conflicts, various religious clashes, and Western adventurism in the name of peacekeeping—witness Somalia—to the kind of corruption most politicians can only dream of in the West, few areas of the world hold a candle to Kenya and Ethiopia.

Yet the music scenes are rich if not wealthy. In Kenya, home of some of the most corrupt bureaucracy in the world, they have a rocking music scene that has made legends of bands like Shirati Jazz.

Again, the expatriate scene is also rich. Ethiopians make up a surprisingly large portion of the population in capitals like Paris and Washington D.C., making food and music there. The exotica quotient his high, but the music is stunning.

The island nation of Madagascar lies off the coast of the continent. In that isolation, some of the world's most interesting music developed, a sign of how important music is to the spiritual life of people all over the planet.

ASTER AWEKE

Ethiopian singer Aster Aweke has been called the Aretha Franklin of East Africa. Like so many African performers, people in her own country know her well, and like so many Africans in general, she became an expatriate, coming to the Washington D.C. area, already home to tens of thousands of Ethiopians. Like Paris in France and London in England, the capital city has become a haven. Unlike other African performers (such as Toure Kunda), she didn't leave her homeland to become a more popular performer. Performing more or less came after her.

Mostly, I write my own songs. I always wanted to become unique in my own style. I'm glad I made it. It took me some time, but finally I've got my own identity. But, it is based on Ethiopian music.

When people hear my voice they say, "We feel it." When they read the lyrics they say, "We feel it. You really sound as if you've been there." I want them to know I am a real storyteller in singing, even though I don't sing them in English. It is so hard to explain.

Before I left Ethiopia, I had recorded five records and I was singing in the major clubs and the big international hotels. But I was worried about my future, what I was going to do.

What concerned me was my education. I could have grown there, too. I'm still sending cassettes. In terms of education. What if something happened to my voice, what am I going to do? On the side, I wanted to do something, because I was only singing on Fridays and Saturdays. I worked only six hours a week, so very thin.

I went to America to study vocal, I went to study business, I didn't know what I wanted. But I wanted to get away from singing. Back home, I wasn't accepted that much among my families, but I was making it. I came here, tried to change, but no. I was unhappy. I hated myself. So I said to hell with everything. I was going to sing. That was the only thing that made me feel good, happy. I wrote songs while I was in America, but I still sent them back home. And I select them. We always do it on a cassette.

I don't know how it did happen that I started to make records in the West. These people from London found me. A guy was selling my prerecorded cassette from Ethiopia. He sold one of my cassettes to an English woman. She took it to this record company, gave it to them.

They heard it, they got to him, "Where can we find this singer?"

He said, "I don't know. She's Ethiopian."

"We've got to find her."

"She lives somewhere in America, but I don't know where."

Then a woman I know went to London. She happened to visit this guy. He knew that she came from America, asked her, "Do you know Aster Aweke? Do you know where she lives?"

She goes, "I know where she lives. I know her."

And these people contacted me. They asked me to send them cassettes that I had, so they could choose and then put it in a record. I told them, "No, I'd rather do it again. We should record it again." So they came, heard a practice. They went home, came back, and that's how it happened.

It was all arranged by Ethiopian musicians. The people who played it in London only copied that and played it. They did not arrange it. They heard it, studied it and then played it over. The keyboardist was covering the horn section. When they took that to London, the keyboardist studied that and played it over.

It is the way I sing, the way I wrote the songs sounds nice with that kind of arrangement. I didn't arrange it for just Ethiopians. It was mostly the songs, I had done it before. I didn't do it just for this record. It's been there.

So when they came to me, we worked on that. We cut it for them. But I didn't write this for a non-Ethiopian audience. It's been there before. We just re-recorded them. They were old. These songs were five or six years old. It was not right to change the music to be suitable for a non-Ethiopian audience. It's been there before. We just did it in a bigger studio.

I re-recorded "Dayim," an old one, for the first Western album. That early album was great. That's when I got famous. That was in the late 1970s.

Now it's even more exciting because I've matured. I know what I'm talking about. I know how when I sing I have control over my voice. It's even more exciting right now.

Before, I'd just sing. I love singing and I'd just sing. I didn't care whether it was wrong or right, I didn't care whether people liked it or not, I was just pleasing myself. But now, I'm careful in terms of what I'm doing, while I write something, while I'm performing on stage. Before, if I wanted to jump on the stage, I used to think, "What are they going to say to me?" If I wanted to shout in the middle of a song, what would people say? "What is she doing?"

Right now, I don't care about that. I feel what I like. I like what I do right now. I give it to them, and they respond. I was afraid, I was shy. Now I know what I'm doing. I believe in what I'm doing right now, so I give what I've got. It doesn't mean that I don't make mistakes. But I don't particularly care.

The east and north of Ethiopia are mostly Arabic. Thirty to fifty percent of Ethiopian people are Muslims. Ethiopia has a lot of Christians. In the history it's very mixed. They sing in Arabic.

We do sing in English, but copy those famous singers in the club. We do have discos that you dance with American English disco music. But they don't want to do it, all over, expose it like this.

I sing in Amharic. It's kind of an international language for Ethiopia. Everybody understands that in terms of the language. You listen to what you understand most of the time. You don't hear Arabic or English stuff on the radio most of the time. Yes, we do listen to English music. We do get films from around the world. But we never wanted to change with it, and open ourselves to another culture and let people here know about our music. I don't know.

Ethiopia has kind of a closed culture. They don't care about the other world. In our culture, for example, when you have lunch, when you eat, you don't eat alone from one plate. If you are a family, if you are like ten, you gather around together and eat from one big tray. On weekends, you don't go shopping, you see one another. All the time, you are surrounded by people. You eat with your neighbor. You see your neighbor every day. You have coffee. Sometimes, if you want, you have dinner. Westerners are fascinated by that, especially the food, the way they feed you sometimes. If you were my lover or my father or my sister or my brother, I'd feed you. You'd just sit there and relax. All those things. It is fascinating. We eat by hand. We don't use forks and knives. People seem to be fascinated by that.

There are big singers in Ethiopia that are not known here, as you might know Nigerians or people from other parts of Africa. There are strong bands, strong singers, strong artists. They're not discovered. Don't ask me why.

The biggest artist I know, his name is Tèklè Tèsfa-Ezghi. He travels to Europe a lot of times. They go. Big musicians go to Nigeria for festivals. All over Africa, whenever they have festivals, they are invited there. I was never invited. But they're not known like West Africans.

This music has been there. For you, it's new because you've just heard it, but it's been there for quite some time. Two, three hundred years. On the flutes, on the traditional instruments and on the modern instruments.

One instrument we use, the kharar, has six strings and you use it like a guitar. It suits "Dizita." We have lots of kinds of flutes and kinds of violins. Lots of them, but this has only one string, they hold it like this [makes a cradle] and it doesn't have frets, either. It sounds good.

This is not typical Ethiopian music. It's based on tradition, but it's modern. For Ethiopians, the sound, the arrangement is modern. We've changed it a bit, as the music grows, but the beat, the scan and everything is based on traditional Ethiopian song.

I am singing. I am trying to introduce my music. I believe it is a rich music. It has different kinds of riffs, scales and the language is fascinating and the melodies are fascinating. That's what I'm doing. The culture, the Ethiopian music. The feeling. I want people to know Ethiopian music first, and after that, Aster, the voice, the melody.

HENRY KAISER

One of the Western artists featured in this book, avant garde guitarist Henry Kaiser is one of the West's great musical enigmas. He seems to have made his career out of being difficult to peg down. Kaiser played on popular cover albums celebrating the music of the Grateful Dead and Neil Young. He was a core member of the avant (savant?) rock supergroup French, Frith, Kaiser, and Thompson. With David Lindley, Kaiser took his longstanding affinity for non-Western artists and brought them to the (relative) mainstream with acclaimed albums of music from Norway and especially from Madagascar. His recording brought international attention to artists like Rossy and Tarika Sammy, making them the generic equivalent of stars. He brings a unique perspective to the non-Western music discussion.

I've been working with non-Western artists since the first day I started playing a guitar. I remember the first day I got a guitar, when I was twenty years old in 1972, putting on an old record of music from Madagascar and starting to play along with a particular track. I didn't realize it until Lindley and I had been to Madagascar, but it turned out that we recorded that same song with that same man over there in Madagascar. In the sense of playing with records and things like that, I've been dealing with that from the first day I got a guitar. I got the guitar to do exactly what I do now.

    I'd been listening to it since I started buying records. That's what I heard on the radio, that's what I was interested in, that's what I looked for in the record store. I found pop radio stations were boring and awful and the noncommercial stations were great and interesting. It was just better music. You turn off the radio and you say, this is better. I'm going to look for this. It's never been a social thing for me. It was new, it told me things I didn't know. It asked questions I wasn't aware of. It made me feel things I had not felt before.

When I first got a record player, I remember buying an Ali Akhbar Khan record, an Albert Ayler record, a Stockhausen record, and some African drumming, which I guess must have been Olantunji, and a Cecil Taylor record. I bought all those at the same time I was buying Grateful Dead records or Charles Ives records. That's the stuff I was buying in the very beginning, when I was a teenager. I didn't go through the popular music, popular culture phase, except with the San Francisco bands that were part of the popular culture I grew up with.

I've been recording with non-Western artists for a while. The first one I recorded with was probably Sang Wan Park, who plays the kayagu. I just tried to seek out the people I'd listened to on the records that I liked. I did the same thing with avant garde music, recording with Derrick Bailey, the same thing with rock music, recording with Richard Thompson and Bob Weir and John French. It's the same thing. I sought out people that I thought would be interesting to work with and tried to meet new ones I didn't know about.

You know there's really no difference working in all these different kinds of musics. People see them as different kinds, but I think that's a marketing thing for record stores, so they can have sections to put things in and so radio can have formats. That's not what music's about. Music's about people, personal expression, people communicating, sharing, creating things together. To me there's no difference in working with Derrick Bailey, with Richard Thompson, with great master musicians of traditional music from Madagascar or Norway or Korea or New Guinea. It's all the same thing. It's just people working together, trying to make a nice musical statement and have a good time.

I kind of feel like show and tell in elementary school. You bring something in and tell the class about it. They didn't know about it. I like serving that function. That's part of it, and part of it is the special magic that two people who have their own musical universes can come together and make something brand new together. That can happen in experimental music, that can happen with musicians from different cultures, folk music. It's a great thing. That's one of the great things about music.

I know I'm an unusual person. I know I can listen to music from Korea or music from the Middle East and I can relate to it. I know the person who hasn't been exposed to a lot of music from around our big, blue planet might not be able to relate to it when they heard it the first time. But if people heard as much of this as I have, they'd relate to everything just like I have. I've spent most of my life searching this stuff out and enjoying it. The more things I hear, the more things I can enjoy, the better it's made my life. That's why I've traveled down this path and tried to find all these things. It's great stuff.

As Theodore Sturgeon said, 90 percent of everything is crap. That's true of anything. You have that process with anything, whether it's movies or music or dishwashing machines. You try and find what's good and what works for you. The more you keep looking, the more good things you find.

To me, the intent is personal expression and communication. That intent is in common with almost all musics. Sometime personal development, too. I look at Chinese Chin music, which is a kind of music developed over two thousand years ago, which was for a musician to play alone, in a room, for themselves, as a solo form for their own personal spiritual development. That's the important function of music. You can take that music and have other people hear it, and it's interesting. To me, that's the thing that's in common in all music. Of course, it can have different purposes. It can be dance music or shamanic music or so-called high-culture music, or farmer's music. Many different things. Those are further refinements of the purpose of music. To me, the purpose of music is communication, personal expression, personal development, sharing.

You try to learn as you go along. That's part of my view of my job as a musician, to learn as much as I can. I take my personal statement, I have my personal statement, but when I do it together with somebody else, both our personal statements change and intertwine into something new. That's what's interesting to me.

The first time David Lindley and I played together in a room was playing for people in Madagascar, the first day we arrived in Madagascar. We got there and said, "Okay, let's play some songs." We were just acquaintances, really. Then we took on this crazy project together. Now it seems like we've been working together for years.

Lindley and I, sometimes in Madagascar and Norway, we'd use our personal language and not vary it at all and make it work and get most of what they're doing. Sometimes we'd come a little bit in their direction, but then it became part of our personal language. It's not melody, harmony, and rhythm. The details of music are not those. Those are the details of Western classical music, which is not the details of 99 percent of the music on this planet. It's little micro-details and musical things and spiritual elements in the music. Those are the things that, intuitively, Lindley and I deal with when we do a cross-cultural project like that.

They're fun kinds of projects to do. You do them every two or three years. Otherwise they take too much time. I do it for the audience, to bring it to the audience. I do it for the people. In Madagascar, we had a tremendous effect in revitalizing the traditional music and the popular music based on traditional music there. I can count thirty or forty CDs that were released because of the success of *World Out of Time*. Lindley and I don't make any money there. All the money goes to the Malagasy people. We're not doing it to make money. We're doing it for love, really.

I could write a fifteen-hundred-page book on what I took away from my experiences in Madagascar. Different spiritual approaches to music, different rhythmic ideas and phrasing ideas from Madagascar, different ideas of tuning and intonation, different vocal ideas and inflections. Just as blues guitarists will put things that have to do with blues vocals in their guitar playing, now there are lots of things that have to do with Malagasy vocals and speech. Frank Zappa had a lot of speech in his guitar playing. Malagasy speech is also in the guitar solo. I could be playing blues one night and say I'm going to play this with Malagasy speech patterns. I'm always learning, always looking for new ideas and ways of thinking.

I know all about being a professional musician in Madagascar on all different levels from talking to the guys about it. It's pretty much the same thing as being a Western musician.

There's a great documentary by Jeremy Mar called *The Left-handed Man of Madagascar* which shows a touring Hira-Gasy band, and you can see these musicians that play at these ceremonies in Madagascar where they dig up dead bodies.

They have the same problems as a rock band on tour of the U.S. or a brass band in a big competition in the 1900s with other brass bands. It's the same things everywhere, I think. Economically, there's just different numbers involved, and some different parts of the game, like if there's MTV involved or not. But gigs and stuff, and the dynamics of bands, it's the same old story everywhere.

When I went through Russia, playing on tour, I met Kuriokhin. He seemed like a neat guy. He was coming to the U.S., so I said let's make a record. I've listened to a lot of music from all over what used to be the Soviet Union. I'm interested in that. It's not my particular area of specialization. He's an experimental artist that I thought it would be fun to do something with, so we locked ourselves in the studio for three days and made a CD we both liked that nobody bought.

I did *Crazy Backwards Alphabet* before I met him. The second and third one might have been around the same time. I'd have to look at the dates on the records. I played it for Kuriokhin and he thought it was funny. I'm sure it already existed. It had nothing to do with him. It's because Michael Maksymenko's parent's are Russian and he speaks Russian.

We recognize that this music does not have a massive mainstream influence, but that's the way music is marketed in America. The purpose is to make money, and it's done by nonmusicians. That's the main thing that's going on with the industry.

It does have an effect. Some advertising agency ripped off and copied Rakotofrah music exactly for an American Express commercial. It has an effect on things. They went to a lot of trouble with their big, scary lawyers to keep poor, seventy-four-year-old Rakotofrah from getting any of the money he deserved from that.

There's some value to that music if they want to copy it so closely to use in a national commercial.

In other countries that's even more so. In Japan and Europe, you get that kind of stuff in commercials a lot.

I'm so lucky to have gotten to play a lot of these people I've gotten to play with, whether it's heroes from my youth or people in other countries, or new musicians younger than me, coming along, inspired by some of the same things I've been inspired by, and by other things too. It's really exciting.

SOUTH AFRICA

I want to join your revolution because it's got so much music. The only thing we had was "We shall overcome." Every time I see South Africa on TV, they've got a new song.
—John Birks "Dizzy" Gillespie, via Hugh Masekela

Absolutely one of my favorite quotes from this book, it sums up the music scene on the Cape of Good Hope, which remains an ironic geographical name if ever there was one. While the revolution was successful, and apartheid became a thing of the past, now the Indian population is bearing the brunt of the brutality in South Africa. While Nelson Mandela went from prisoner to the highest office in South Africa, under his watch Mzwake Mbuli, one of Africa's most politically outspoken musicians even during the Botha and de Klerk reigns of terror, languished in jail.

The music, however, remains vital. The West actually revived it, with artists like Paul Simon "discovering" the wonders of isis-cathamiya and mbaqanga, and translating them to a Western audience at once leery of new sounds and hungry for something different.

Yet, in his wake, the westernization of South African music slowed down. Suddenly, people outside the country gave the stamp of approval to these old forms of pop—it was kind of like someone "discovering" Buddy Holly and the Beatles and giving them a new twist that made them acceptable, desirable, and *current*.

Not that the West hadn't had hits like this before. Both Miriam Makeba's "Pata Pata" and Hugh Masekela's "Grazing in the Grass" were mbaqanga. We just didn't know it back then.

Photograph: Ken Nahoun, Warner Bros. Records

PAUL SIMON

An inveterate folkie, Paul Simon has a long history of using music from other cultures toward his own ends. Even as far back as Simon and Garfunkel, their last chart hit before they initially went their separate ways was "El Condor Pasa," an eighteenth-century Peruvian folk song that Simon adapted and played with South American folk heroes Urubamba, introducing mainstream America to Peruvian pan pipes. Similarly, "Mother and Child Reunion" rode a very cool rock-steady riddem recorded in Jamaica. So, when he needed a smack of musical insight, who would wonder that it would come from something other than American music? Inspired by Zulu jive and mbaqanga, Paul Simon recorded one of the most remarkable albums of the eighties based on original South African songs with his own lyrical sensibility. Cultural imperialism or pop genius? Or maybe just a bit of both?

I didn't do "El Condor Pasa" because I knew it would become a standard. I didn't know it would be a standard. I just did it because I was interested in it. It just happened that in those times there was more acceptance of what was unusual or nonmainstream music. Now we're in a more primitive phase. I think I was fortunate in those days that radio and audiences were open to listen to that kind of music. Now I think it's more difficult to reach that kind of an audience.

The experience with Urubamba was great, too. This was an entire album that was one song. Similar experiences, because, again, learning about another culture, interacting with other musicians is very liberating for a musician. You get a lot of information that you wouldn't otherwise get.

I hope I'll be able tell you something about what was a tremendous adventure for me, both musically and on a personal level. This project began quite by accident when a friend of mine gave me a cassette of an album called *Gumboots: Accordion Jive Volume Two*. That was in the summer of 1984. I listened to the album all summer. It was an instrumental album, accordion, guitar, drums and as the summer went on, I was scat singing, improvising melodies over these tracks. I didn't have any intention of recording. I hadn't even thought about that.

I was just driving along and playing a cassette and singing along with it. But towards the end of the summer, I began to think that maybe I could record with this group, except that I really didn't know anything about them, where they came from, who they recorded for, because what I had was a copy of a copy of a cassette—I'm sure the recording industry would be pleased to hear that. Basically, I learned all of this from a bootleg tape.

I went to track down this recording, and it turned out it came from South Africa and in fact it was township jive, mbaqanga, music of Soweto and the black townships of South Africa. My first thought when I heard that was it's too bad this is not the music of Zimbabwe or Nigeria or Zaire, because life would be much more simple if that were the case. But then I began to think, this is the music of South Africa, and it's extraordinarily beautiful. So I began to pursue this musical train of thought, and I was put in touch with a man named Hilton Rosenthal, who produced a group called Jaluka. Jaluka was well known in South Africa because they were the first racially integrated band to play there. They have since disbanded, but they had quite a significant success there, and they had records released here, which are not very well known here, except among members of the music community.

Anyway, Hilton Rosenthal was the producer, and asked me, "When did you begin to get interested in South African music?" I told him that I didn't really know that much about it at all. This is my first experience with it, this township jive record. So, he asked if I would like to hear more music, and of course I said I would. He sent me about twenty albums of different styles of music and different groups and different tribes. The more I listened to the music, the more fascinated I became with it. I began to wonder if it would be possible to go and record with these groups. So, again I called Hilton and I asked, "Is there any restriction against me recording with these groups? Can I travel freely there? Can the groups record with me? Is there any problem with that?"

He said, "No, I'd have to check with record companies, I'd have to check with management. If it's okay with those people, then it's entirely possible for you to do this."

In fact, that's what happened. We set it up, I traveled.

Early in 1985 I went with Roy Haley, my old friend and the engineer who recorded all the Simon and Garfunkel records, and we flew to Johannesburg. The first night I was there we went to a reception at Hilton Rosenthal's house that they had for me and for Roy and most of the music community was there. It was an integrated group, it was a mixed group, and the discussion was pretty open. Mostly about music, but also about politics. They wanted to know what the American people felt about politics in South Africa, and I told them that the country was absolutely unified in a sense of moral outrage, and frustrated as to just what could be done about it. There was a divergence of viewpoints: that the Regan administration was in favor of constructive engagement and many people felt that stronger measures should be taken.

As the discussion got further into politics, and our views were clearly shared, they told me—several of the guys there were well known producers and musicians—that the black musicians union had voted prior to me coming there as to whether they wanted me to come. I was unaware of this vote. What they decided was that it would be beneficial to the music community there to let me record, because they felt what they were experiencing was a form of double apartheid. They were living under a repressive government, and when they tried to exploit their music and have their music played to the outside world, the music was often rejected on the grounds that it was South African. What they were experiencing was being blocked on all fronts. There was tremendous frustration, because the musical scene is very rich and very much modern. This also could be said for the other artistic fields: playwrights and poets also had a lot of trouble getting their work heard or seen. So they thought, since I was an artist whose work was popular internationally, I would be a good vehicle for them to show their music, an album of South African music.

Obviously I'm not South African. I went to make an album of my music and the music of the musicians that I hoped to interact with. I didn't know when I first went out there whether I would be able to achieve this, because I didn't know the musicians, I didn't know the conditions I would be working under, and I hadn't written songs. I was just going to see if I could create the structure of songs and then later on write it. I had done this occasionally in the past. Songs like "Late in the Evening" and a few other songs of mine where written that way, where I cut the track first and then wrote the song.

In this particular case, I intended to do all of the recording and all of my writing that way, cutting the tracks, then writing the song. How I went about doing that was, with the various musicians and groups that came in, we'd sit in the studio, I wouldn't play, because I wanted the musical backing to be what they played, so what I would do was sing into a microphone and improvise melody and meaningless words, phrases so I could hook them on to a melody and try to form the structure of a song. In my mind I thought later on I would actually write the song, about a subject matter that I didn't know at the time it was recorded.

I became friends with a lot of musicians. I had a chance to go to Soweto, I had a chance to hear many different groups that I was unaware of when I went there. I knew of three groups when I went over. When I was there, more and more groups would come forward and say they'd like to play and since we had block studio time, it was kind of possible to just bring people in and see what kind of music we could make.

Eventually I found a rhythm section that I really liked working with. They are extraordinary musicians and they're all Soweto guys. They are English speaking, they are thoroughly familiar with American music. They knew who I was, knew my music. In that sense they were different from the groups I went to record with originally, who really didn't know who I was, who didn't speak English—we had to communicate through an interpreter—and essentially they didn't know what I was doing, and since I myself didn't exactly know what I was doing, I couldn't explain it.

All of these songs where I used elements of music or thoughts that originated from these records or thoughts that came out of these sessions that were not my own thoughts, on all of those compositions, I consider that we were co-writers. So this is the first album that I've ever done where over half the songs are co-written.

Joseph Shabalala is the lead singer and composer for Ladysmith Black Mambazo is a very well known group in South Africa. I had first heard of the group and seen the group a few years ago on a BBC documentary called *Rhythm of Resistance: Music of South Africa*. When I was over there on this trip, Joseph came by the studio to visit and we met for the first time. I wanted to find a way of singing with Ladysmith, but it actually took me several months to get up the nerve to ask if he would consider doing it. I was very much in awe of the group. I was intimidated to ask whether they'd want to sing with me.

I'm pleased to say that they said yes they would, so now the question was how to write a song that would fit Ladysmith Black Mambazo style and also was a Paul Simon song. That took me a couple of more months, to figure out what that song would be. I had to listen to Ladysmith recordings and eventually I wrote the melody to "Homeless," the English words and the melody, and I sent them over on a demo to Joseph. I said change any words you want, change the harmony, add words in Zulu, continue the story, feel free to just take this as a sketch.

We met in Abbey Road Studios, of Beatles fame, in October of 1985, and Joseph had added considerably more to the song in Zulu, then we wrote one of the verses together in English.

They are known for each of the albums having a particular ending for each of the songs. I chose one of the endings that I liked and that I was able to phonetically sing, and we decided that that would be the very end of the music. When we got finished with the "Homeless" section it was going so well that we decided to enlarge the piece, and basing the next section on another Ladysmith song, I made up English words that led into that vocal riff, and that actually led into their song, and when that finished we went back to the English and then put the ending on. That was our first day of work in the studio.

On the second day, Joseph said that the group had been working until late into the night on an introduction that was a traditional Zulu song, and they changed the words to fit into the story of "Homeless," and all that it implied.

I didn't pick Joseph because we're the same size. I picked him because I liked Ladysmith.

Photograph: Shanachie Recording Artists

JOSEPH SHABALALA | LADYSMITH BLACK MAMBAZO

Ladysmith Black Mambazo are not the only group performing their particular brand of choral South African music. They are among the best, and the way they came up is so reminiscent of the way any musician in a capitalist society succeeds: They played talent shows, winning them more often than not, got a big fan base and started making records. Their talent and the utter beauty of their sound carried them internationally. Their show, full of cutting dance contests between the members of the group (without missing a note and with out instrumental accompaniment) as fierce as any seen on stage seal the deal.

This has church roots. At Christmastime we would sing a cappella music for our parents. And then when we got older we would sing in competition. The prize was a goat. The one who won would get the goat. That was dinner. We've been together since 1961, but then we would only sing like twice a year. But from 1964 we were very hot.

This type of music, isiscathamiya, will develop like that, just going through competition. We were lucky to be popular, we were lucky just to have this attention from the people. There are many who make this type of music. They are still doing competition. With Black Mambazo, we are the first a cappella group to get attention from the people.

I'm from Ladysmith. Ladysmith is in between Durban, by the ocean, and Johannesburg is west. Now Ladysmith is in-between. When you drive from Ladysmith to Durban, it's about two hundred kilometers. When you drive from Ladysmith to Johannesburg, it's about three hundred fifty kilometers. Now, I was born in Ladysmith, I grew up in Ladysmith, I spent my life in Ladysmith. And then, I just went to the big city, to Durban, to work there. It was 1960, it was my first time to go to a big city. It was 1960, January. My first year, I was working in a weaving factory.

I worked there for one year, then I came back home, because when we come back home, we work the land, we are farming. We are plowing there, producing maize, coffee, corn, pumpkins, milking cows. Stuff like that. We spent one year working in the city, and then come back for one year of working on the farm. If you want to take three years in the city, you must take three years on the farm, then go to the city. Until I moved there in 1964. Then I worked there, full time, in Durban. Now, I developed our music. We had enough time in Durban to develop our music. From 1964 to now.

In 1973 we were full-time in music, from 1973 until now, because of our people. Because people just support us. They love our albums. When we finish recording, and then they called us, they said, "We have this album. We want another one." They used to push us like that, all the time they'd demand. And because of the demand, we were full-time from 1973 until now.

You see, in South Africa, if the people like you, they demand you. When they have the record they demand another one. I think if they thought, "Maybe he's going to leave this job, let us get all he has before he leaves this job." Because they push you. I remember one year I was making three albums a year. I remember that. Because of the people.

Now, in South Africa, I have twenty-five albums. Shanachie has some of our albums here. They license them from South Africa. I think they have maybe three or four. Let me say that Shanachie was the first record bar (company) that started to sell our records here. They were the first one. But we take a long time to find out about them. We started to know about them when we came here, and we discovered there are records out here!

We perform mostly in Zulu. Now, because of different people in South Africa who love us, we have another record in Sotho, another one in Xosha, and then some in English, another one in German, just mixed there and there a couple of songs in German, because we like to share our ideas with all the people who love us.

In South Africa there are many different languages. Zulu and Sotho are very, very different. Even myself, I don't know how to speak Sotho. I just hear a little bit and know how to speak Sotho a little bit. But Xosha and Zulu are not very difficult. A little bit. Many words are together. And Ndebele, too, they are different a little bit, but not very much. But Tswonana, is very difficult, Tswanana, Sotho, Vendi, you see, Vendi and Sotho are similar, but Twanana and Sotho are very different. Even myself, I don't know those languages, I just touch them a bit.

There are many groups. In South Africa, we have many, many things. Because Tswonana, they have their culture, they have their traditions. Xosha, they have their traditions, their way to dance. Sotho, they have their way to dance. They all have different things. Zulu, they have their own dance. And then the regions, you see, they are different. Like, where I grew up, in Ladysmith, this type of music, isiscathamiya, is born in Ladysmith. This music of Ladysmith Black Mambazo is born from traditional Zulu songs, dances and then Zulu song is done in the form of call and response.

That's what we call mbaqanga (pronounced: mmm-ba-[click]anga). Mbaqanga means that now they mix their voices. They got an original voice from South Africa, now they mix that voice with instruments. Now they change the instruments to their beats, now they call it mixed, or in Zulu, mbaqanga. Because when you make mbaqanga, mbaqanga is a porridge, a Zulu porridge. When you mix that, you first boil the water, then you put in salt, then you put in millet meal. Then you stir it. Now we call the music that is mixed, we call it mbaqanga. When they dance, they're dancing we call it mqashilo. Because now they are jumping, they are jumping they are doing their thing, they call that mqashilo. That's why the type of music we sing, they call isiscathamiya, because the way we act, we are just touching the floor softly, which means isiscathamiya.

The names came from the action. The way we act. It was born from the way we dance. When we dance a mqashilo dance, we strike the floor hard. When we do this dance we strike the floor softly. The name for striking the floor softly is isiscathamiya. Now we call our tiptoes guys. They are just tiptoe, they are not hurting the floor because we used to stomp the floor hard.

Before isiscathamiya, we worked with Zulu dance. Now, because we were together at home, not away from home to act, we did this type of music together, ladies, young boys, young men, just together. The high parts were sung by the ladies. The next parts were sung by the young boys. And then all the rest, the older men were singing the deep part. Now, when we were away from home, going to work, we left our families at home, and now we assembled together, because now we felt homesick, because at home we'd always sing. Now, at weekend time, when we were doing nothing, we assembled and when we began to sing, we discovered that there was no high part. They are all singing deep voice. And then one of them said, "Well, maybe I can try to imitate the ladies at home." And the music changed itself. It just changed itself so much.

This music is heart to heart. I don't know how to put it. Because even at home we were just singing, we were praising our lady, praising our father, praising our kings. Truly, I can say these are the songs of peace from South Africa. Although you're heart is sorrowful, you can say, "Be calm my heart, because even here you are at home." Because you are away from home, but even when you are at home, you feel there is something missing somewhere.

We first recorded in 1972. We started selling records in 1973. We are very lucky, we are the first people who got the demand from the people, they wanted an LP from us. Before that, all other groups, the ones that played instruments, they used to just make seven-inch singles, then after that, they combined just to take those good ones and make an LP. But Black Mambazo, we sang for the people first, for a long time, in competition. Now the people knew us. Because we started to take this thing into competition in 1966. Then from 1966 to 1969 we recorded a tape for the radio, and then we got a demand from the people, and then the record companies started to look at us. And then we recorded.

In 1971, we started to make a translation on the radio, ABC. When everybody heard that, they all demanded that we make records, so we started to make records in 1972. We made seven singles. Then people started to say, "We want an LP of this group, because we know many songs by them." People tell us that Black Mambazo was the first group in South Africa to sell LPs. They tell me that. I don't know.

When we first recorded in 1971, it was just a seven-inch single. Then the people said, "No! Only two songs from these guys?! We know all of their songs. We want them."

And then the record company comes back to me and says, "Joseph, do you have twelve songs?"

And I said, "No. I have more than twelve songs. I have more than thirty songs."

And they said, "The people want an LP."

And I said, "What's an LP?"

Because when I went in to make the record, I didn't think they were going to put it out, because I didn't see any records. All I saw was tape.

Even then, I thought we were just rehearsing with the microphone, because when we were there, our mind just went back to this chap, there was this chap who came up to me, I remember, he said, "All the people who sing on the record are people who died, because the people who record them steal their voice. They are going to take your voice."

My music was loved, because in my mind it was always with me that this music was good, it came from the heart, from grief, from loneliness, but there is something missing somewhere. Because of that, then God helped me in my dream. I always listened to music, until I saw the people who were singing for me. I caught the humming from them, I learned from them how to teach. Because only one thing, among the people, if there is no teacher among a group, nothing will happen there.

Before *Graceland*, we had toured West Germany, Cologne, Hamburg, Frankfurt, but London, we had never been there. This was our first time to come to London when we made the tour with Paul Simon. And the United States.

After Paul Simon, when we finished the *Graceland* tour, because of the demand, we began our own tour, about eighteen shows, and then come back again for the United States, Canada, Holland, and London. And then come back again for Australia, New Zealand, Switzerland, Spain, Italy . . .

What has changed is that, after Paul Simon's *Graceland*, there are many people who started to know Black Mambazo. In and out. Especially at home. There are the white people in South Africa who don't know us. They started to know Black Mambazo, through the *Graceland* album, and they started to know us and support us.

I remember the day I met Paul Simon in Ladysmith. He was wonderful. When he chose Black Mambazo to make a record with him, that was wonderful, but I can't forget the first words that he said to me. He said, "Are you Joseph?" I said, "Yes." He said, "I'm your fan! I want to do something with you, but I don't know when or where." It was wonderful to me. But all along I knew that this thing was my gift from God. I remember 1975, that this is my talent from God. It made me very, very excited. And I went to London to make a record with Paul Simon. It was very good.

Today I'm proud to introduce Paul Simon as one of Ladysmith Black Mambazo. Ladysmith Black Mambazo has ten members but now we have eleven. Many people were waiting for this album in South Africa.

Let me just say that when we first compose our songs, we were just composing our songs for each and everybody. But we know that maybe those don't understand our music. But today it's amazing. It surprised us, because they started to support us. Even themselves, they tell us, "We don't know you. Where did you come from?"

What I know about it myself is singing music. When you see somebody crying and you sing for them they have to laugh, because you sing for them.

WEST NKOSI

Like too many African musicians, West Nkosi died way too young, succumbing to injuries from an auto accident in 1998, in his early fifties. One of the chief architects of the mbaqanga and Zulu jive sounds, West Nkosi was also a remarkable saxophone player. His work with Mahlathini and the Mahotella Queens remains as fresh as when it was originally crafted thirty-five years ago. Nkosi started out playing pennywhistles in popular South African kwela groups in the early sixties, before moving on to sax as pennywhistle music faded in popularity, leading to the rise of mbaqanga, a much harder version of kwela. He also began producing recordings, and that is where his real contribution to the noise of the world comes in. He brought the world some of the first and best recordings of Ladysmith Black Mambazo and Mahlathini and the Mahotella Queens. We spoke in that nether time between Paul Simon's Graceland *album and the fall of de Klerk and apartheid.*

South Africa is very rich in music. You will find all the Michael Jacksons, all the Lionel Richies, all the jazz players. It's like New York when you get to Johannesburg. You get a lot of different music. But we more, because we have traditionals, which you people don't have. We have traditional tribal dancers and different songs. The way of performing is very different from the Western style.

With Mahlathini and the Mahotella Queens, we mix our music for all the different tribes that live in South Africa. We only specialize in the attire. The Zulu tribe is the most popular language, so what we use from them, we use the costumes to identify with it. It's so simple for us to use that. Some other tribes have costumes, but they are a little bit heavy for the stage act, so we just decided to use the Zulu traditional.

Mbaqanga is made from a lot of different rhythms. It's not actually a stew, as you translate it in English. It's a food, a very strong food. I don't know if, in the USA you have this type. It's like when you do mashed potatoes, but a little bit thick, strong. When you eat it, it stays in your stomach for the rest of the day. You don't get hungry.

Because of the boycott on South Africa, if we had made the music in South Africa, there was no way that the record could have been obtained by the European market. We recorded in France because that was the only way for me to get our music across to the European people.

When I first came to Europe, I discovered that the French people were the first to establish anything musical from Africa. It begins from the French market, and from there it develops outside, to the U.K. and Italy, Germany, and Spain.

The French have colonized a lot of black African countries. So they want to pay back what they did to the black people. It is the only way to pay back what happened in the old days.

It was difficult for us to get the right record company. We had to negotiate with the British company for a long time to take this music up. The recording companies are selfish. Everyone wants to sign the group up for themselves. They do not want to license it from somebody else.

A lot of our younger generation has been influenced by American music since the television was introduced into our country. When the television was introduced, they did not have regular material to show the audience. What they did was get videos from all over the world. That alone has got a very, very big influence to the people. You press your button and on the screen, there's Michael Jackson. Then everybody thought, if you want to appear on that box, you have to dance like Michael Jackson or sing like him.

That was true until Paul Simon came in. Then things started to change. Paul Simon, when he came in and did *Graceland*, it was reflected back to South Africa. Then it was played on television. People started to realize, "Oh, our music is also good." A lot of companies started to do local production, to show people these sorts of things can be done.

We don't hear much African music from outside of southern Africa because of the diplomatic relationships. We don't have them. They can get us, but we can't get them. All the African independent countries have that problem, from Zaire to West Africa. We have relationships with Zimbabwe, Mozambique, Lesotho, and Botswana, Swaziland. Anything north, there's no diplomatic relationship.

I'm here right now, so I don't know what's happening. From what I could see on "South Africa Now," I could see the whites fighting to retain apartheid, that apartheid must be there. But I don't think that apartheid is going to last very long. Those days are long gone. We leave it to the politicians for the time being. We can't get the real answer.

If you structure your song as a direct hit at the government, it can be dangerous. But if you structure it in a clever way, to tell people that it's important to live together, that can not be dangerous. It depends how you put it. It is dicey. Not that there can be big problems, but you may lose publicity. If your music is not being publicized to the audience, you end up not gaining anything from it. You need to have publicity so people can buy your music and you can live on it.

Musically, South Africa is more advanced than the rest of Africa. We have a lot of studios down there, twenty-four to forty-eight tracks and also Synclaviers. If you go to Dakar, Senegal, Zaire, very poor studios. Not like South Africa. We have forty different studios.

The problem in most of Africa is that most of the big guns don't invest their money in those countries' studios. Most of these countries, the musicians don't make money. I went to West Africa just recently. I found my tapes. They had been brought from Paris, and they are selling them as pirates. They get them on the charts as pirates. We don't get a cent. There's millions of dollars for musicians there. Not my group alone. Even the Americans are losing. That's why the companies are not willing to invest their money. They can't get it back. There's no control over piracy there.

Photograph: Earthworks

HILDA TLOUBATLA | THE MAHOTELLA QUEENS

Traditionally, women have a much tougher time of it then men when it comes to maintaining a career in music outside of Western culture. The Mahotella Queens supplied the backing to the late king of the "groaners" Simon Nkabendi, otherwise known as Mahlathini, the Lion of Soweto. They were big in South Africa through the mid-sixties and early seventies, with West Nkosi electrifying (literally) traditional mbaqanga music into something more pop, kinetic, and danceable for the group. However, the Queens wanted to get married and start families. Performing while the women were home raising kids was perfectly acceptable for men, but it didn't work the other way. So, the Mahotella Queens took a decade-long hiatus. "When the girls laid off, we tried to substitute for them with other girls," noted Nkosi. "When you look at the picture on the cover (of albums made during that period), you will find that it's completely different."

We got married. We had children. In our culture, they believe when you are a married woman, there is a time you must go live with your mother-in-law, father-in-law, all the family, to prove that you are a real housewife. You've got to prove that you can cook, that you can mend, that you can bring up your children on your own. You can do the housecleaning, you can wash, you can do all the things that are supposed to be done by a married woman.

Performing is still a bit difficult for the families, but there is no other way. They have to get used to it. There is no other way. This is our profession. Even if you have a BA degree, there is nobody who can take your profession away from you. We have got to take it. It may be difficult but they have to take it.

Photograph: Lance Mercer, Epic Records

ROBBI ROBB | TRIBE AFTER TRIBE

There's more to South African music than mbaqanga. As West Nkosi pointed out, until Paul Simon came down and relegitimized the music, Western sounds prevailed in Pretoria. Beyond that, there were groups that did interesting modernizations of traditional sounds. Guitarist Philip Tabane started playing with the healing drums of South African, the Molombo drums in the long-running group Molombo. Both Western and traditional sounds informed Robbi Robb's musical gestation. A white South African during the time of apartheid, his group Asylum Kids would preach ending the racial segregation from the stage. This resulted in a subtle repression of the band that made them so unpopular with promoters that few would risk booking them. Robb ultimately moved to Los Angeles where he put together Tribe After Tribe with fellow Botha refugee Robby Whitelaw and an L.A. drummer simply known as PK. He went on to work with Pearl Jam bassist Jeff Ament in Three Fish.

It wasn't a matter of banning. It was very silent, concerts suddenly being cancelled and stuff like that. It was never like an official banning. It was just like, they would pull you off stage, bring the dogs in, disperse the crowd, and your next five or six gigs get cancelled.

Now the government is getting trickier than that. Friends die in car accidents and stuff. On the way to some political meeting, people are killed. People who don't drink alcohol wind up dead with alcohol in their bodies.

It's a tricky situation, because the right wing is so strong that every time he makes a move, the right wing gets stronger, and every reform he makes, the right wing gets stronger.

I lived in the Orange Free State for a while, which is like probably what you would call the Midwest. But very, very redneck. It was a mining town with a lot of Afrikan-speaking people, which is the language of the oppressors in that country. There, I'd get called a redneck, because they are calling English people rednecks. When the English came to fight, they wore these silly little helmets that would let the sun burn their necks. So, in South Africa, I'm the redneck, but in America they are.

Being in Los Angeles is like taking the lid off the can of our creativity in a way. In South Africa, a lot of good music didn't come through. I had a very turned-on mother who brought home music like The Flock and Led Zepplin and stuff. I would get exposed to this music through my mom. When I started forming bands, I would be playing this rock and roll. I was always very active. I love dancing and stuff, and people wouldn't get it back home. They were like, "What is this music?" Until later in the game.

Arriving in America, the things that we were doing, people had seen and done before. So it was like, "Okay, now I can go deeper in and look for that thing that I really want."

And it was always to somehow combine the ceremonial, magical music of the Africans, rather than the township stuff, with rock. The first Deep Purple album I had heard blew me away. I wanted the power of that and the passion of the drums.

Philip Tabane is my main, main, main man. He is my Jim Morrison. I walked into a venue one night and three thousand people were stomping and clapping and yelling "Quah! Quah!"

And I thought, "Fuck, this must be a good band. Who's here?"

I look, look, look, and there's Philip Tabane walking around with this big smile on his face, and the drummer is just standing there beside the drums, not playing, just standing there, and this power is just oozing into this crowd. Then Philip would play this incredible riff, and he'd stop, and the people would just go "Whaaaaa!" and then the drummer would start, just go, go, go, go, go. And then he would stop. And so much of the power was in that stopping it. It was like coming and then pulling it back and the fucking power was just going to the people and the people would just fucking rock. And I saw that, and I said, "Okay. I know. I know something now." It's taken me a long time to get back there.

Arriving in L.A., people would see the band and say, "Hey, this is the U2 from South Africa." And the A&R people would come down and say, "Yeah, you guys are like U2 meets the Fixx, and INXS. Write us a song like 'In the Name Of Love,' and we could make a lot of money."

We got a little bit sucked in there. And it was like, okay, go home and try to write a song like that. And before I knew it, I couldn't write a song. It was like, "Fuck this. What's going on here?" And I thought, "Wait a minute. Let me get back. Let me go out and buy all the records that I grew up on."

I went and got my Johnny Winter record, went and got my Deep Purple record, and got myself the Philip Tabane record. And okay, here we go, let's get back to it, break free of this think and make our own record, release it on our own independent label, try and get some sort of a trust. If we can sell fifty thousand records, that would be fine with me. Just to win that trust, so that when we go to a record company, we can say, "We know what we're doing and we know what we want to do." As you can see.

In South Africa, when our records weren't being played, and the television wouldn't support us, and stuff like that, we had a band called the Asylum Kids which became the only band that could fill the city hall with no radio play or no television. So I had this thing in me, that I knew I could do it in America, too, that way. I didn't need the radio, I didn't need that net. I could do it without. And people would say, "Oh, go back to Africa. This is America. You will never be able to do it."

But I fucking thought to myself, "I know I can do it. Just get me on the road, let me play to the people, I know I can do it."

We made a video of our song "White Boy in the Jungle" because Africa is very interesting in the way that people dance and the colors and the costumes and the stuff, and it could be very interesting. The director interpreted the thing in a very natural way, whereas someone else might have turned it into a curio shop. It was not the African curio. But the video is spooky. It is so fucking spooky. People gasp. When girls watch it, they say, "I can't believe this. You can't do this."

The whole concept of the video is we're dancing around a fire, and there's this old man looking into the fire, and in the fire he sees the rainforests falling. Trees are falling and he sees the bulldozers and stuff. We dance, dance, dance until we get ourselves into this feverish situation, where we move into this state of epilepsy and we fall down to the ground and start banging our power into the earth, symbolic of like giving the earth the power to resist this destruction. At the end, you see the trees upright themselves.

It looks very pagan in a way. Have you ever seen any photographs of a tribe called the people of Cau? There's a stunning book called *The People of Cau*. It's this beautiful tribe, they do these creations where they paint the whole body yellow, and just the face will be black, and the hands. And they'll just groove around like that for the day. They don't wear clothes, but now their government has told them to put on clothes.

They live in North Africa, south of Morocco, north of Zaire, around the Sudan. So we used the makeup concept from them. The night after the gig, we had the people from Atlantic over to the place, and the response to the video was super.

I don't have much faith in some of the black leaders from the rest of Africa. I've seen the corruption they've fallen into. They've taken on white men's values and stuff like that, like making the people of Cau wear clothes.

I love the way Fela talks about it. But then you look at the world, the amount of money that's spent on grabbing and spoiling and raping and pillaging. Every man in the world could be a millionaire if you were to dish that cash out. What did you come for? We've come for the jungle, to cash in the jungle. I think now, from living in America now, I'm getting more of a world perspective of that greed, that pig on the wing. I'm getting like, "Okay, I see it there, too."

There was a time when I started seeing it, and I would say, "Blame it on Botha." A bomb would go off in Lebanon, and I would say it's Botha's fault. Because of people coming down so heavy on South Africa, and now I'm thinking they're missing the point. I started seeing that they were missing the point. It is the greed that we have to look at.

The thing about Africa, also, that I want to find more meaning in, is this thing Fela said at a concert: "You've got to treat Africa like this garden, as soon as the world can start treating Africa like a garden, the whole vibration of the planet will change."

I really believe it is true. It's almost like the same way I feel about what America should be doing with Indians. If we had arrived here and taken the lesson that these guys were natural environmentalists, that they had a harmony with the give and take of the environment, we wouldn't have fucked it up that badly. But we wiped them out, and it's there. The blood and the karma is that. It needs to be acknowledged. Like Fela says, it's the garden. If we can look after the garden, the whole vibe will change. I want to explore that a little bit, and see what kind of feelings come from that. There are a lot of people who say that somewhere south of Zaire is where the Garden of Eden was, where the Nile starts.

You had to have a permit to go into the townships. I was very fortunate. One of the other fortunate people was Johnny Clegg (of Jaluka). In my days learning how to play jazz, I met this black keyboard player who was like another McCoy Tyner, a Herbie Hancock type. He could play. He taught me a lot. We would talk a lot. It was really strange, because I would be impressed by what he would say, and it would be a surprise. A black man talking science and everything. I was really impressed with him. He was with another band, and the guitarist left. He asked me to join the band, and it was my pleasure. It was an eight-piece black South African jazz band called the Muddy Bridge. So, I moved to the township to rehearse with him, and I went to the gig that they had set up in the Homelands, in Botswana, which is one of the evils of South Africa. I lived there. I was like the only white guy around for about five hundred miles in this township.

I was about seventeen, eighteen. Something like that. So I got exposed to a lot more than the average white South African could ever be at that time. Suddenly, I started seeing these personalities. Black people were usually just this cloud of people that were there and were dangerous. They could probably kill you for no reason.

We're just not getting the information. We're not being exposed to it. We don't talk to them. But now, because of living there, I picked up on a lot of words that will open up a black South African to me in a very friendly way. The black people in South Africa are amazing. They are absolutely amazing. You can walk past a group of black people and say, "Hey, six mabone," and they will say, "Hey," and they'll smile. They're like so spontaneous. That's just street talk. Six mabone is a really cool saying that I love. It means that everything is so cool, but what it really means is that you have a car with six lights on the back. Like an American car with six lights. It's a status symbol. It's the best thing to have. If a black guy in South Africa says, "Hey, that is six mabone," he's saying that is the coolest thing that can happen. You can walk past a crowd of blacks and say, "Hey, six mabone," and the agreement is on. You are somebody who knows something about them and everything is cool.

I never got to speaking any language while I was there, but living in the location for six months, and these guys talking all the time, it's amazing how much I learned to understand through listening and feeling, even though I didn't understand the words.

Another interesting thing that happened there was that the bass player and I started having a little ego vibe. We couldn't deal with each other. We were irritating each other. But I would never give him the verbal vibe that I would give another band member if he were white, because I didn't want to feel like I was a white guy whacking a black man. He also had some problems giving me the truth. What he really felt.

That's another weird thing about apartheid, the overcompensation. You're always on tenterhooks around the situation. You don't want to be honest, because you don't want to come across racist or anything.

So we found some boxing gloves one time and I used to be a boxer. I was showing them some moves and we got into a little interband championship. And there were guys I had a really good vibe with, it was like three points and the fight was over.

Tata and I got together, and the anger was there and the strange apartheid thing was there. We started this fight, and we started going for it. It got to the point where we started really fucking each other up, and everybody was like staying back and going, "What is going on here?" Well, we fucked each other up really good and proper and after that, I felt that I wrenched a real mean part of apartheid out of me, because after that I could tell him, "Fuck you!" and he would tell me, "Oh, you're just like every other white guy." We would just say the things, and now I could learn from him, the way he sees white people in another way. It was great. I felt that was a very valuable thing in my life, in terms of bridging that gap between me and the native South Africans.

I miss the black people that I've been with and I miss thunderstorms. I need to see a proper thunderstorm, one where you can almost move into the space of fear. This could go wrong, this could shatter the fucking house.

I don't really miss South Africa, though. The learning process I'm going through now is wonderful on all levels, musically, spiritually, everything is just growing, growing, growing. So, I don't have a missing vibe.

Can I tell you something? One of the most impressive things about America is the telephone. I love call waiting, I love answering machines. Try getting a telephone in South Africa.

MZWAKHE MBULI

Calling Mzwakhe Mbuli the Fela of South Africa would be unfair to both of them, but the similarities are inescapable. Both were outspoken opponents of their governments. Both spent considerable time incarcerated (or as Fela liked to put it, "as a guest of the state")—as this book goes to press, Mbuli is serving fourteen years at hard labor on a spurious bank robbery conviction. Both were poets of the people. One key difference: where Fela flaunted his defiance of the Nigerian government, largely on the basis of his family ties, Mbuli, the son of a mbubi singer, didn't have that luxury and spent a good deal of his time underground.

There was this two-year experience when I was underground. They eventually got hold of me. But there was an advantage in that there was so much pressure called, so much international pressure, that the state of emergency was supposedly uplifted. When I was released, I was released because it was the end of term of the official state of emergency. Then I was released. What happened was, because there were all these overseas invitations that kept pouring into the country, I started applying for a passport. Each time I was supposed to get a passport, something would happen to me. It was all predictable mishaps. Either detention or something terrible would happen to me. And, indeed, in 1987, when I was supposed to leave for a conference in Amsterdam, I think the police looked for me all over. They intensified their search, but they failed. At one point in time, they invaded a student residence when some students created some problems in the central part of Johannesburg, in the city. Then maybe they thought they should raid.

P. W. Botha went on television saying all the nonsense the students were doing would come to an end or they were going to combat that. At that time, I had many places to hide out. One of them was a university residence. Now, it was too late one evening, because it was announced in the newspapers and on the radio that the president was going to give a "special talk." I went elsewhere to be able to listen to what he was going to say that evening. Because the whole program ended up late, and I was in Soweto and supposed to drive to town, now I realize my hideout place was far away. So I decided to go to the nearest one, which was a student residence. When I was there, the police raided that evening. That was how they were able to get hold of me.

That was in late '87. Now, when they released me in '87, I thought it was over. I didn't think it would happen soon again, the next arrest. I knew that they still were going to arrest me. But when you're out of prison, you don't assume that they will come tomorrow again.

After my release, I tried to apply for a passport. This time, they again looked for me. They even went to my other home. I was no longer staying in my place again. Right after my release, they picked up my brother and threatened to beat him up, etc. Then I sensed there was trouble, but I continued to apply for a passport. So there were two different applications that were turned down.

I didn't give up. Before they arrested me in '88, check what happened. We put a lot of pressure. The lawyers for human rights, they put pressure that I should get a passport. They made an arrangement with the minister of Home Affairs, to introduce me to him, introduce my case. When he agreed, a week before my arrest, he turned down the appointment and said he doesn't know about my case but asked someone in his department to look into the case of Mzwakhe Mbuli. The lawyers for human rights thought it was still necessary to push for the meeting. I went to the eastern cape, before Capetown. I was in Port Elizabeth. It was like being in Philadelphia when the minister was in New York. When I was supposed to fly, that particular morning, the lawyer called and said, "No, the meeting has been called at the eleventh hour."

I was in P.E., I was supposed now to fly back to Johannesburg and go back to Soweto. It was another big disappointment. But the following day, they raided my home, and they got me. For us, we were able to guess that because we were putting so much pressure, they were able to pick me up.

I thought since I was surrounded by lawyers I was pretty safe and about to meet the minister of home affairs. I was actually a target.

All of them were involved. PEN International, even the United Nations, when my home was bombed. Even Artists Against Apartheid. I've got a lot of letters and faxes of people who pledged to go to Zimbabwe. A lot of celebrities were drawn to my attention by a campaign from the outside about my plight.

When I recorded *Change Is Pain*, I was exactly underground. I thought, rather than rotting underground, let me do something. So I did something and it became a success here.

When I performed, I was always unadvertised. The person who was MC, or the person who was in charge of the party or gathering or the rally, wedding or funeral would say, "Ladies and gentlemen, we have a surprise for you," maybe after a particular person or speaker or a particular act, and say, "Can you guess? The people's poet!" The thing that was outstanding about this is that when they announced there was going to be a poetry item, people naturally assumed maybe it was Mzwakhe. After all, it did not appear on the program, then who is this person who came out of the blue, unexpected? It was always considered and assumed that maybe it is Mzwakhe. Sometimes, they would guess correctly, and I would appear and get a big welcome.

On *Change Is Pain*, it is like music and poetry is parallel, but people don't see that or don't notice that. In this case, in particular, I composed everything to arrangements, words, voices, where to start, where to stop, etc. Maybe I needed to do what I have done even previously. But it had to take Mzwakhe to compose the appropriate music for Mzwakhe's poetry, whereas previously it was like a joint venture and I was not in control of these session musicians. In this case, I've worked with this band, they became used to me. Now, I conduct rehearsals or compose. I'm happy. The music, everything is different. It was forty-eight track, compared to the twenty-four track that I've used in the past. I was there, even during the mixing period, tiring as it was, throughout. It was taxing but fruitful.

There is something significantly important about the second album, because it is the product of prison in the sense that most of the poems and the songs, I composed that stuff when I was in solitary confinement. I was not allowed to keep a pen and paper in the cell. I was compelled, therefore, to use my mind as a memory bank and when I was released I went straight to the studio to record.

For me, it is still very vivid and very fresh. That is why I'm saying, maybe after a couple of years it will be something else, but at the moment, I still regard myself as not fully recovered from the experience, the nightmares and other things. There are other things that still happen while I am asleep, but I've recovered. It's not like I'm sick. There are things that still make my body just shake or jump.

If you talk to me, you talk to me right here in South Africa. I'm here in Soweto, and I can tell you, people around me, we are more disillusioned than having the hope for freedom. In the past three days on television, de Klerk himself and other cabinet ministers, the things that they're saying are quite appalling and discouraging. It's like people struggling for no apparent fruitful cause. For me, I get the sense that when I watch them on television, it's a question of how to keep what they have. They don't give you the sense that they are willing to resign themselves from power or be part of the interim government that should be created or the constitutional assembly. They speak like they're bosses or masters.

Ten people have died today. Yesterday, it was eighteen. It's so sad that there is violence around us here. In spite of what I told the people while I was there, this thing is going to just continue. I don't see an end to it now, in the near future. I mean, we'll have a black leader, there's no doubt about that. Everyone now, the newspapers were blaming the police and the army. Where do you see a situation where eighteen people are killed? When you have a confusion of police, and they all are underground and two helicopters are hovering around and still no one is arrested in connection with all these murders. For us, it's a mystery. But we know that the agents of the system are involved in this whole thing.

Right now some people think that it is foolish or stupid for me to be here, but I'm here. They think that it's because it is clear that there is no hope that things are going to be okay. There is no peace here. People are at war. The government is still responsible for all the massacres that have been in this country. It is unfortunate for me, it's sad. For my writings, my point of view, listen to my albums. That message is appropriate exactly contextually even to the situation here in Soweto or here in South Africa.

I'm a self-taught composer musician. I always work hard. I wish to do ten times what I want to do. Those are efforts of hard work. That is why the music is different. Even the manner in which we recorded the whole thing, it was like live in the studio.

"Do Not Push Us Too Far" is a song that is similar to maybe ten of the Mahlatini songs. That would definitely be pure mbaqanga. But the way that I do these things now, of late, is that I compose a song—take "Imandulu"—I sing the part to the guitarist, or the band as a whole. I do that to the end, and involve the backing vocals. I do it without giving a person a chance to breathe, to think and say, "Let's go for it, go for it, go for it."

When it happens, the process is very fast. It's like everything is boiling in me and I want everyone to boil. When the song is played, after even two or three hours, then people who know music better will begin to say, "The drumming is in 6/8, the speed of the song, G is this and that and that." When I do it, people will say they hear a little bit of mbaqanga, jazz, marabi influence. But when I do a thing, I compose by singing the parts. The player should obviously listen to me, listen to me even if I have to do it ten times, and try and play it like I'm doing it for you now, for example. Then, later it gets different definitions and manifestations.

I don't agree with the people who say, "It's like Afro–rock and roll with a jazz beat . . . ." No, no, no, no, no. Sometimes it's best if you say it's like township jazz, etc. But, I'm saying these things, because sometimes if you take it to a rock and roll situation, I don't agree. But, the guitar is loud. For me, I even say it should be rock loud, but this is not rock and roll. I worry about definitions after I have actually done the song.

The recent tour was, for me, among other things, an assessment. I was able to evaluate during the tour the response of the people. Say from Denmark or Canada or the U.K. or Finland or Germany or even here at home, the response has always been the same. Here it is a technique of whether people understand certain ways or not. Take the song about brain damage, "Uyeyeni." That song appeals to people who cannot understand Zulu in this country. In the far northern end, next to the Mozambiquan border, you have people who don't understand those words properly. But because of the music, how it is done, it makes a person anxious for some more. It happened throughout the tour. That therefore means it works.

It is supposed to find a wide audience, but for me, I regard this music like a boxer combination. It's an uppercut, punch, jab, left hook. Whether I'm in the States, in the Caribbean, in Africa, the impact of that is the same. I'm confident of my punches. Irrespective of how big or small the room is, the ring, how tall or short my opponent is, it's the same for me. It works. I'm saying this because we've performed in places like SOB's, where the stage is extremely small for us. For me, it was like a restriction, but it worked. Elsewhere, it's bigger stages, like a stadium situation, and it still works. I think I'm sure of these facts, the formula, the recipe, there is something that makes me more confident that wherever I can perform, whoever is in front of me will feel the heat.

There are people who put their families first before they sacrifice. There are people who put their families, their treasure, etc, before they can actually talk of justice and plead on behalf of the people. Fortunately, there is something I believed in, that if you put your life in the service or dedicate your life for the service of other people, then you attain true happiness.

I have lived a life as though I didn't care about my self or soul. But the people who cared so much about their soul, their life, their families, their properties, some of them have died many years ago before me. I happen to be alive. Not that I was reckless about my life. I have always regarded my well-being as precious.

There are people who care about others, and people who do not care about others. So I do not care about the set of people who do not care about others. There are people, who when they become successful in this world, do not care about the plight of other people. There are those who care about other people. It's my wish to prove this practically about the plight of people all over the world.

There is so much pain in the world. I've seen many programs that were disturbing to me, how children were tortured in Chile and Guatemala and elsewhere in the world. It's painful, it's painful. I couldn't take some of the things. Other people are victims of death squads, their families have disappeared, not only in Argentina, but in Chile and elsewhere. But people are not prepared to mention that. Just to raise a finger about somebody doing wrong to someone else, it's sad. I'm saying, this country has always created problems for some of our people who elsewhere would be regarded as giants.

We have people who I think, because of their stature, cannot be easily arrested or put into prison. But these people are afraid to make statements. A person could even be in the position of Bishop Tutu and still not be able to make statements. But Bishop Tutu is able to make statements against apartheid. So, for us, those are the people who have courage at one point in time, in history. Now we have musicians who are able to make statements.

Take a singer like Stevie Wonder. Blind as he is, he is able to see about apartheid. But there are people inside South Africa who are actual victims of apartheid who have failed to make statements about apartheid, because at one stage they wanted to pursue their career, they didn't want to be arrested, they didn't want to test prison. Sometimes, when you can no longer be arrested by singing about Nelson Mandela, now they jump on the record, they can sing about Mandela. We have people like that all over the world. You must always expect such people until a Mzwakhe will be matched.

In South Africa, at the moment, for me optimism has lost meaning. When I left the country in June, I had seen enough corpses in my life. I had never seen so many corpses, dead people, black, like

I did this year. Then I left for three months. Now, I'm back in this country, I'm seeing corpses again. During my tour, there was a lot of suffering in Slovenia, Serbia, Yugoslavia. It continues to take place, but the rate of people who have died was far less compared to what happens in my country in a week's time.

At the moment, I know that the tide of history will catch up with apartheid and it will go, but I don't want to say to you that it's going to happen soon. This thing is still going to take a very long time, because the people are not yet in power. The world should not think—and the world has been misled to believe—that by definition this change is not bad. When you release somebody from prison, there is change. There is, as a result, a struggle.

When Nelson Mandela came out of prison, the world was led to believe that was a blow for freedom in South Africa. It's not like in Zimbabwe. We don't have our own flag; we don't have our president. There are one million people out of twenty-six million people, one million people are ruling us. The president is white, everything is white. So, unless we have a people's government, elected by the people themselves, maybe things will get better. But at the moment, we have a government that is using all possible means to frustrate the efforts, the mechanism, the freedom wagon from reaching its ultimate destination. It's sad, because, even if tomorrow, it could be openly said that apartheid is dead, it will take generations to do away with prejudice because of the damage apartheid policies have done.

The Berlin Wall, you know, is gone, but when you talk about apartheid, it's still intact. It's there in the textbooks. If, from the United Nations resolutions, apartheid is a heresy, it's an evil crime against humanity. It's a system that should not have been allowed to exist for a day, not for six months. Now, we still have apartheid being spread in dribs and drabs, and you have the spreading of the apartheid system, which is the homeland system, and the land taken from the people. That land remains in the hands of the government puppets, and who will strip the citizenship of urbanists like myself who are still here.

I am still obviously not a citizen, because I cannot vote. What we see on television is people signing, not signing over power, but maybe signing peace accords to do away with the violence underground. But that is rubbish. It is meaningless because the violence continues before and after the peace accord.

I am one person who believes that in the end that things will come right, but it is sad. People are bitter in this country. The more people continue to die, the more bitterness arises. You must think of vengeance.

This world is a different world. I mean, what is happening in Slovenia, I didn't know people could be talking about problems that occurred forty years ago. Even in this country, you will have people who will rise up and fight for massacres that have been committed from time to time against the people by agents of the government and the members of the death squads.

It is a terrible state of affairs. I don't see any light at the end of any tunnel. I don't see a tunnel. If it's a tunnel, all that I hear are wailings and cries.

I am not as yet a person who is able to see light. It is false. When a person appears on television wearing beautiful suits and speaking beautiful English, they blast the world and blast us. During the night, there is too much sound of gunfire. I have never lived in this country where every evening there is the sound of gunfire. This is happening now, as I talk to you.

There are more police on the streets than before. It's like the same state of emergency. Then, unless something is done, then I will be fair enough to say that now things are okay. Now, it's bright, I can hear the singing of the birds in the sky. At the moment, it's helicopters and other things.

I'm not sure why things should be like this. But one day, like I said in one poem in the *Unbroken Spirit* album, I had a beautiful line there that went, "I am seeing how hard and tormenting it is to write about pain and not joy, how hard and tormenting it is to write about slavery and not freedom. When shall I write about the beauty of nature? When shall I write about the daffodils? How can I write about the beauty of nature when the ground is daily soaked with the blood of the innocents? Nevertheless, no oppressive kingdom is eternal."

The life here is unpredictable, but I always say I have something in me, I have gone through the worst problems in my life. I have tasted all forms of torture. I always say I will survive. I will live until I see freedom. I will live until I see the downfall of all the tyrants and dictators in this world. So have that hope that I have that we will meet and shake hands in the near future.

MIRIAM MAKEBA

The Grand Dame of World Music, "Mama Africa," Miriam Makeba had a pop hit with "Pata Pata" (also called "The 'Clicking' Song" for the tongue clicks that characterize Zulu languages) in 1967, bringing a leavened version of mbaqanga to Western ears for the first time.

When I came here, I was something completely new, because I sang my songs. I sang my "clicking songs," so it was something completely different. It opened the way for many South African artists, including Hugh Masekela, Dollar Brand, what's his name now? Abdullah Ibrahim. At home he was Dollar Brand. He was best known at home as Dollar Brand. Everyone is in. Paul Simon has opened it even wider.

With Harry Belafonte, I had another vehicle, because when I was performing with him, I was reaching more people. His audience was wide, so is Paul's. So when I'm with him, I'm reaching different people. It is an audience that we might never have reached on our own. Paul's audience is completely different. And they like it, when we came on stage, even those who had never heard us before, they were happy to discover and hear. And people left happy: they came backstage and said they liked our music.

I think artists should be like that, should help each other. I've always liked to perform with other artists, because I think I'm contributing something to them as well as they're contributing something to me. Paul's record was big, but in the show, all of us contributed something to make the show the success that it was. I'm very grateful to him, because I feel, through his show, I was able to come back here and renew my old friendships and fans. People are quite happy that I'm here.

Even though Paul Simon used South African township musicians and South African township music, he has a style all his own, and his style and my style are completely different. I don't want to measure anything I do against what Paul Simon does, or any other artist for that matter. I think that is the spirit of competition that I never was used to, and will never get used to. I always feel that I am going to do what I'm doing. If it works, it works. If it doesn't, it doesn't, but I'm not going to measure myself according to so and so.

My door was open before I sang with Paul Simon, before Paul Simon did anything. With his style and his mixing of our music with his style, it worked for him. It was very good. Maybe more young people are talking about South African music because of Paul Simon.

That doesn't mean that it opened my door, because my door was opened before that. I never sold millions, but my first performance in this country was on the first of November 1959, on Steve Allen's show, which was viewed by 60 million people. Then, I opened at the Village Vanguard the next day. I've stayed here for the next ten years, when in fact, I was only supposed to stay for four weeks. So my little door was there, because I came from nowhere to stay for four weeks, and I wound up staying for ten years and working everywhere.

I've never sold records like Paul Simon has, because it's not the same thing. That's why I don't like the comparison. I cannot dispute the younger people, simply because I was not here from 1969 until I came back with Paul Simon. I was completely off the scene in this country. So children who are the age of my grandson, who is twenty-one, most of them do not know Miriam Makeba, except for children who have parents who are my fans, who heard the music in their homes. That was not because of anything else except the fact that I was not here. And coming back with Paul Simon in 1987 was very good for me, because I came back then, and coming back in a show like his was just wonderful for me. I hope that I will not be erased again.

"Pata Pata" is the song that really took off for me in the sixties. I wasn't very happy about it. Like, man, let me move away from "Pata Pata." But they say, "Hey, people like 'Pata Pata.'" You have to do what people like.

I remember, I did an interview with Al Jackson on the radio in New York, and when "Pata Pata" played, the phones were blinking and blinking because people were calling. There is a friend of mine, Duma, who said, "You see, when 'Pata Pata' plays, all the phones light up." I always say to him, "Get me away from 'Pata Pata,'" and he says, "You can't do anything about it, because that's the song that became big for you, and because the people like it. You've got to keep singing it."

It's the language. Many of my compatriots say they're from South Africa, they hear, "Can you click like Miriam Makeba?" It's like this language is mine. It's not, but they heard it first from me. It's like the short haircut. Some people would ask me, "Why do you wear your hair natural?" and I said, "You want me to wear my hair unnatural? You answered yourself. It's natural."

One cannot just stay in one place. You have to grow, you have to change, without changing your basic style. I think if I completely changed my style and went to sing jazz or something else, people would be shocked, maybe, unless I put just one song of a different type within my usual type of singing. Then it wouldn't be too much of a shock. We're always afraid to do that, because you don't know the reaction you're going to get from the press, from your fans, from everybody else. I think working with Sipho Mabuse brought something a little bit new from the younger generation in South Africa, because he is still in South Africa, and he came from there to Brussels to work with me on the album.

I always wanted to leave home. I never knew they were going to stop me from coming back. Maybe, if I knew, I never would have left. It is kind of painful to be away from everything that you've ever known. Nobody will know the pain of exile until you are in exile. No matter where you go, there are times when people show you kindness and love, and there are times when they make you know that you are with them but not of them. That's when it hurts.

I was banned from going home. I still am banned, but in the past year, I got phone calls from home from people saying that the government said I could come home if I want to and I apply for a visa, just like anybody else, because I'm not South African any more. I told the newspaper guy who called me, "Well, you can tell them that I consider myself South African, always South African." If I have any other travel document that I am using, it is an honorary one, because I never renounced my citizenship of birth, and secondly, we have leaders who are in prison; we have a state of emergency that keeps our people in prison. If they say we can come home, then lift the state of emergency, release all our people from prison, and let all our exiles come back home and be free, to come back home and vote for whomever we want to vote for. We might surprise them. We might vote for one of them. They don't know that. They should give us at least that opportunity. For me to just be told I can go home, why was I told that I couldn't go home in the first place. I never understood that.

I must say I was the first person to come over and let people discover a little of our culture, not only of South Africa, but of Africa. That's why they call me Mama Africa. I always knew that it was possible. All I needed to do was be here. I'm very confident about that because I know I have something different and special to give. There aren't too many Makebas.

HUGH MASEKELA

South African expatriate trumpeter, Hugh Masekela is known for fusions of Zulu Jive and jazz that led to the chart-topping hit "Grazing in the Grass" in 1968, and four decades of remarkable music. He considered it all a holding action.

People try to imply that mbaqanga is getting popular now, but "Grazing in the Grass" was an mbaqanga record, it was number one. People tend to forget that in 1967, Miriam had a top five record, an mbaqanga hit, it was her own composition, "Pata Pata."

Miriam's first album was mbaqanga based, but the musicians were not there. It was an environmental thing, because there really weren't any musicians to play what she could do. We had a long compromise, a musical compromise era. It's like when the first Brazilians came over here and they tried to teach the subtleties of samba and bossa nova. I think Stan Getz got the closest to it. But the reason it sounded so good was that he was playing with an all-Brazilian band. We didn't have the opportunity. If we had had the right people, we would have been doing this kind of album long ago.

There's a certain amount of growth to mbaqanga in that now we can change keys, use minor chords, but basically it's a resistance. It's like samba. It's a music of the people. It's like salsa. It might change a little, but it's more than an artistic or classical music. It's a folk music. Mbaqanga actually constitutes a great part of our resistance to the brutality. The thing that makes us happy, the thing that the government doesn't understand about us, is like when they are shooting at us, and the people are demonstrating, they sing mbaqanga. It's like the people's music.

Over the last ten years, I've had a renaissance in my life. This is the first time I've gone back to Southern Africa. I've been able to put together members so that we could do the rawest kind of African music we could ever want to do. It has definitely become easier to do the township music.

If you look at it from a realistic point, I don't consider my career as having started yet. I'm like an activist on hold to become a musician when my country is free. It's really like being in a prison camp, like being a POW.

Paul Simon couldn't have done *Graceland* unless he went to South Africa. That's how he made *Graceland*. It confirms the point. To do good mbaqanga, you have to go to the source. It depends on the source's accesibility. He was able to get to the source. He couldn't have done that album here. He had to go to the people.

This is a thing that we can't do, because we have sworn that we would not go to South Africa unless South Africa is free and right. The day Mandela says, "Okay, everybody is out of jail, I'm out of jail," I'll get on a plane. That's when my career will start.

If South Africa was a normal country, I could have gone back after I graduated from music school here in 1964 and formed the bitchingest band and done this album then. But by then, I had established myself—I was not the only one—we had ensconced ourselves heavily in the resistance movement and the anti–South African government movement. There was a war in Mozambique, there was a war in Angola, there was as war in Namibia. The place was very impenetrable, and the government was at its most paranoid.

When I arrived here in 1960, Eisenhower was president and Nixon and Kennedy were doing the mud slinging, McCarthy hangover was really heavy, and Africans were basically just categorized as communist. Any one who was anti-West was considered a communist.

We had a secret file with the FBI that was sent over by the South African government. I didn't know it, but I knew that there was an FBI car outside my house. And when I went to get my residency permit, my green card, I found out I had a secret file. So, like the immigration officer who was going to interview me didn't know what was in the file. Fortunately, my lawyer was a former immigration officer. The guy opened the thing in 1965 and the first thing he says is, "Wow, you're a communist."

It's funny, when you see where communism is going today. I'd always thought it was a failure anyway, so to be accused of something you're not . . . but this guy is really scared. My lawyer looks at me.

So I say, "Look man. This is a secret file. Read the rest of it. Who says I'm a communist?"

They had it in there from the special branch in South Africa that this man is a communist. I said, "If you can believe the South African government, then your shouldn't even be in this gig."

Then he turns the page and says, "Did you know that you were being watched all the time?"

And I said, "Yes."

What I'm trying to portray, when we arrived here the West was so paranoid of us it was like being in enemy territory. But it's the marketplace. So it's amazing—notwithstanding all the resistance we got—it's amazing that a person like Dollar Brand, Abdullah Ibrahim, or Miriam Makeba, have gotten to where we are able to sustain in South African–allied territory.

I met Abdullah in 1958. We were playing with a group that was like the Mills Brothers of South Africa, like the Ink Spots. They were the most popular group ever. We were out on a tour. I was a young guy, about eighteen, and we were going to Capetown. It was mbaqanga basically, this group, the Manhattan Brothers. They were like the pioneers of vocal mbaqanga. They were the biggest group. They also did a lot of Mills Brothers songs, like "Marie" and "Paper Doll." They wore tails and stuff. Miriam Makeba actually started her career with them, sort of like the Platters.

Our piano player was a guy named Todd Matshikiza, he was working on a township opera, about a heavyweight boxer named Ezekiel Dlamani, his boxing name was King Kong. He was like Tyson. He just hit everybody. But he was also a street guy. And he got into the same kind of trouble that Tyson got into, but he went even further. Some guy was messing with his woman, they had a clash, he killed the guy's ass. So he was sentenced to life. He wanted the death sentence but the judge wouldn't give it to him. So there was a lake at the prison, and he drowned himself. It was a national story, everyone knew about it. It was also the first musical ever in South Africa.

So Todd was trying to raise the money, and we were going to Capetown with this tour. They called Todd and said, "We've got the money for the music." So he had to leave the tour, and we needed a piano player. We went out to look for a piano player, and somebody told us there's a guy who plays cocktail piano in this lounge.

So the leader of the Manhattan Brothers, Kippie Moeketsi, he was our mentor. He knew everything from Bach to Charlie Parker, he was a real militant, but Abdullah Ibrahim and myself use a lot of his sounds and methods. He was one of the kingpins of mbaqanga. He died in 1983, at the age of fifty-nine. A great guy, and real activist. I can only compare his political attitude to Miles Davis, but he was even more intellectual, more scholarly. He was very clear about us being exploited. He always told us, "You are being exploited. Remember that. I'm going to teach you that."

He taught us everything about Charlie Parker and Duke Ellington. He knew everything: "But remember, even the guys I'm teaching you about were exploited. You will never be free until South Africa is free." He was real radical.

Even when we did the musical, some rich white folks who were liberals and like activists raised the money for *King Kong*. So when it came time to discuss salaries for the band, because it was big money, was going to be a big hit, had a cast of eighty people. They wanted to pay us some menial money, and Kippie was the one to stand up and say, "You've been exploiting us all our lives. This is our big shot." And he asked for ten times more than what they were offering, otherwise the band was going to walk out. He was our representative. And the other guys were trying to calm him down, and saying, "Kippie, be cool man."

And he said, "No, even you have been exploiting me. I want to get as much as I can out of this, and as much as I can for all the guys."

We ended up getting the most money we've ever been paid. Kippie was really fantastic.

He was one of the guys who went out and he chose Dollar Brand to replace Todd Matshikiza. He was the musical mentor of the group. So I spent five months on the road with Abdullah.

The tour didn't go so well. These guys were not so popular anymore. Not as popular as they thought they were. So we got stranded on the road. We lived together under very dire conditions. Africans were not allowed in hotels in those days in South Africa, so every town you went to, you lived with families that were into music, and were relatives of people in the group, and stuff like that. There was actually a time in the tour when we had nothing to eat. But Dambuza, the leader of the Manhattan Brothers, wouldn't give us our railroad tickets back. He kept saying, "The next town. The next town is where we're going to make it."

Five months later, Kippie had been drinking, and he pissed on this guys pants. The audience couldn't see, he said, "Dambuza, I want to go home," and pissed on his pants.

They were doing these steps and you could here the water go slosh. Dambuza looked back and said, "Kippie, I'm going to kill you." And we're all dying of laughter.

So the tour was over, and we finally got home, because Kippie pissed on the guy's leg, and the guy was going to kill him, but the guy finally saw the sense. And my parents, they gave me a rough time about playing music. They said, "We told you, don't be a musician, stay in school." I came back weighing 110 pounds.

Abdullah went back to Capetown. I went home and formed a trio.

We went and did this musical, *King Kong*, which was a smash, ran for about a year and a half. By the time we were finished, Dollar had this trio, and they were playing a place called the Ambasador Jazz Club. We called each other, and myself, Kippie, and another guy decided to go to Capetown to join Dollar's trio, and we became the Jazz Epistles. We played at the Ambassadors for two months, and you couldn't get into the place. That's when we did all our compositions. Then we moved up to Johannesburg. We were the first group, first African group to do an LP. And then we became a household name.

We were about to embark on a national tour when Sharpeville happened and gatherings of more then ten people were banned.

I'd been waiting for a passport, and my passport came through during that waiting period. The band came on in March, and in May, two months later, my passport came through and I left. Since then, I've never really played with Abdullah. I've seen him, but I've never been to his shows. We've never had the opportunity to play together, partly because we're never in the same place, and partly because we've grown in different directions.

He was like the free spirit musically. Him and Kippie. They'd go into an avant garde spin. They were heavy into avant garde. Dollar was really the biggest, I would say he's the authority on Monk. Dollar is Monk right up to lifestyle.

I think it was the inconsistencies and conditions in the environment that made it impossible for me to do the kind of albums that I'm doing now. When I came here, I was alone, and I didn't have access to people who were familiar with the South African dance band medium. So, I ended up with a hybrid, because the musicians that I was playing with when I started were Americans. So I had to write everything down and explain to them. The groove was difficult for them.

I think that today people have become more universal, and that the younger musicians I usually work with are Americans. They're graduates of the Berkelee school of music. But they know as much, and sometimes even more, about African music than I know. And they are as much scholars of African music as I was of American music when I came here, because I came here as a bebopper.

In South Africa what's amazing—Dizzy said, "I want to join your revolution because it's got so much music. The only thing we had was 'We Shall Overcome.' Every time I see South Africa on TV, they've got a new song."

I said, "I don't know when they rehearse, who writes the lyrics, when they compose the songs, but it's topical. Everything is topical. And they have the choreography down, too. Where do thirty thousand people get together to rehearse something like this?"

But South Africa is such a musical place. It's like the Caribbean or Brazil or Zaire is a lot like that. It lives by music.

Music in Africa is a ceremonial thing. It's used for every occasion. I think it's one of the things that frustrates the colonial mentality. And it saves us. If we were like the Native Americans, purely like a warlike people, I think the music has saved us, because we always go back and sing about what's happening to us. It is the thing that has sustained us. Sometimes, instead of fighting, we'll just sing about it. Most of the time, I think that is what sustained the African American. They were brought here as slaves, they were shackled and whipped, but they sang their asses off. And today, the African American influences 80 percent of popular music. They may not get the returns, but they definitely influence it. And it's a thing that under the conditions and brutality that Africans internationally have had to develop behind, whatever they are given the opportunity to do, they excel in it.

I've also spent a lot time in southern Africa, in Zimbabwe. I lived for four years in Botswana. There are more Botswanans living in South Africa than there are in Botswana. The borders are artificial colonial borders, so it's a great mbaqanga area. And I was able to stop writing music on paper. I found a band that just knew everything that I'd ever done, and every other classic.

I'd sooner be in Botswana now. The reason I left Botswana, there was a South African commando raid on Botswana, and they killed all my friends, all my friends, including the fellow who encouraged me to come to Botswana. Our mothers were friends. We were childhood buddies. And when I was in Lesotho to perform in 1980—I had gone with Miriam Makeba to perform there—we hadn't been in the area in twenty years. I was supposed to go to Botswana to perform, Lesotho and Swaziland. And the governments of Botswana and Swaziland cancelled our concerts. There was a "cholera epidemic." The government was so scared of the impact of our return. So the Lesotho government said, "Fuck it. There's no cholera here." And we played to seventy-five thousand people, Christmas Day 1980.

I was going to stay for three days, but I wound up staying for three months. I had to catch up with all the time I'd been gone. For example, when I had left, my youngest sister was seven, now she was twenty-seven and she brought her three kids with her. I had to catch up with friends. So my friend called me from Botswana, he said, "Come to Botswana." I said, "They cancelled us in Botswana." He said, "Come anyway." I said, "It's a desert." He said, "Come anyway. Come and see." Because he was in exile from South Africa. I went to visit them. I was going to stay for a weekend, I spent six weeks there.

I met Kalahari, the band that he introduced me to. They happened to know everything that I did. The minister of home affairs, who had cancelled my show, he said, "Man, we're sorry. Could you raise funds for this and that?"

I don't know if you remember the raid, but they showed it on the TV. That was his house. They said they were attacking a terrorist camp. It was people's homes. He owned a bus company. His wife was like assistant secretary of social affairs. The only reason that they didn't bomb my house—they bombed a house six doors down from us. My wife and I said goodbye to each other. It was like that close. They didn't come because they couldn't prove to the world that my house was a terrorist den because I was too well known.

So it has been all those things that have made it difficult to get down and get into township music. If South Africa was a normal society, I'd be making these records from way back. I would have been living there. I wouldn't have to come from overseas. I'd go overseas by choice.

We have a big network of musicians, like I worked with Mbongeni Ngema who lives in Paris. We did *Sarafina* together. He's coming to stay with us for a week and a half.

The South African government uses everything, even successful music and theater, to trick the world into thinking that they are really okay, because no other African country can evidence as many successful musicians and theater acts as South Africa. But actually, what we're seeing is just a drop in the ocean.

But they use that. They say, "If we are so bad, would we allow *Graceland*? If we were so bad, would there be a Miriam Makeba, Dollar Brand, Hugh Masekela?"

But what the world doesn't realize is that we are just one percent of one percent, and probably not the most capable, of the artists. But now, we've got a little network, there are a lot of artists who go home, who go in and out.

I think that the only other stage now is to be able to go to a free South Africa and play with guys like Philip Tabane. Philip Tabane is one of our most talented musicians. I'm looking to do an album with him, to produce an album. He is somebody I really admire. He has been doing what he is doing for thirty years.

There are so many great musicians in South Africa. I think that the main problem is that the great artists who are not mainstream in South Africa, guys like Philip Tabane, should be very popular artists internationally, because of what he does, but is not known because somebody has to recognize him, identify him, he has to get an international deal, the record company has to believe that he means something, and give him exposure. When he played at the Apollo, it flipped out the audience. People were on their feet. And they had unbelievable reviews, and then nothing happens after that.

Being a sangoma doesn't necessarily make you a great artists. It makes you a member of a certain cultural tradition. I think that more than being a sangoma, Philip Tabane is a great artist. I think that if he just got the right kind of attention, he would fly. But he is one of thousands of people who need a shot.

The main thing is, not only South African artists, but African artists, shouldn't have to come overseas to get recognition. But we're living in a situation where we still have a postcolonial structure in Africa, where anyone who is in recreation or entertainment was originally looked upon as a lazy native, so an infrastructure for the music industry was never really formed in Africa. It is now in its infancy. I would like to help to hurry it up. African artists should not have to come from overseas and grovel for attention because there are enough people in Africa to support them, and they can live as well as salsa musicians or samba musicians who come overseas by choice.

A person like Philip shouldn't be different from a Milton Nascimento. He should be able to come over here and go home to a normal society and be appreciated for what he does. He is prevented at home from the people hearing him. The mainstream there is not created by the people. It is created by a record industry that exploits the cheapest desires of African music consumers. In that place, they don't have a space for a person like Philip.

It's the same here in a lot of respects. They go for what's popular, exploit it while it's popular, and so a lot of great African-American artists making African American classical music, what the media here calls a few things, one of them is jazz, don't get a shot. I don't know why. There's something sick about this country. Jazz musicians in this country should have a national endowment, because it is the classical music of this country. If it wasn't for jazz there wouldn't be rock, but racism is so rampant in the industry, that the people who make the music industry what it is get the least benefits from it.

We were in Paris, getting ready to open *Sarafina*, and we played a month in England. Last Saturday, *Sarafina* opened in Paris, so I went from London to Paris, and I was in the theater, and someone said, "Fela wants to see you." I saw Fela, and he was doing his new album, *Over Takee, Don't Over Takee, Yaa*. He's great.

I met Fela, because I had heard about him from a lot of friends when I first came to school. They'd say, "There's a trumpet player just like you in England, his name is Fela." Because he started on trumpet. He picked up the sax when he formed Africa 70.

What happened was, when I peaked here in 1968, I had the number one record in the country for about six weeks. It was incongruous to my political position that I was making all this money, but I came from 27 million oppressed people. And there was something unfulfilling. I had a house in Malibu, I was driving a fancy car, I was living the life, and there just seemed to be an emptiness to success, the way it translated into conspicuous consumption. I felt I wasn't getting enough of what I was about, so I decided that I was going to leave the country.

I wanted to go to southern Africa, but I couldn't home, because I was at the height of my activist period. It was the time of the anti-Vietnam war. I was very active. My friends were like Peter Fonda and Crosby and Stills when Crosby was still with the Byrds and Stills was in Buffalo Springfield. The Grateful Dead, the Jefferson Airplane, the Doors, Big Brother and the Holding Company. We were always doing antiwar concerts. Then there was the Black Panthers and Black Power. I was very involved in that.

There was a void in my live. It was great to be involved with American politics, to be antiwar, to be into black power, but still, I was like a Hollywood-type celebrity. I had the fancy car, the fancy house by Malibu. I felt I had to get out of the stagnation. I decided to go to Africa. I gave myself a pilgrimage. I bought myself a ticket to about fifteen countries.

I studied in Zaire, and while I was there I saw Franco. I got a house right opposite from his club, and I jammed with him a lot. I was really looking to play with African musicians. I had written to Fela, and he said come over and we'll take it from there. I spent a month with him, and I played with his band a lot. I didn't record with him, but he was helping me find musicians. It was still the same quest. To get closer to the home sod. He said, "The best thing you could do is tour with me. Be a guest artist with the band." So, I did that.

When we got to Ghana, a group called Hedzolleh Soundz opened for him. They really knocked me out. I stayed with that group for about five years; we did about six albums. When I got there I said, "This group knocks me out."

Fela said, "I thought you'd like them. I think you should stay with them."

So he left me in Ghana. I still travel on a Ghana passport. I'm a Ghanan citizen. I speak the languages. I spent seven years, on and off, in Ghana.

FLAMENCO

Usually, flamenco conjures up images of a guitarist, vocalist, castanets, a woman with a rose in her teeth, and a man with large loud heels. A reality check reveals that, while that plays for *las touristas*, the current state of flamenco is something else again. Take Jose Miguel Carmona of Ketama and La Barberia Del Sur, who often eschews the typical nylon-string acoustic guitar of the *tocaore* in favor of a Stratocaster.

Despite the new trappings, the flamenco sound remains unmistakable. Two important elements underline the new flamenco that burst out of Spain in the early ninties, most visibly touted by the Gipsy Kings, who reflect both elements of the sobriquet new flamenco.

The new comes out of the desire among the younger players to incorporate various strains of popular music and culture that bombard them every day in this global village where MTV reaches billions of households around the world. In any other context, it might seem unusual to see a player J. M. Carmona's age on stage with anything but an electric guitar.

The other side of this, of course, is that flamenco is a traditional music, one with roots traceable to at least the eighteenth century. Some contend that the tradition is older, that it in all likelihood Columbus was entertained by some early form of flamenco. However, we know that by the mid-nineteenth century, travelers to Spain were writing about this music of inns and cafés.

As ephemeral as the musicians who play the music, it is likely that the roots of flamenco lie in the inns of Andalusia where people from all ends of the economic and social strata, from shepherds to shopkeepers, from tailors to thieves, would gather at the end of the day. The style grew out of the local folk songs, played on acoustic guitars for singers and dancers. The sources of these songs are traceable to places as far afield as Indian and Middle Eastern folk music.

Photograph: Gilles Larman, Elektra

CHICO BALIARDO | THE GIPSY KINGS

Mixing the fire of Gitane Gypsy music with the recognizable rhythms of rumba and salsa, the Gipsy Kings became one of the biggest world music acts ever, playing on Spanish radio and even more adventurous pop stations. The Gipsy Kings's first show in America was a showcase for the late, lamented New Music Seminar. They were sandwiched between African rockers Toure Kunda (see page 159) and the Ohio Players—two very funky bands. They blew the audience away—those familiar with their imported debut and those who were totally unaware of them before they took the stage but for the buzz going around among seminarians—with their wall of guitar virtuosity and flamenco passion.

It was our first American concert. A long time ago, we used to play in New York at private parties. So we had been in New York before, playing for people and it worked really well. So we were not that surprised by the city.

We were surprised that the show went so well, especially with New York being such a competitive city, and the news being that it is very difficult to make it in New York. We were surprised that people went so crazy over it, but we were very happy about it.

It had been much more difficult at the Palladium, because there were so many groups playing and they were pressured for time. They were not the best conditions. We were happy it worked well.

People are getting more and more interested in music that is a reflection of different cultures. We had been playing for sixteen years before we were signed in the U.S., and it is very nice to know that we are part of a movement, finding ethnic music again.

So I am not surprised that people like the music. I'm happy about it. I'm not surprised at the success that we are having in the States, but I am by how quickly it spread out. For example, we are on tour of sixteen different cities.

Since people in radio and the music business in general reflect what the American audience want and like, I'm very happy when people like you like the music. If you don't know the music, listen to it. That's very important. The music is very emotional. Once you've heard it, if you like it, talk about it. Just being very personal, honest, and emotional about it. If you like the music, let people know about it.

Playing flamenco is first a question of emotion, playing the guitar. Plus, I like the sound of it. Guitar is one of the best ways to express yourself. The sound of the guitar by itself suits us very well. We are very grateful to the man who does our sound in concert. We were afraid that we would lose the quality of sound that we have when we play with the family. We were afraid that we would not be able to get that tone and quality in concert.

Not that there's a specific sound that we are looking for. It depends on the song. When they want something very soft, they want a soft sound, sometimes they want something very dry and cutting.

You don't have to study for fifteen years with a professor to do something very nice and very emotional with a guitar. We played at classical guitar festival a couple of years ago. All the classical players came by after the concert, asking who taught who and who were our professors. We told them we don't even read music. We learned by ourselves.

We don't have to work on the tradition, really. It's a part of us. It really isn't difficult to find a balance between new stuff. What is more important is working on our harmonies, and being more subtle in our concept of flamenco.

Flamenco, the beginning, was really a family affair. You would just play it in the house together and in the field outside. It was mostly within the family. It is great to be able to mix music and work and family. There's something about love and being together, producing something together.

There's an old saying among the Gypsies that you learn to play before you are born. You learn about music in the womb.

Music is part of our environment. Women having children are around music all the time. For example, when my kid was just two years old, he was already carrying around a guitar. They get used to that. It helps you learn how to walk.

What's important for us is to play music. Certainly, we started playing with our family, but we were determined to get away from that as soon as possible. We were playing in cafés and in the streets, for money, since we were fourteen.

Mainly, typical flamenco music doesn't have to be in the form of a regular song. It can be just anything. There is no specific structure. What the Gipsy Kings did is integrate the typical flamenco principles, but change it so that it would be in the classic format of a song, with words. Flamenco music didn't have to be with words. We're keeping the idea of a combination of guitar and singing, but we're trying to bring it together in a more subtle way, so that it's easier to listen to.

The very difficult thing was to harmonize with what Nicolas [Reyes] was singing. The guitars are supposed to follow the singer. At the same time we wanted to add new elements and new sounds. That was my job when I came in. One problem was that we think in two beats, while the rest of the world usually thinks in four beats. We had to work together a lot to agree on that and to keep the real principles of flamenco music, but at the same time to arrange the music and make it modern.

We don't feel that we have to define some kind of music. We don't feel that we are leaders of some specific movement. We just want to play. That's most important. We're very happy people like it.

JORGE PARDO

Creating a remarkable fusion of jazz and flamenco, wind player Jorge Pardo, along with bassist Carles Benavent, has been at the heart of many "Nuevo Flamenco" recordings, beginning with Paco de Lucia's "flamenco fusion" period.

The music I play has influences from many different musics. It's not the flamenco language, it's not the jazz language. I grew up with all these influences. I can not really be objective about my music.

There are Gypsies all over Spain, but of course the flamenco was born in Andalusia and passed around more there. In the last thirty years it's reached the big cities like Barcelona and Madrid. A lot of flamenco is happening there. Still, this is not popular. It is traditional maybe, but not popular. The music you hear on the radio in Spain the stations is maybe about the same as here with maybe some differences.

Flamenco is a music that will open a lot of people's ears. That means that it gets in closer to other musicians all over the world. I think that in twenty or thirty years, there will be Japanese flamenco bands, German flamenco bands. There are now even some Japanese flamenco bands, with singers and guitar players. But I mean that it's going to grow more and more.

It's not that hard. It's like the first time somebody listens to jazz and says everything is the same. Somebody who listens to jazz for the first time can't tell the difference between Sonny Rollins or Michael Brecker or Charlie Parker. After you have listened to it for a while, you develop the differences. Flamenco is about the same. At first it sounds like the same dancing, clapping, guitar, but when you get more into it, you will recognize the different styles.

Flamenco, up until the last thirty or forty years has been music from the countryside, really. It was made in small villages in Andalusia. It's really when the big cities grow up, like Seville, Madrid and Barcelona, then flamenco comes to the big city. That was when flamenco met the rest of the world of music, in the big cities. So, that makes the flamenco bigger. It's known that some other sax players played flamenco thirty or forty years before me, but it didn't have the same kind of success at the time. When flamenco went to the cities and met other instruments, out of the flamenco at the time came other harmonies and other rhythms.

I think anywhere you go, New York or Germany or Italy or Japan or a small village in Spain, whatever, what you have to do is make the music you feel and take it out from your heart and your mind.

If you do that, I think the audience will take that as it is. I don't think the audience is so expert that they're going to say, well, this is flamenco, this is more like pop. They see a good feeling on the stage, that's it. Whatever you do.

I think it's very similar to what happened with the blues in America. It's smaller here in Spain because Spain is smaller than the States, but it's like the same kind of thing.

The way I record is I use a lot of recordings out of my own improvisations that I put onto a hard disc. Then I used my own improvisations as proper melodies. Then I re-harmonized them and orchestrated them. It's not very typical. That's something I liked the first time I started working this way. The melodies that are played on this record, they are played for the first time ever. It's nothing that is played twice or three times. Everything is played the first time. I'm working with my brother. He's a genius of these things. We use a Macintosh with ProTools and an Audiologic sequencer. Starting with the rhythms I play, everything is a bit of a coincidence. I used a lot of coincidences.

I found a lot of coincidences in the patterns of the different rhythms, in flamenco and out of the flamenco, in some Caribbean rhythms and some African rhythms. Much music I've been very close to uses the same kind of patterns, this 2/3 or 3/2. In a bularia, it's a rhythm that's in three parts, but it's ordered in five different accents. The ronroco, which is burning in Cuba, is in four parts, but the accents are the same. There are some other rhythms, like the Cajun music from New Orleans. They use the same type of pattern of five different accents. Some music from Northern Africa and then add fandango to it, and soliero, buleria, and segueria. I found a lot of coincidences between them. That's why I tried to put the buleria and the fandango together, and it works, and soliero and a ronroco together and it keeps working.

After I did that, I brought everybody together, and we decided about the arrangements, the way we usually do. It's like an electronic jam session. Instead of everybody playing on the rhythm, everybody played on the melody. Usually when you make records, you first put down the rhythm section, then you build the arrangement on top of that. This is like starting a house from the roof. Everyone plays just from the melody.

Ornette Coleman does that. He is one of the greatest musicians of this century. I play a piece by him called "Law Years." It's a very short melody of Ornette's that I put right on a bulerias rhythm. He would be shocked, because it's very different. Maybe he'd like it.

Before, the tunes didn't have a shape to the compositions. Now the compositions have a good shape to play anywhere. We are playing this stuff live. It really works.

Sometimes, it's just a matter of time. You can't do something big in two days. We keep working in this kind of music that is a new sound. We're building this up. It's a lot to do, still.

I think we are now closer to flamenco than jazz fusion. Any, all those terms like flamenco or jazz fusion or straight jazz, all those kind of words, they start to have no sense to me. What we really do is our music; it is born of a new thing. I wouldn't say it was more jazz or more flamenco or more fusion. I don't know.

CARLES BENAVENT

Carles Benavent's work with Paco de Lucia, Jorge Pardo, Ketama, and so many others has made him the flamenco bassist of record. Like so many other bass players, he is a man of few words.

We don't have any records as a duet, like Jorge and me on the cover. I play on his records and he plays on my records. I've made three. I also played on the first Ketama record.

    We play what we feel. I think it's natural. It's not one thing, premeditated, you think about it and you do it. I think it's the natural way.

JOSE MIGUEL CARMONA, ANTONIO CARMONA, JUAN CARMONA, JOSE SOTO | KETAMA

The offspring of noted flamenco guitarist Pepe Habichuela, Ketama have taken their traditional and familial roots and brought them into the twentieth century by adding rock. They became founding musicians in Spain's Nuevo Flamenco movement with a version of flamenco combining Latin percussion and electric guitar with more traditional flamenco instruments. It is a blend that intrigues Spanish audiences and adventurous rock fans alike. While they opt for the purer strain of flamenco whenever possible, they are also ultimately flexible about it. This flexibility led them to one of the greatest cross cultural music projects ever recorded, the monumental Song Hai, *featuring their flamenco guitars matched with Danny Thompson from Fairport Convention on bass and Toumani Diabate on kora.*

JUAN CARMONA: *Song Hai* was a beautiful thing. In spite of the fact that we couldn't participate as much in the recording and production end because we couldn't understand the language [English]. Of course, music was the language we understood the best among us, with Toumani and Danny Thompson.

JOSE SOTO: We had very little time. We saw them four days earlier, so it was maybe a little forced. We talked about the base of the music that each person wanted and what we were going to do and the themes, and we had moments where we improvised. We used instruments related to flamenco and also we used bass guitar. The result was real original. A good mix of musics and a good experience. The language was the rhythm.

JOSE MIGUEL CARMONA: We're going to tour Europe with Toumani.

ANTONIO CARMONA: When we were in Barcelona for three days, we decided to play with Don Cherry, another branch of music. We enjoyed playing with him a lot. He used piano and an instrument that looked like an arch. It was good and it mixed well with African music as well.

I also love salsa. Salsa is like a fountain for me. In salsa, I always hear and can take many things. I like to borrow things from it because there is a specail rhythm, a rhumba that is close to the music from here, from Spain. So we can work with it. Mix it with everything, a little jazz with Morrocan.

J. CARMONA: In addition to guitar, I also play an oud, an Arab instrument. It has ten strings, five sets of two. I've played it since the time we first recorded with Pepe Habichuela. It is a typical Arab instrument that goes really well with the music we play.

J. M. CARMONA: Flamenco is a thing of real roots, a traditional form of music that has many years of history. It's not just another form like any other form of music. You have to know it. Learn about it. If you want to truly appreciate its subtleties, you must learn about its roots to know what it is.

A. CARMONA: In my family, for example, everyone plays the guitar. We have a long tradition of guitar in my family: grandfather and great grandfather, my aunt, the women played the guitar, too. Everyone has played the guitar and danced, too. We have been playing for centuries.

J. SOTO: In the young flamenco groups, because Ketama is, as you call it, new flamenco, we came more from this modern musical epoch. We have many musical influences. What we do carries influences of many types of music. But always with the base influence of "Gypsy Music."

This movement has not been around very long, about five or six years. The movement has branched out from Andalusia during the last year and a half, two years.

J. M. CARMONA: Look, all of us are flamenco musicians. More than anything, we all have our roots strongly based in flamenco and in our lives we always play flamenco and we always played flamenco with our parents when we were children, but music has to evolve and we have to find new forms of music to mix with flamenco—with salsa, jazz, and African musical forms. But above all, it's our flamenco. I believe it continues to be flamenco, because there are the same elements of happiness and fandango. We incorporate other forms, but it doesn't come out as salsa, rumba, or tango. We use those things, but we always have flamenco roots. It's the flamenco we're living now.

J. SOTO: We have been playing together for about five years. But we haven't been able to dedicate as much time as we would have like to the group Ketama because of financial reasons, the currency, etc. But for the last year and a half, it's been better and has really allowed Ketama to live. We play flamenco guitars, acoustic guitars, we incorporate conga, cajon, electric piano, percussion, and acoustics. It's really very acoustic music, flamenco. We use bass sometimes, but it is essentially acoustic.

J. CARMONA: I believe that the music we do is really based in flamenco, because we have played together for five years and originally we played more pure flamenco than anything else, one of the inseparable components of our music. We had mixed flamenco since we were children. Now we play it with a bass, drums and other modern instruments.

A. CARMONA: I play percussion, conga, cajon, nylon guitar. We play everything. Juan plays guitar and percussion, Jose sings and plays guitar and percussion. Live we use two guitars, I play the conga, another percussionist, cajon, a bass, and drums.

J. SOTO: What Ketama performs in relation to the musical components is maybe purer. Pure flamenco has four guitars. Pata Negra, Ketama also uses this. We share and project the happiness that is always part of flamenco. The Gipsy Kings are an extraordinary flamenco group and they are excellent musicians, but the music they do, the Gipsy Kings are only one example, which is a type of music that has been part of Spain for a long time and is part of our customs. We try to use our customs. There are dozens of styles of singing within flamenco. But the music is not purely Gypsy but is a distortion. Ketama performs a different kind of music. The other is more commercial, for mass consumption. We have, of course, a much smaller audience.

J. CARMONA: The music of the Gipsy Kings, who are really great artists, who have brought flamenco to the attention of the general public, is very distinctive from ours. Because our music is more based in flamenco. It's not better or worse, but we remain closer to flamenco roots. All of us, Jose, Antonio, Juan Habichuela, Pepe, we all have very deep roots in flamenco.

PACO DE LUCIA

One of the great players of flamenco, Paco de Lucia has brought his style to jazz and classical without compromising what he does and how he does it. People work with Paco on Paco's own terms.

I started to play before I got the guitar. I'll explain. I grew up in a family where my father and all my brothers played guitar, so before I picked it up, I was listening; before I could speak, I was listening; at the same time I was learning to speak, I was listening to them play. So, before I started to play, I knew every rhythm of the flamenco. We have complex rhythms in the flamenco. Not 3/4 or 4/4. Not only like that. We have long passages, long kompas—kompas means bars. Before I start to play, I knew the feeling and the meaning of the music. So when I started to play, I went directly to the sound I had in my ear.

My family grew up with the Gypsies, so we grew up listening to this music. Any party, any birthday, any fiesta we have singing and dancing and playing and stuff. For any occasion we have the excuse to make a fiesta. As children, we grew up with that all the time. That was a real big part of things that help you a lot to grow up to have an important base to be a musician, a player.

The Gypsies need flamenco for living. It doesn't matter if it's popular, or people like it or don't like it. This is not a problem. The Gypsies spent many years playing only for themselves. It's only from about one century ago when the Gypsies started to make money with the music. Before, they made music only for them, to have a good time, to realize themselves as human beings. They are basically artists, musical people. They need the expression to realize themselves. It doesn't matter if people like them. They don't care.

The guitar traditionally, for many years—and now it still is the same—was to accompany singers, to accompany dancers. Solo concertos of flamenco guitar are relatively new. When I was a child, until I was eighteen years old, I played for dancers and singers all my life. I came to the United States when I was twelve years old playing in the Ballet de Jose Greco. I spent one year the first time here, and the second time I came with Jose Greco, I spent another year. After that, I played with all the dancers and all the singers until I got my own name to play alone.

I respect the tradition very much. The tradition is very important for the emotional message and meaning of flamenco. At the same time, in the darkness you have to reach for something. I don't know what. On the one hand, you have the tradition. On the other hand is looking for something else. Something to incorporate the old tradition and a more recent tradition. It was not easy. I don't feel free when I compose new things for flamenco. I have to take great care with the tradition. It was not easy to evolutionize this music. All the pure flamenco people don't accept any movement, so you have to be very subtle, and do it very carefully.

The limits are because of the tradition and the purists. Plus, the Gypsies are people who sit down in their antique culture. They don't like evolution. They only accept evolution of a high quality. A very high quality. That's why I work very carefully. I didn't want to be out of the flamenco. My idea was to grow up in the flamenco, to continue to be a flamenco guitar player without losing myself, without distaste, without any capitulation. That was my fear. But I was very happy when I realized that all the things that I did, it stays with the tradition. My best success, my real success in life was that.

Flamenco has four chords, more or less. No more. There are four chords in the cadence of the Spanish music. Four chords. It depends on the key, but for example A minor, G major, F major, E major. That is the flamenco cadence. That's the key of A minor.

I don't change the basic rhythms. The basic rhythms stay the same. It is a kind of 3/4, but there are other tempos. There are twelve measures. It's kind of like Indian music where one bar is a long one, like an Indian raga. The buleria is like that, one fast, one slow. I change the chords and the tension of the rhythm, but not the basics. If you change the basics, it's not flamenco.

I am a curious flamenco musician.

EDUARDO BAUTISTA GARCIA

Eduardo Bautista is the head of the Spanish government's Division of Music Publishing Royalties, SGAE. Unlike the U.S., where the extragovernmental organizations ASCAP, BMI, SESAC, and the Harry Fox Agency distribute royalties to songwriters, in most countries there is only one rights organization and it falls under the direct aegis of the government. One of the champions of any music in Spanish, Bautista has actively recruited Spanish-speaking composers from all over to have their rights administered by SGAE.

Being from Latin origins, that's the reason this was scheduled an hour and a half ago. This is how we Latins interpret punctuality. But this is one of the good things about the Latin way of life. Time doesn't count, so lets take it, let's use it, and when we have too much of it, we say bye.

SGAE is the Spanish society that holds together all the writers and publishers in Spain. Like you have in America ASCAP and BMI, in Spain we have SGAE, in Mexico we have SACEM, in Venezuela they have SACVEM, in Colombia they have SICO. In every country there is a society of authors and publishers and writers. It's a good thing that each one of these societies should revise their policies on how to help their national repertoire. A better understanding of each other could help us create a mesh and help each other with the experiences of all that.

I don't want to create any polemics about this, but the European market may be more open than the American market. I think that the American market is opening. The are leading acts like Luis Miguel or Luis Guerra who sell three hundred thousand records here, in the States. You will never see them in them in the *Billboard* charts. You can have a hit, sell one hundred fifty thousand records and make the charts. You can sell three hundred thousand Latin records and never be in the top forty. Why? Because those records are not sold in HMV or Sam Goody or whatever. They are sold in little department stores and different places. But the fact is, they sell, those records. So I believe that the market would open. If we try too hard and it doesn't open, let's try Europe. We have a big market in Spain. It's a 60-million-record market.

We had a broadcast concert of the opening of the World Expo with Celia Cruz, Tito Puente, Oscar D'Leon, and Ruben Blades. We didn't need Prince. We didn't have Bruce Springsteen. They broadcast this concert to 400 million people across the world. They didn't have to have Placido Domingo and Jose Carreras. They had salsa. You have to read the signs, and if you read the signs, Europe is ready for Latin music.

When people say "Latin music," we immediately see Tito Puente and Celia Cruz, and we all believe that's how it all started. That's part of the region, but Latin music is such a large spectrum, such an enormous spectrum nowadays. We have rock and roll, we have all firmness of rock and roll. We go from rock and roll to folk Latin music.

We have Latin jazz as we all know. This amazing community that spread across the ocean from Spain and Portugal over to the USA and down to the Tierra del Fuego is probably as wide a spectrum as any other in the world, perhaps second to Anglo-American music. Latin music exports such a wide spectrum of styles it would be worth it to the record industry to keep an eye on this wide variety, and do not simplify the thing by thinking that Latin is just Jose Jose and Julio Iglesias. It's much more than that.

I think there are tremendous, amazing groups in Spain and Mexico and Argentina and I think the time has come to make some effort and set up some strategy and come over here and say I think I'm good enough and I deserve a place over here. They're not going to give it to you for free. This is what an open market is like. Now that we have the EEC, the European market, we have a market of 400 million with highest income and revenue. That is 40 percent of the worldwide sales. Luis Guerra has been number one in Holland, singing in Spanish. Luis Guerra wouldn't sing any other language. He's too in Spanish to try singing in anything else.

The Gipsy Kings have been number one all over the world. Luz has been in the French charts, Duncan Dhu have been in the French and English charts. If the Anglo-American is too difficult, too close, too exclusive, try Europe. Spain could be the gate of Europe.

Carles Benavent and Jorge Pardo have been playing with Paco de Lucia for a long, long time. They are responsible for the most amazing fusion experiment in Spain, which brings together flamenco, jazz, and Mediterranean music. These two guys are the fathers of the fusion of Spanish music. They've been investigating for a long, long time. That shows in the music. Carles and Jorge are tremendous musicians

Gerardo Nunez is—some call him a flamenco guitar player. That's saying about 20 percent of what he really is. He's a phenomenon. The music speaks for itself.

Celtas Cortes play Celtic or Gaelic rock, but they do much more than that. They are not a second division group or a struggling group. They sell records by the hundreds of thousands in Spain. We're not talking about a group that happens to do Celtic rock because it is "arty." There is a big market in Spain. To prove it, they have been number one in the Spanish charts recently. People love to dance to Celtic rock in Spain.

We have rap groups in Spain. We tried to bring over some of the Spanish rappers, but we have so many styles and we couldn't bring a sample of each one. This is what's more popular. Rap is not a big thing in Spain. We have groups like DNI, which is the Spanish acronym for the identity card. There are many more. There are good Latin rappers.

This is what the future might look like, a cooperation between all the artists in the Latin American countries. We have to convince our record industry, we have to convince the media people in our countries that this product is good enough and it can go to any place anywhere in the world and sell. From a philosophical point of view, we convert this into a strategy, then we have to get together and talk it out. Not too much, just enough so we all know where we stand and how we can blend together.

You have to knock on the door and say, all of the money doesn't have to go to classical music and big auditoriums where they hear opera. Music is rock as well and some of the money should go there. Any of you can hear the music, and music says much more than words.

MARIO PACHECO | PATA NEGRA/NUEVOS MEDIOS RECORDS

Mario Pacheco is the professional scion of the nueva flamenco movement. His Nuevos Medios record company in Barcelona has released most of the key acts in the genre, with the notable exception of the Gipsy Kings. One of those key act was Pata Negra, who along with another Nuevos Medios act, La Barbiera del Sur, mixed their flamenco with rock, using electric guitars—anathema in Gypsy circles.

We went to world music festivals around Europe with artists from Africa and Pakistan and the only ones who couldn't read or write were Spaniards. I don't think you'll see that many illiterate Gypsies any more, except for the women, but fifteen years ago it was very normal. For someone born in the sixties, they didn't go to school.

The funny thing is no other flamenco musician has every gotten into rock. Jazz, they all like, fusion, salsa, or Cuban music. But rock and roll, Pata Negra and Barberia del Sur were the only ones. They were very influential, but not among the flamenco musicians. More they were influential in the world of Spanish rock and roll. That's why they always had huge audiences, because they were rock and roll people.

I remember when Cameron was at his peak, there were a lot of people going to those concerts. They were playing arenas. When it was a double bill with Cameron and Pata Negra. When Cameron finished and the electric Pata Negra set came, all the Gypsies left. They couldn't stand the volume and all that. The rock and punk fans came in.

Definitely, Pata Negra were the first flamenco artists to use an electric guitar. And not so many artists did so since then. The way they started was not like, "Let's play flamenco on the electric guitar." It was more like, "Let's play the blues," and they discovered the blues were already electric, via B.B. King and Albert King and Eric Clapton and all those guys.

The electric guitar just doesn't work so much from the point of view of a flamenco-trained musician. There are a lot of piano players like Keith Jarrett that don't like to play electric keyboards. They are trained in a tradition, but also a technique, which is very different from the technique of electric guitars.

The Habichuelas and Jose Soto, the guys from Ketama, they started playing at home and with professors. The first job they had was playing for traditional singers in a tableau, which is like a flamenco club. They had that training for years, from when they were fifteen until they were nineteen or twenty, they had that job. Raimundo and Rafael, they never had that job, really. They played in the street. They also started recording very early for Polygram.

Their father was a flamenco guitar player for a while, but he gave it up and started selling clothes in the villages. He didn't think that was a job for maintaining a whole family. Juan Habichuela and Pepe Habichuela and the father of Jose Soto, Manuel Soto Sordera, they stayed, all their lives like professional artists. Raimundo's father started as a guitarist, but when he became an adult he didn't play anymore, except at family occasions. But they have relatives who are guitar players.

The others are more like, the families came to Madrid so they could work properly. All the dance companies and the shows were here. Raimundo and Rafael from Pata Negra, their family didn't do it that way. They stayed in the Gypsy quarter in Seville, just living out of selling things around. They weren't that professional.

Raimundo and Rafael started learning how to play flamenco, but they didn't take it as a job. They didn't play that much for singers or take it like a career when you are hired by a certain singer to go with him, like Cameron did with Tomatito. They always had a reputation as being something special, not a straight flamenco guitar player.

The full story is, they started when they were very young. They recorded a record with a family called the Montoya Family. That was their first record. They must have been fifteen or sixteen. They weren't related to the famous Montoya's Carlos, who went to America, or Ramon Montoya. He was the legendary guy who invented modern flamenco guitar. Carlos Montoya was like his nephew. Montoya is a very common Gypsy family name.

This family from Seville, they were known, but they weren't in the professional circuit. They always recorded with the same producer, Ricardo Pacheo. After that record with the Montoya family, they did a trio with a songwriter named Chico Veneno. He was like the Andalusian Bob Dylan. He's very popular now on his own in Spain. They did just one album, very influential, called *Veneno*, which was acoustic, but it wasn't flamenco. It was very punk, acoustic punk. After that, they did the first Pata Negra Polygram record with more electric instruments and all that.

Ricardo Pacheo was the producer for the Montoya family and also the producer for Pata Negra, and also the producer for star flamenco singer Cameron. He was like the third member of Pata Negra. He chose a lot of the repertoire, a lot of the lyrics. Some of the lyrics and the music were his. He was very important in making that music happen.

They never played proper flamenco. They always played bulerias. The thing was, they had a new modern sound for bulerias. There are many styles that Raimundo can't really play for a singer, like taranta or segueria. So they were always more flamenco from the streets, not the more elaborated, theatrical brand of flamenco, but more like what the Gypies of Seville sing and play at their weddings mixed with hippie rock blues.

They were hippies. That was the difference. At the same time they were very inside the Gypsy community. That means that when they were very young, they were married with the Gypsy girls that their family chose for them, very much in the Gypsy wedding tradition, but they didn't hang around with Gypsies. They were all the time with the hippies, and those hippies weren't only Spaniards. There were also a lot of Americans. All of them were in Seville, and all of them got their records from the American bases, from the American servicemen. That was funny, because in those days you couldn't find those records in Spain. Janis Joplin or Jimi Hendrix, those LPs were never released here. So they got them from the American soldiers.

They had them in Seville, because near Seville there are two important bases, one in Marrone for the Air Force, and the other in Rota, which is like the biggest Navy base in the south of Europe. So they'd hang around with hippies and American soldiers.

Pata Negra take their name from a type of Spanish ham. Spanish pigs, at least in the Seville region, are black. The best ham comes from those Spanish black pigs. That ham is called *pata negra*. By extension, they use *pata negra* for anything good, like good tobacco imported from America or good dope. Whatever is the best is called *pata negra*.

JORGE STRUNZ & ARDASHIR FARAH

Jorge Strunz is from Costa Rica. Ardashir Farah is from Iran. However, in perfect global village style, their flamenco chops are so unimpeachable, they've worked with genre heavyweights like Gerardo Nuñez.

JORGE STRUNZ: Although the people in the industry would always say, "You guys play great," they would always ask, "Where am I going to sell this? Singapore?"

That kind of comment was common until the Gipsy Kings came along. Although they're a pop phenomenon and a vocal group primarily; nevertheless, the sound is related to what we are doing. As far as the pop industry and the music industry is concerned, they are the closest thing to us that they had seen. Once they established this great success, which they did, all of a sudden there was this tremendous interest in what we were doing around here locally from the industry. Largely due to the Gipsy King's success.

Today, if you sell over one hundred thousand copies of something in instrumental music, you are something of a phenomenon. In those days, despite the fact that they weren't getting large radio airplay, some of those records sold almost gold. *Friday Night in San Francisco* I think went to nearly a million sales worldwide.

ARDASHIR FARAH: With *Primal Magic*, we decided to make the music a little more accessible than it had been in past years. So one decision we made was to lean on the rumba rhythm on the Latin side, make things heavier.

STRUNZ: Rumba is something that's Latin American in origin, and it's a really good place for the guitar. In any case, rumba is really a whole world of music, the same way someone would say blues or jazz. It's almost as broad as that. It's one of the main pillars of Afro-Cuban or Afro-Caribbean music. It became popular in Spain. The Gypsies adapted it to the flamenco style of playing, but it's not a European style of playing by any means. It's an American invention. By that, I mean it's part of the Americas. It's an Afro-Caribbean invention. It's one of the great danceable rhythms, the perennial danceable rhythm of the planet. It needs no introduction to the rest of the world.

The original rumbas, they were recorded and conceived in Cuba. They were originally played with stringed instruments, not with brass or piano. They were more like tres and guitars with bongos and small ensembles. As the bands got bigger and there was more dancing and more people involved in the salons, they had to replace the strings in those days, with brass and piano. The guitars were simply not loud enough to cut across the additional percussion they were adding. Originally, the rumba and the son were started with fretted instruments and skins. In a sense, that part of what we do goes back to that tradition.

That's sort of like Yomo Toro. Yomo Toro is Puerto Rican, but he's sort of an outgrowth of some of those traditions, of which there were many recordings made in Cuba, notably in the twenties, thirties, and forties.

FARAH: We did use rumba right from our first record. We just emphasize it more on *Primal Magic* and *Americas*.

STRUNZ: That's right. All the records have at least one or two rumbas.

FARAH: We did get into some Middle Eastern composing and arranging and even instruments on the two Milestone albums, *Frontera*, 1984, and *Guitarra* in 1985.

STRUNZ: In that period, Ardashir and I actually hand an ensemble that was all Middle-Eastern. We had zampoña, dumbek, and santur and the two guitarists. The band now is primarily Latin-American.

FARAH: The Iranian pop community, all the pop singers and Iranian producers and musicians still work in Los Angeles. Every now and then, I get a call from one of them to do a session.

There are about three hundred thousand Iranian people in Southern California. Virtually every Iranian pop artist lives in Los Angeles, and a lot of classical. Classical music has a place in the old country. A lot of people are still active producing and composing back there, and a lot of them are hits. But the pop market is centralized in Los Angeles and in New York.

There are concerts that take place before two, three thousand people featuring all Persian artists. In fact, Strunz and Farah, we did participate in one of them at the Shrine auditorium not too long ago.

Pop music, it's evident. When you listen to popular music, no matter what country it comes from, it's evident. Basically, it's the same mainstream pop instrumentation like synthesizers, drum machines, bass guitars, electric guitars.

STRUNZ: Instrumentation is one thing. You don't usually hear acoustic or ethnic instruments in that context, with the exception of Latin pop, which will sometimes use a conga or a bongo. Even a lot of Latin pop stays away from that. It would sound too much like salsa, and salsa is not considered a pop kind of thing.

FARAH: In the case of Iranian pop music, it's become very American sounding, because they are using a lot of the influences that are available to them here. They are very versatile. Sometimes they use the Latin influences, sometimes they use rock influences, but there's not really one thing that characterizes the sound, except for the language.

STRUNZ: The first time we used a singer was a famous Persian singer, who has since died, named Hayadeh. Would you say, Ardashir, that she was one of the best-loved singers from Iran?

FARAH: Maybe the best.

STRUNZ: One of the greatest voices on the planet.

FARAH: Singing in Persian, of course, which is kind of unusual.

STRUNZ: But she loved the idea of singing with guitars, which she had never done in her career. So she was very open minded and adventurous about doing it, in spite of the fact that some of the people around her, I understand, were critical of the idea of her doing anything of the sort. She went freely into it with a great spirit and did a great job of it. It's the last cut of the record, called "Mirage."

On the other hand, we did a record for a small audiophile label in Santa Barbara. It's run by Kavi Alexander, a Sri Lankan, who specializes in Indian classical music recording with the old boom-mic method, two stereo microphones and an all-tube chain. He presented us the opportunity to do this very low-budget recording. We had to record it in two days. It was going to be recorded in this live ambiance in a church, actually St. John's Seminary in Santa Barbara, California, which has a beautiful natural reverb. The idea was to compose the music that would suit the medium, in a sense.

"The less commercial the better," he said. So that gave us an opportunity to really get involved with another side of the guitar, which we'd always had interest in. Actually, we had some material already developed in that side of the guitar.

FARAH: It was also a very live approach.

STRUNZ: Right. No overdubs.

FARAH: Everything is performed the way it sounds. No mix-downs or punch-ins or anything like that.

STRUNZ: It's all mixed on the spot. We did some editing, but mostly it was the performance and the rehearsal, taking the live tape and selecting the best of three or four takes on a tune.

The idea that Kavi Alexander, the producer had, and this again is sort of esoteric, but he wanted one side, he said he saw in both of us the Hispanic and Middle Eastern strains of string instruments. So, he said, "Why don't we dedicate on side to the great Ibn al Arabi, who lived in the Middle East, in Turkey, and traveled to Spain, on the other side, we'll dedicate that to San Juan de la Cruz, Saint John of the Cross, a famous Spanish mystic of the early middle ages."

That was sort of the setup for the record. Using those inspirations, in a sense, we proceeded to compose the music. One song was called "Zyriab."

FARAH: It's the name of an ancient Persian musician who traveled to Spain.

STRUNZ: He traveled to Cordoba. Cordoba was a big center of learning in Spain. He arrived in Cordoba around the year 820. He had been to the califi of Baghdad and played there. Apparently, there was a rivalry between him and another great musician at the court. The court wasn't big enough for both of them, apparently, so Ziryab decided to move to Cordoba in Spain, where there was a flourishing artistic scene. He subsequently became very influential and one of the founding fathers of Andalusian music in Spain. Ziryab was his name, which supposedly means black bird. That was something we had read about in a book called *Memorias De Flamenco*, which means Memories of Flamenco. It was written by a great Spanish flamencologist named Felix Grande.

He talks about Ziryab there, and we thought that would be a perfect name for that tune that Ardashir wrote. We found out that two years later, Paco de Lucia decided to use it in his record, too. Which makes perfect sense, also.

STRUNZ: It's the one he plays with Chick Corea. It's similar. They're both frigean modalities. They both were trying to evoke a similar shadowy historical figure, an artist that made an impact well over a thousand years ago.

Spain was a mixing ground, a fusion place for North African and Middle Eastern musical strains that mixed with Celtic and Iberian Spanish strains for hundreds and hundreds of years and eventually evolved into flamenco, which is currently the art form of southern Spain and of the Gypsies. It's the oldest form of guitar playing on the planet. And also, I might add, the most intricate and most complex, in my opinion at least. We are not flamenco guitar players, although I have played flamenco, myself. I played it as a teenager and with Spanish dancers and singers. What we play now is Flamenco influenced in certain areas. That aspect of it is emphasized more by the fact that there are Middle Eastern strains in our music because of Ardashir, and also because of the fact that I've always been interested in exotic scales, many of which are from the Middle East and from India, and for the guitar.

You put all those mixtures together and it gives you, on some pieces the gestalt is like that of Andalusian music, although, strictly speaking it isn't Andalusian music at all. It's a very different animal from real flamenco. We play with picks. We improvise linearly, freely. Those two things are significant differences between what we play and what is really known as flamenco guitar.

FARAH: We use flamenco guitars, basically. We had a builder by the name of Pedro Maldonado build a whole bunch of guitars for us in 1986, about seven or eight of them.

STRUNZ: He's from Spain, from Malaga.

FARAH: He shipped eight guitars to us. We took three of those giutars and let some of our friends that were interested have the rest. On the last record, we did use some others.

STRUNZ: Esteso, who is another builder from Spain, he's Paco de Lucia's builder. We have an Esteso in the arsenal here. But mostly we use the Spanish flamenco guitars. We find for the sound that we're using, they provide the most of what we need.

We use a lot of Latin American folk influences. A lot of the records have a lot of Latin American folk influences. Luis Conte, who is an old friend of ours, does all the hand percussion, the shakers and light percussion on that stuff. Luis has got quite a collection of the oddest percussion instruments that anybody has. Mexico has such a florid Indian culture, what with the Aztec, the Mayas, all those other high Mexican Indian civilizations. They developed quite a number of musical instruments that they used. Luis has collected quite a number of facsimiles and authentic pre-Colombian instruments. He has a huge collection. His house is like a museum. We select what we need for our particular repertoire at the time, and he brings along a trunk of that stuff. They had a wide variety percussion and wind instruments. Strings were not known to them, of course, until the Spaniards came.

Plus, there's all the other international influences that Ardashir and I are open to. Then there's jazz things, and other forms of music, classical music.

FARAH: We emphasized some Indian influences on the first record, collaborating with Indian violin virtuoso L. Subramaniam. He played on two pieces with us at the time when he was taking lessons from an Indian music teacher in Los Angeles. We used to get together and practice a lot of the Indian motifs and ragas. They've been incorporated into some of the compositions on the first record together with the Middle Eastern influences and the frigean modes. The third record, *Guitarra*, is very heavily influenced by Latin American folk.

STRUNZ: Jazz was a big influence. I spent a long time studying Pat Martino and George Benson. I remember two, two and a half years where I got very involved in their playing. Then, there came a point where I said I didn't want to use any of their licks any more, in spite of the fact that I went through them simply because I was trying to find my own language. But they were nonetheless. Those are the guitar influences. John Coltrane was also very influential. Miles Davis, also. Primarily, the idea of free linear improvisation on top of a groove was one I thought was a very liberating concept for any musician.

That idea of free linear improvisation is one that we still value very much in our music, and it's always been present in all our records.

Although we use a very different language from jazz, it's a language we've had to develop ourselves to reflect our own background and the sort of internationalized guitar playing that we do. We couldn't use a language that wasn't our own. Otherwise, we would have to speak it with an accent, if we're not being legitimate. What we wanted to do was develop a language on the guitar that we spoke in fluently. We had to create our own boundaries and our own phrases and so on. I think in that sense of linear improvisation, jazz was an important influence.

In our particular case, I think we've been able to find a happy marriage of virtuoso guitar playing on top of a world-beat kind of base, which is the rumba, although modified by international influences such as our Latin drummer and of course the Middle Eastern strain in our music and our otherwise progressive inclinations in certain areas of guitar playing. That showed that virtuosity, if it's placed in the right context, can be very, very commercial. People appreciated it.

We were able to develop work and play the repertoire locally, here in Los Angeles, where we always had sort of a grassroots support among a circle of hardcore fans. Nonetheless, the industry, at that time, was very closed to what we were doing. Generally speaking, they found what we were doing too exotic.

What the music business doesn't appreciate is that among the masses, there's going to be an intelligentsia, or the sophisticated listeners who understand what good musicianship is and what the demands are and what creativity and imagination is in a piece of music, even if they are not musicians themselves. In fact, I think they might be better equipped to judge that than the musicians themselves.

EASTERN EUROPE/KLEZMER

"Don't your people have any music?"
—An old Appalachian fiddler to "songcatcher" Henry Sapoznik

On such statements do revolutions rise. Because Henry's people have music, and few people were more uniquely equipped to know that than Henry, now a Jewish music archivist and member of the klezmer group Kapelye, and Hankus Netsky, New England Conservatory of Music professor and founder and leader of the Klezner Conservatory Band. Both came from musical families, albeit they had very different routes to their music.

Since the mid-seventies, largely due to the influence of older players like Dave Tarras and older recordings by artists like Naftule Brandwein, musicologists like Sapoznik and Netsky, along with curious players like Frank London, Andy Statman, and Don Byron, have started exploring klezmer. The centuries-old music of the traditional Eastern European Jewish wedding has developed a contemporary underground following of players and fans around the world. Klezmer can now be heard on hundreds of recordings by dozens of groups from places all over the world. One of the most poignant moments in the interviews that make up this book found Netsky playing klezmer in Poland, where religious and racial fervor had all but eradicated the indigenous culture that made this music there.

Yet Eastern Europe is a hotbed of indigenous music. The Balkans have their own distinctive harmonies that have caught Western ears by surprise, whether in their "natural" state as presented by groups like Trio Bulgarka; in a highly stylized form like the Bulgarian Radio and Television Choir, a.k.a Les Mystere Des Voix Bulgares; or filtered through Western ears as in 3 Mustaphas 3.

HENRY SAPOZNIK | KAPELYE

Henry Sapoznik is deep in klezmer. The son of two Holocaust survivors, he went through yeshivas and, upon graduation suffered from a familiar syndrome among religious school graduates: yeshiva backlash. This, and his interest in music, sent him to North Carolina to study Appalachian music. While he was collecting fiddle tunes, one artist took a look at this Jewish city kid and asked, "Don't your people got music?" This question led him to klezmer. Sapoznik's father, Zindel, was a fairly well known cantor. In the mountains during the summer, Henry would sing in choirs along with his father by day and see the big name Yiddish entertainers like Dave Tarras in the evenings. As the curator of the Max and Frieda Weinstein Archives of Sound Recordings of the YIVO Institute in New York City, he maintains access to thousands of recordings relating to the Eastern European Jewish experience. Many of these recordings chronicle the Jewish dance musics popular in the emigre Eastern European Jewish community from the turn of the century until around the Second World War. Under the auspices of the Archives, Sapoznik produced a collection of Tarras's music, Yiddish American Klezmer Music 1925–1956 *and earned a Grammy nomination as the producer of the album* Partisans of Vilna. *As an almost incidental sideline to this work, Sapoznik plays stringed instruments with the klezmer band Kapelye.*

I first started playing this music after beating a hasty retreat from living in North Carolina and trying to pass for white. When I first started my group, Kapelye, there were two other groups in the country that were playing this music. That's about ten years ago. As of a week ago Thursday, there were seventy-three groups playing this music.

For a subgenre in Jewish music, the highly unexpected rise of Yiddish dance music in post-Holocaust America has caused a huge change in the perspective of nonaffiliated Jews or Jews who have trouble understanding what they like about the music in their heritage. More importantly, non-Jews find it exciting, invigorating, and spiritually tied-in to a rich history.

This music has not only found a new audience. Younger musicians who were playing other forms of music, classical, rock, country or funk, perform it. These musicians made up—and still make up—the overwhelming majority of players for the genre of klezmer music.

For a long time, if you had said "klezmer" to a professional musician, it would have earned you a black eye. It was a negative image. It denoted a musician who could only play the old music of Eastern Europe, or as a hip friend of mine once said, "It denoted round men playing square music."

The YIVO Sound Archives were originally formed by accident. The YIVO collects all manner of material relating to the experience of the Jews of Eastern Europe, which includes memoirs, photographs, books, histories, ethnographic studies, and so forth.

One of the things that was a by-product of this collecting was the 78 [rpm record]s. So when I came in and was doing research in the mid-seventies I came across a collection of 78s in a place that didn't have a 78 player, didn't have an amplifier, didn't have speakers. They had no policy. They had collected them, but they didn't know what to do with them. I would come into work and bring my old Garrard 40B and play these 78s through an old Sony stereo center quarter inch tape recorder and feed it through the amp. I made the first set of transfers from these old 78s and started to archive this material so that someone who was interested in music could find it. Almost coincidentally, they decided they needed someone who could take a very disparate collection and give it some sort of vision. What I've been doing since 1982, when I was hired, is work on creating a discography of the 78s.

People want to play this music and they don't have the material. Very little was published.

The archives has approximately seventy-five hundred to eight thousand 78 rpm records. They're not all here. A lot of them are duplicates. Up here, we have about three thousand or so 78s, in the albums and lots of LPs, lots of field recordings.

We do not have the largest collection. The Hebrew University has a much larger collection. Lincoln Center has a larger collection. The Library of Congress certainly has a larger collection, but none of them can compete with our accessibility. We have over two thousand 78s on cassette, ready for anyone to use.

Our scope is very broad. We have cantorial materials from the turn of the century, Yiddish theater material from both Eastern Europe and the United States, klezmer materials and comic recitations. There are a number of records not to be found in any other places that we are making a commitment to re-record on fresh tape and make accessible.

By default, I suddenly find myself as one of the leading experts on Yiddish radio of the twenties, thirties, and forties, partially due to this collection we rescued from [New York City radio and TV talk show host] Joe Franklin's archives, and partially due to my knowledge of the recording materials of the period. It worked very well in tandem. But the only way for the material to make any sense is to get it out, and to do a history and contextualize the materials as much as possible. To give people a sense of what people were listening to then, and compare it to what's going on now.

The bands and playing of the music became the instrumental foundation of the Yiddish theater. This then was the instrumental foundation of Yiddish music in America.

It gives an amazingly good idea of the growth of the community. These records were made years before any ethnomusicologist took an interest in recording traditional music. These are commercial records, and the only records we have of the emerging ethnic community, of what the Jews were listening to and how they changed and adapted.

What it still says is that the Jewish community was not adverse to co-opting popular music forms that were going on in vaudeville and burlesque and uptown on Broadway. There was a very strong sense of preserving the culture, but not at the expense of interacting with other music and theater forms.

What's really great about working with the discography is to be able to find the recording of the Yiddish version of "Yes, We Have No Bananas" and to find out it was a knockoff of the Irving Kaufman recording done three weeks before. Someone at Columbia or Victor was going through all the ethnics. He knew he had a hit with "Yes, We Have No Bananas." So they'd get someone in, write out the music, get someone to translate it, and end up with "Ya, Ve Hab Nicht Kine Pananas."

That happened with most materials. Invariably, it was American popular music that influenced the Jewish world, as opposed to the Jewish world having a significant influence musically on American popular entertainment. When Irving Berlin wrote "Yiddle on Your Fiddle Play Some Ragtime" in 1909, he was writing a piece that sounded like any of the pieces written by other pop composers who were not necessarily Jewish. Really, what it shows was that for all the assimilation of American popular music forms, the Yiddish theater and Yiddish popular entertainment managed to maintain a very equitable balance of ingroup Jewish identity by external American influences.

I've been able to work with people who need scores for theater or movies, who need actual period material. So, it's basically being a caretaker for the collection, but it's also application of the materials. It's been very important to take it out of the realm of archiving, out of the museum and preservation, and apply the materials to an everyday use, such as klezmer bands or documentary filmmakers or television.

There's a per item charge for every recording they use. It's really our only funding.

We had someone come in a couple of months ago, doing some work on a TV show in Germany on the anniversary of the Anschluss. They needed some material. I pulled out one of the tapes, and because of the vagaries of the humidity and everything, the tape had fused together. I was horrified.

Now, what we're doing is trying to get the tape on ten-inch storage reels. We've put in a grant application to at least pay for a certain amount of staff time to run these tapes once a year to prevent moisture from building up. This is the kind of stuff that hasn't happened because there was no policy for the collection. We've gotten some cylinders recently, and some were mildewed. The wax is better used as candles. It's just too depressing.

We really can use the expertise of people who have experience in record transfer, in sound restoration, because until that happens, that whole, very vital history of Jewish music in America is on hold. We do what we can do, but we're still growing. There's a lot more room for growth.

HANKUS NETSKY | THE KLEZMER CONSERVATORY BAND

Formed by Professor Hankus Netsky as part of the Third Stream Music movement at the New England Conservatory, the KCB helped revive this old music of the European shtetl and fueled a growing movement in the Jewish roots music of Eastern Europe that has spread back to Eastern Europe and beyond.

We recently performed at a WOMAD Festival in Australia. We were sandwiched in between Youssou N'Dour, who is a very popular artist from Senegal, Le Petit Prince de Dakar. Boy was he great. I love that "Try To Be Strong" ("Miyoko") song.

He had a very nice entourage. They were a nice group. It's also neat, these Afropop groups that get up there with two instruments and twelve drummers. It's sort of mind boggling. It's nice to be in these kinds of festivals and accepted on that level.

The problem with world music as a label is we do get bookings with Youssou N'Dour. The audience might be his audience, they come and hear us and don't know what to make of us. Obviously, as a category, it's absurd. It puts everybody in one bag, as if these musics have something to do with each other. It's a very silly category.

On the other hand, what it says to me is curiosity. It says that if you're curious about exciting styles around the world, of various types, you can find it under world music. It says that people are looking for sounds that are different than what they grew up with. It definitely helps to bring the music to the attention of people who never would hear it otherwise, and a lot of them are very turned on by it.

I think it's definitely helped. What I'm glad to see is that we are included in world music, that we are part of the world.

I grew up in Philadelphia. It's a hotbed of all kinds of music, especially this music. A very cultural place. I was interested in funky music and ethnic music. I played some Greek music. I played Middle Eastern music. Whenever somebody came along who had some interesting music, I'd try to learn it.

I was interested in Irish music, but I couldn't find the right Jewish music. There was some reason that it was being hidden, and I didn't know what that was. I personally got interested in the music in the mid-seventies. Actually I had been interested in the music all along, but I had no idea where to find it. I had been interested in the music ever since I started playing music. I knew I had some relatives who played Jewish music, but they really didn't tell me much about it.

It wasn't until about 1974, when I finally met my great-uncle Sam, who had played the trumpet in my grandfather's band when they played Jewish music and jazz and all kinds of things, in the 1920s. I had grown up with a photo of that band in my room, a big photo from about 1920. I always thought, "Gee, if I can get in touch with one of the people in this band, then I could find out what Jewish dance music is." When I got together with him, he actually had a record collection, and when he played me those records, I knew that was the music I had been looking for all along.

I actually had always been a working musician, from the time I was thirteen or fourteen. I had been playing gigs of varying types on piano and saxophone. I had also been in synagogue choirs and was interested in cantorial music and Jewish music. There were even some Chasidim that I played for when I was young. But I just didn't know what to play. When it came to playing Jewish music, there were the Israeli songs that I leaned in Hebrew school and there was "Hava Nagila" and *Fiddler on the Roof*, and that was about it.

I'd ask my uncles. I even went to see my uncle play at a Jewish resort and one or two Bar Mitzvahs. My uncles are all musicians. I would say, could you teach me some of that Jewish stuff, and they'd say, "No, that's dead. Forget it. Nobody wants to learn that."

Whatever music my grandfather had written down, I had in my closet, but it was like finding the Dead Sea Scrolls. You also have to know the language. You find a book of music and it's just shorthand. You don't have any idea what the rhythm's like or what all the various instruments would do, what it would actually sound like if it was played, what the phrasing was like and everything unless you have someone to help you or have an actual recorded example. I really had no idea how to figure it out, what it actually was.

I finally called up my uncle Sam. He had it and he was willing to talk. He was willing to sit down with me and play me the records and tell me who the people were on them and tell me stories about what it was like to play and what a wedding was like in those days. He really introduced me to the music.

He introduced me to it. I taped a lot of the old 78s that he had. A lot of them had belonged to my great grandfather, actually, who was also musical. Then I would bring them into my classes at the conservatory. I taught then, and teach now, in an ethnic music program, which is called Contemporary Improvisation.

I'm actually the chairman of the Contemporary Improvisation Department at the New England Conservatory. It is a program that acknowledges all kinds of ethnic traditions. So I would start bringing them into my classes; I'd bring the records and ask any students if they wanted to play. Then I would organize these informal jam sessions that would get together people from all over Boston who were interested.

I was inspired by Mick Maloney, who's a very wonderful, pioneering Celtic musician in Philadelphia. He really went out of his way to teach the music to everybody by having these great parties on Friday nights. I tried to do that with this. I tried to have these sessions where we'd get together and listen and learn the music.

Finally, we had this opportunity to do this concert at the conservatory. It just worked out that way, that we could get a hall and actually put together a Jewish music concert. Being the only faculty member that was real involved with it, I was put in charge of it. I decided to formalize the band, to put together something a little closer to the instrumentation on the old 78s I was hearing, which was a sound—I didn't realize it—that hadn't been heard anywhere very much for about sixty years. We closed that concert with this band.

I called it Klezmer Conservatory because here we were at a conservatory playing klezmer. It was sort of a joke. Klezmorim didn't go to conservatories traditionally. So I called it that, the Klezmer Conservatory Band when we finally did the concert. The audience went wild when they heard that band. They just really responded.

I thought we were just doing that one concert, but the phone kept ringing. I kept getting requests for this band to come play performances. We only knew three songs at that time, so we had to keep learning music and finding sources.

Now we've been around the world several times and played in places like Australia and New Zealand and Poland and Holland and Germany and Switzerland.

Poland, in particular, was a very emotional experience for the band. It's really, really intense. It's pretty amazing. There were a couple of feelings I had. I got the feeling that it was very close to Polish music. Klezmer is an offshoot of the Eastern European music.

Jewish music in Eastern Europe, it's the Eastern European frame, the music is in the Eastern European style, but the Jews obviously went through a whole other situation in Eastern Europe than the people from the predominant culture. It has all of that, the extra sort of wail and cry of the Jewish experience, plus all kinds of other things that are traceable to its Jewish origins. Because of that, when you go back to a place like Poland to play, they're hearing their own music through this special kind of filter.

The fact was, when we came out playing Jewish music, it was like we were playing Polish music with a certain *je ne sais quoi*—if I were Henry Sapoznik, I'd say *Jew ne sais quoi*—this special edge and this special emotional impact that they hadn't heard for years. It was like, "Oh! Oh yeah! Wow! That sort of sounds like Polish music, but it's a little bit more exciting than Polish music."

It was more exciting than the usual thing that they hear. It had this extra kind of energy, this extra kind of wail to it that made it stand out. The audiences responded to it like crazy. They danced quite wildly and we got three encores. We always get three encores when we play in Poland or Germany. It's amazing. The audience was very special. They seem to be hanging on every note.

We make sure that we always play Holocaust music whenever we play in Europe. The message of those songs seem to really reverberate well. The audience seems to take those songs especially seriously, and to really think about them. There would always be a moment of silence whenever we did anything from that repertoire. It was like it wasn't proper to applaud right away. It was important to think about the message of the song for a while.

There's also a feeling that the songs had come home. I remember doing a song, "Oyfn Veg Shteyt a Boym," "On the Road Stands a Tree," which starts out, "On the road stands a tree, standing bent over, and all the birds have flown away from the tree." There we were, in Krakow, playing this song, and all of a sudden I realized this is the tree. This is the tree that's been abandoned and left all alone. You go to the Jewish neighborhood and you really feel that. It's a ghost town. It's this incredible, just centuries and centuries of Jewish history right there, with Yiddish writing on most of the walls, shuls everywhere you look, but no Jews. It's very, very eerie.

Munich's got other ghosts. Munich is one weird town. There is, of course the foundation for Jewish culture in Munich, but it was so important for the Nazi Reich. It was strange. Playing in Germany, I got a lot more of these feelings playing in Munich than I did playing in Bremen and these places in the North that seemingly were not the fountainhead of Nazism, but were just involved in their own way.

Another thing about Munich. You went to Dachau and, my God, it's like it happened a thousand years ago. There's nothing there. It's like visiting the ruins of a medieval castle. They tore down all the barracks and left one standing, kind of like Colonial Williamsburg or something. My God! I couldn't believe that. You see this huge field, this wide-open space, and you can't picture a concentration camp. This is not klezmer music, but it's some of the things you get to see when you go to Europe on tour.

We've been to Germany three times already, so we've been all over. We've really gotten the feel for the different parts of it and the different attitudes. It gets pretty weird when you get to the small towns in

Austria. Boy, nothing's changed there. You have your Hitler commemorative stamps. I found Austria a lot scarier than Germany.

Internationally, at least two or three hundred bands are playing klezmer. Maybe more than that. When we were in Hamburg, Germany, there were three bands in Hamburg, one of which was led by a Jewish Holocaust survivor.

In Europe, it's totally up from nothing. There have to be fifty, sixty bands in Europe. There have got to be one hundred fifty in the United States. There are bands in South America. Every community seems to have identified its klezmorim, who entertain at functions and things. It's very healthy at the moment. There's a lot of action.

It's funny, the four groups that started it, and there were four groups that started it in the late seventies. They're all still doing it. They're all still pretty much top groups. The only group that's really come in there since then is the Klezmatics. You can draw your own conclusions and make your own opinions.

You know that it's not just a fad within the Jewish community, but actually becoming something that's recognized as our contribution to music. It's really a tradition being taken seriously when you see that the mainstream, popular media are picking up on it. I remember the feeling I had when the singer called me and said, "Hey, turn on Miami Vice. They're playing our record."

Or we played five times on *Prairie Home Companion*, with Garrison Keillor. That was very exciting.

We are not like a museum piece band or anything like that. We do a lot of original music. We do it our own way. We have three or four members of the band who are very strong composers. The whole score to the Rabbit Ears children's project that we did, *The Fool and the Flying Ship*, was all original music. So the music is progressing, and we're hoping that we're a part of that.

FRANK LONDON | THE KLEZMATICS

Several former students of Netsky's formed their own klezmer bands. Erstwhile Klezmer Conservatory Band trumpeter Frank London now plays and does much of the arranging for The Klezmatics. London also played and arranged for the Les Miserables Brass Band and has done session work with artists ranging from South African guitarist Philip Tabane to alternative rockers They Might Be Giants. One day might find him with jobs like an afternoon gig at Carnegie Hall with an Estonian music ensemble and an evening jazz date at Fat Tuesdays, downtown. His "alternative" feel and attitude take this traditional music to another plateau.

Just going out and singing "Oy, Romania, Romania" is just not enough for me. It doesn't say anything to me as a person. Nostalgia doesn't say much to me. How can I be nostalgic over a land I have nothing to do with? So, we try to make our song lyrics, even though they are in Yiddish, pertinent to our lives, so someone can either read the translation or understand the words, and they'll say, "Oh, yeah." Why do you think our first album is called *Shvagn=Toyt* [Silence=Death]?

The music is supposed to be for Jewish weddings. Therefore, what you're playing at a Jewish wedding is klezmer music. We do the real Jewish weddings with the real dancing. Without understanding the purpose of the music is for dancing at a real wedding where they dance the traditional way, then you lack something.

However, by that kind of formal logic, any kind of music you play at a Jewish wedding is klezmer. So, if I'm playing Michael Jackson's "Thriller" at a Jewish wedding so people can dance and enjoy themselves, then that's the klezmer thing. By that kind of logic. Frankly, half of me could agree with that, if you take that definition: that klezmer is music for Jews to dance to at weddings.

But the other definition that I use, which takes that into account, is that klezmer is the Eastern European music that Jews used to dance at their weddings during the late nineteenth and early twentieth centuries, and later came to the new world with those Jews and was played in New York in the early part of this century. Klezmer, then, is the repertoire and the style of playing that was used in those specific Jewish weddings.

Let's expand the phrase "dance music" to mean "functional music." Even the rubato stuff had its place in the wedding. It certainly was not concert music. I've been to concerts where people got up and played the klezmer music all night. I just got a little bored because I wasn't dancing, I wasn't moving. It's like sitting down for a Youssou N'Dour concert at Carnegie Hall. That's not what it's about. If you do that, you'd hope they'd play it straight and not take really long solos, right? Whereas, if they're at SOB's you don't care what they're doing. They can groove on one chord, and you don't care. You'll shake all night.

At the very beginning, for the first two or three years, we were copying other bands, copying old records. Regurgitating. We were a repertoire band. Where we're going? I'm not quite sure. I know how we're getting there. We're getting there step by step. We're getting there by keeping the tradition, but by moving in very slow steps in ways that seem natural. There are a lot of different ways the band plays klezmer on the record. It's based on what the tune leads me, as an arranger, or the whole band to hear.

For example, I play a lot of Chasidic weddings. All of a sudden, I'm hearing a lot of what sounds like Arabic, Middle-Eastern music at Jewish weddings. Now, I didn't know anything about it. I found out now that it's very popular. What they do is dance a hora, like a circle dance. I love that beat, and that's where the "Fun Tashlikh" arrangement came in. This is what contemporary Jewish weddings have. That tune is traditionally played as a bulgar. I changed the rhythm to a contemporary Jewish dance beat. Sometimes, I'm working on things now, just the beginning, kind of in dedication to

Aster Piazzolla. In like an homage to him, I've been working on taking a straight bulgar, a pretty straight rhythm and reharmonizing the melody. Kind of using more progressive harmony.

Part of the way we work is by project. We don't know where we're going, but we do these things that expand us. For example, let me give you four or five projects that we have done or are doing. We do a lot of work with Ray Musiker. He's like a second or third generation klezmer, first generation in this country. His older brother, who passed away at a young age, was Sam Musiker, who was a really famous klezmer. To make it even better, Sammy Musiker, married Dave Tarras's daughter. They recorded an album in the fifties called *Tanz*, which is Sam Musiker and Dave Tarras, father in law and son in law. Ray plays third clarinet and tenor sax on some of the cuts. That's his lineage. In the sixties, he recorded probably the only Jewish jazz album, with this vibe player, Terry Gibbs. What this guy did his whole life was teach music in the public schools and do club dates. I found out about him, met him on a couple of club dates. I found out that over the last ten years, he's been writing his own original klezmer stuff.

The last point klezmer got to, before it metamorphosized into other kinds of Jewish music, like Israeli and Chasidic music, from a functional point of view, is really the style that Tarras, in his later years, was playing. That became the style and the repertoire of how it was played. The more idiosyncratic guys like Naftule Brandwein and others, that isn't what made it through to the fifties and sixties. The next generation of players, like Musiker and Max Epstein and the other guys that were around, kind of play in that late Tarras style.

So Ray has actually begun writing some tunes. We played a show with him at the Knitting Factory, and we brought him to Krakow for this Jewish festival and played a concert with him. So, that's one way the Klezmatics work. Our special project with this guy is intergenerational. It's old music but it's new music, his composition and traditional stuff. Really doing that.

As a band, Ray would be our mentor. I know there was a very wonderful fiddle player that both Alicia and Michael Alpert spent a lot of time with. He lived in Queens and was just wonderful. He was the other old guy in *A Jumping Night in the Garden of Eden*. He was just wonderful and sweet. I would say spiritually and musically, it's Naftule Brantwein is, because the tunes he played and wrote, the way he played and everything, he was the cat who does it for us. More than half the tunes that we wind up writing arrangements of turn out to be his tunes, just because they have this energy in them.

Hankus Netsky has a real strong communication with Ben Galing, who was a radio announcer in Jewish music for years and years. Henry has spent a lot of time with Sid Beckerman, who's still alive. Michael Alpert had spent a lot of time with Ben Bayzler, who passed away.

You know what's beautiful about this? The old person that the young person hangs out with also reflects on the young people. At the end of this concert in Krakow with Ray Musiker, we did all his music. We did this huge freilich jam session. We had been up on stage for about two hours and finally after two hours of this burning traditional music, we get into this klezmaticy space Arabic freilach jam, and Ray took a solo on the clarinet and it was the most modern solo you could imagine. And none of the other old guys that people hang out with could have done that. They don't do that. But Ray just does it because that's the kind of guy he is. That's why he works so well with us.

He and I talked about it on the flight back. His music sounds modern because he's not a stylist, except maybe for klezmer. He doesn't play bebop, he doesn't play swing, he doesn't play Dixieland. What he plays is music as he hears it. Because it's not instantly recognizable in a certain style that evokes a certain era, therefore it becomes timeless and personal. If he were a bebopper, his solo might be great, but you'd say, "Oh, he's an old bebopper." Or if he were a Dixieland player, you'd recognize that.

That cuts both ways. For me, what makes the best players recognizable is either they are like that or they so strongly define an idiom that you can't think of the idiom without thinking about them. Witness Diz and Bird. Diz and Bird are like that, whereas Miles is the other kind.

In terms of mentors, Dave Krakauer, our clarinet player, spent the last years of Martha Schlamme's life playing with her. She was a very famous Yiddish singer.

By our contemporary definition, that's part of what klezmer bands do, is Yiddish songs, even though Yiddish songs aren't really klezmer. Klezmer is an instrumental music. It should be klezmer and Yiddish songs.

One thing that makes klezmer klezmer is the repertoire. The repertoire we play is the repertoire of that period, either through old recordings or through books.

You know what's fun? You can find on recent klezmer albums a lot of the same tunes. You can back to back, you can hear five different versions of the same tune. It gives you an idea of what different bands are doing with it.

The second thing that defines klezmer is style and ornamentation. You can play non-Jewish music using klezmer ornamentation to make your point, like Benny Goodman's "When the Angels Sing," when they break into the bulgar, the freilich, and you hear Ziggy Ellman really play. There's rhythm and ornamentation, and that's very specific.

Things are not as general as they may seem. The thing that I really lay into a lot, more than a lot of other bands or other arrangers, is the rhythmic element. The beats are different, both the way the drums play and the way the ensemble plays and approaches the rhythm.

One of the things that the Klezmatics have fun with is like the very last part of the suite on *Rhythm and Jews*. It is kind of like what I think of as punk klezmer a little bit. What we've done is, we've taken the rhythms of the klezmer, or the old things, and play them on other instruments, a lot louder. More amplification, more guts; it's taking the rhythmic impetus and letting that motivate it. That's something that I find very important. When a lot of young klezmer bands think they're playing klezmer, they're playing two-beat stuff, and klezmer's not two-beat stuff. Or what people call the Romanian hora—there are two or three different names for that—is anything from a waltz to a 5/8.

Can I tell you a great thing someone said about the Klezmatics? It sort of sums it up. We have a lot of fans all around the world. We are definitely their favorite klezmer band. But there are a lot of people who don't like us and people who walk out on our concerts because we're too loud and too weird and stuff.

This woman was talking to us in Switzerland. She said, "A lot of my friends walked out on the concert. I guess people don't like hearing jazz mixed with Jewish music."

And she stopped and I'm thinking to myself, like, what a jerk, and then she goes on, "No. That's not true. They don't mind hearing Dixieland mixed with Jewish music. They just don't want to hear *modern* music mixed with Jewish music."

As soon as she said that, I knew she was absolutely correct.

People say, "Oh, you're not traditional." Yet they love to hear these bands with the Dixieland and swing things. It's got that same kind of corny nostalgia. Certain people have a problem with the fact that we are mixing it with modern music, and yet, the tradition of any living folk music always includes that it grows. Otherwise, it's not a living folk music. What Andy is doing and what we are doing is absolutely the living, traditional klezmer music, because it's in the tradition, but it's alive now.

We had one of the most poignant moments in our career in Budapest. There was this guy about our age, very hip looking. He was hanging out with the band. I didn't know what his function was, but he was very cool, a little sarcastic. After the show, we're being interviewed for Hungarian TV. He's acting as co-interviewer and translating for the interviewer. And he turns to us and he says, "You know, you people did something to me. This is the first time in my life that I ever felt that being Jewish was something you could just feel good about and enjoy." We almost wanted to cry.

I still say we're a band in process, because we don't know where we're heading. We're trying to really be pure to the tradition and yet really be alive now. I don't want to go too far either way yet.

ANDY STATMAN

Modern klezmer seems to attract renaissance musicians, and Andy Statman is their king. Earning early status as a bluegrass mandolin player, Statman moved on to become one of the preeminent klezmer clarinet players and band leaders working today, yet he is also a truly fine and accomplished jazz player. Any wedding Statman plays is worth crashing.

I was a protégé of Dave Tarras. Dave grew up with this music; he lived this music; he came from the community that the music came out of. I think that Dave was the last of that stature who really had those roots and that depth.

I spent lots and lots of time with him. I've had the good fortune to study with a lot of fine musicians. What happens between the teacher and the student, there's this very subtle transfer of attitude and energy. It's something I can't put into words. It's sort of an attitude and approach that you get, not just from spending time with the person but from body language and talking with the person. It's a very intangible thing that I can't put into words, but it's really there. It has to do with spirit, a particular kind of spirit.

My studying with him quickly grew into a friendship. I first saw him around 1975. From then on, basically.

A lot of the study was nonmusical. After one or two clarinet lessons, it quickly changed into a friendship. Everything at that point became completely informal. Sometimes we wouldn't play at all, and sometimes we'd play. He wound up giving me his clarinet, so I'm playing his clarinet, and he wrote music for me, so he wants me to continue for him, so to speak.

The music is reflective of a community. Dave came from a Chasidic family, and a great deal of the music is Chasidic music. The real fountain of the music, the great source of the music has to do much more with very slow, heavy, nonrhythmic pieces, many of which are of a religious nature and deal with exploration of the modes and hit a lot of deep Jewish feeling. It's very deep stuff. The dance music is the more superficial realm of the music.

I spent many years studying. I spent a lot of time with Dave Tarras. I know what the music is. I have a good sense of what the music is, how it should be played and what the roots of it are. From the knowledge I have and the experience I have of playing it, it's obvious to me that there are certain parameters to the style. It's not this hodgepodge, it's an actual style. It expresses certain things in certain ways, just as swing is a style. Bebop is not swing and swing is not bebop. They are two different styles. Klezmer is a style.

Listen to the old recordings. It has to do with ornamentation, types of melody, the feelings that the melody is expressing, and the types of rhythms that the melodies are built on, as well as a certain type of nonrhythmic songs. Songs without rhythm, songs that are played over a rubato.

I play a lot of Chasidic music, and I play klezmer music, but by the definition of what I consider klezmer music to be, I don't do a lot of it. It's a matter of how it's played. It's a stylistic definition. Klezmer is sort of a style that had a number of styles within it that developed over a number of years, but is no longer really a living style. The community that it came out of is basically gone, and the roots that nourished it are really not there. It's really not serving the needs of a community in the way that it once did. It's serving certain functions now.

Klezmer music is a particular style that came out of a culture. It's basically certain types of melodies and ways of presenting those melodies, which has to do with ornamentation, types of accompaniment to the melodies, the melodic structure of the melodies, types of tone used in the instruments and the types of rhythms played along with the melodies. Klezmer, as a form, there's a real definition there, I would say. It was a form that developed in Europe, and as a real, living form is really dormant at this point.

Klezmer music was part of a particular culture that was wiped out in Europe and that pretty much died here. The only element of the traditional culture that remained are really in the Chasidic community and the Orthodox community. It's really not a living form in any to those communities. In Israel more than America, it's more of a living form, and it's the makeup of a general type of music that comprises what is being played there in the religious community. As a functioning part of a living community, which is what it was, this community no longer exists, because that whole culture was wiped out in the Holocaust, and the Jews in America completely assimilated, by and large.

So the culture is gone, that style of life is gone. The roots of where that style of music is coming from are still existent, but in a lot of other ways are gone. What you have is the first generation musicians in America, who still had those roots, and their music, as far as I'm concerned, was the real klez music.

After the immigrant generation, by the time you have the first generation Americans, a lot of the power and depth of the music was lost. They were much more American than they were Jewish. Those things don't transfer.

In other words, you have revivalists in classical music who play Mozart and Bach on original instruments, and it's very beautiful. I'm not talking in terms of the musicians, I'm talking in terms of the general flow of the music.

It's a form that has sort of had its heyday, and was reflective of a particular culture and environment. I'd say even a point of view. All of that is, by and large, gone. From my perspective, the first generation Americans, going back to the twenties and thirties, they just didn't have the same understanding of the depth of the music that the immigrant generation had. The immigrant generation was from that culture and absorbed the influences that made up this music.

What happened was, it sort of degenerated into a type of dance music. Klezmer was much more than dance music to begin with. Dance music was just the tip of the iceberg. The dance music is just one part of it. It was one of the lighter parts. That's not to say that the dance music couldn't be profound. That's just one element of it.

It just got more and more Americanized. The first generation that was playing it were more interested in playing like Benny Goodman or Artie Shaw than playing Jewish music. It lost what it was.

I find most of the reinterpretations of the klezmer music that I've heard don't compare in any way to the original. The original recordings reflect much greater depth and understanding of the styles. The reinterpretation of this, in many cases, aren't as good as the records they are getting it from. A lot of the reason for that is the original recordings were made by people who created and lived the music. We are a few steps removed. It's something different. It has to be something different in a lot of cases, anyway. It could be different and just as good, or it could be people trying to do that and not really hitting the mark, certainly on an emotional level, in terms of understanding the music.

In a lot of ways, you can't. You're not from that culture and you don't have the same influences. Technique is just a by-product to serve the music. You can have great musicians. A lot of the guys who are playing the music now have a million times more technique than the guys who were playing the music eighty years ago. But the guys who played the music then were much better musicians. They could play music with much greater depth and deeper feeling. It was deeper music. I'm saying this very generally, but if you listen to the old recordings and you listen to the new recordings, you'll be struck by the difference.

In terms of real klezmer music being played, what I would consider real klezmer music, I think it's pretty much gone. I think what's happening is people have studied the style to varying degrees and are using it as a springboard for their own musical exploration. I think it's developed into something else.

Photograph: Corinne Turner, Rykodisc

BEN "HIJAZ MUSTAPHA" MANDELSON | 3 MUSTAPHAS 3

The crowned clowns of klezmer, the wildfolk of worldbeat, 3 Mustaphas 3 underpin their sense of humor with solid musical chops and in-depth knowledge of the noise of the world. Playing a twisted version of Eastern European folk musics that fuse elements of Bulgarian harmonies, rhythms with elements of African percussion, klezmer, and Mediterranean and Western pop, this idiosyncratic band is led by music entrepreneur Ben Mandelson, the guiding light of Globestyle records in England. Their sense of play is demonstrated by a small typographical accident that they thought was funny enough to keep, changing Naftule Brandwein's "Where Were You Before Prohibition" to "Where Were You Before Naftule Brandwein."

On Ryko, they made a mistake. The title is "Vi Bist du Geveyzn Far Prohibish'n," which is Yiddish. On the contract, they translated that as "Where Were You the Night Before Naftule Brandwein." They put that extra couple of words in there. They made a mistake in the contract. I don't know why. It's their sense of humor.

Naftule Brandwein is a very interesting person. He was a very famous reed player from Europe. He was Jewish. He came to live in America in the 1920s. He had a very famous klezmer orchestra. He was a clarinet player and alto sax. He even had an illuminated sign that used to flash saying, "Here Today, Naftule Brandwein." Very amusing, and a very good musician. There were several clarinet players like himself and David Tarras. Naftule Brandwein was his contemporary. Very similar. Maybe more ornate than David Tarras.

David must be around ninety-seven or something. I know people know him, and they were telling me all about him. Another Hank, Hank Sapoznik. More Hanks. He was telling me all about him.

I think klezmer is often a collection of different tunes put together. In traditional music, people do compose, but they also take motifs and fragments and take three bits and stick it together. If you work like we've worked, as wedding musicians, or a bar musicians, sometimes you don't compose. You don't play anything original. You take five pieces from somewhere, and we'll play that, it will do because we need a fast one at this point. I think, when these people like David Tarras and Naftule Brandwein were playing record sessions in the 1920s, they were like that: "Oh, we need two more songs, so we'll put this one in."

So they comprise it more than compose it. It's the same with us. Sometimes we'll take a song that we know, we'll make a version of it, and by the time we've played it a few times and said, "Oh, take that bit out, put that bit in." We make it like a custom car.

We were playing that with tabla. We had a very good Indian musician, Bondo Fernandez was playing with us. We like that.

Other instruments on our records include the bagalama, a little, tiny stringed instrument from Greece. It's like a mandolin, but much smaller than a mandolin. If you listen to Greek music, you hear a thing going "chin chin chin chin." That's the bagalama. It's like a stringed high hat. In Turkish music they also have an instrument, baglama saz, that means a large saz.

In Greece the bagalama is a prisoner's instrument. They used to make them from a hollowed-out wooden spoon, put some strings on it. It would go under the coat. People used them to play a music called rambetica, in the 1910s, 1920s, 1930s in Greece. They were sort of underground musicians, burglers, drug addicts, thieves, pimps, and streetniks.

A maultrommel is German. It means mouth drum. It's also called a chang. It's like a Jew's harp.

The kaval is a flute, an endblown flute of the Balkans. It's the most expressive flute of the Balkans.

Gajde is a bagpipe, a sheep body. With one drone from general Balkan use. Sometimes two. It's a widespread word. It's the same in Spanish, you get it. North Africa. It's a reed instrument bagpipe.

Tapan is a big drum, like a parade drum. One side you play with a big stick for the boom, the other side you play with a thin stick for the tac. I think, even the word tapan is onomatopoeia.

A nay is a classical Arab flute. They're a beautiful flute.

Zil is the little tiny cymbal, used by belly dancers. When you buy American-style drum cymbals, you get Ziljian cymbals. That's Turkish Armenian. Zil means cymbal. Ziljian is the person who makes the cymbal. It's a trade name. Mr. Ziljian is like being called Mr. Cymbalmacher.

A hardingfele is a violin from a region of Norway called Hardangerfjord. It has nine strings. There are four on the top and five sympathetic strings. You know sympathetic, like a sitar, or a violin de amour in the European baroque tradition. It rings, it rings. It's a beautiful violin. I bought it for myself. I play that.

Daira the madman. Daira the madman is like a large tambourine. A kind of a tambourine with little zils around the edge. You find them in Central Asia. It's a very nice sound.

A guiro is a type of percussion instrument used in merengue. It's metal, like a torpedo, or something. You scape it. We call it scratchy.

I mostly play stringed instruments. I don't know how many. Twenty? Thirty? It doesn't matter. All instruments are the same with strings. Two or three categories. There's a difference between playing them and making sound on them, I think. Some instruments I can play adequately, some instruments I can imitate somebody playing them. I wouldn't say I can play a lot of things. But I can make some noise on some in a session kind of way. Make noise. It would be pretentious to make a claim to be a thirty-instrument man.

We are very serious, though. We are the hard news, Reuters Agency of world music. That's right, that's what we are. Very serious. We just made a new record, just finished mixing it a week ago. Maybe that's even more serious. Just has some funny moments. We have a kind of difficulty with the humor and serious thing, because with 3 Mustaphas 3, they are the same thing. Aspects of every day life are humorous and serious at the same time. So there are some leg pullings and leg pushings and there's real music.

On *The Heart of Uncle*, there were not so many gags, gags, gags. On *Shopping* there were more gags. I don't think the quality of music was bad on *Shopping*. The quality of music was good on *Shopping*. The gags come and go. I think if they don't appear on the record, maybe we make more in the show. In a live show, it's for the moment.

You find, with a comedy record or a novelty record, you can hear it just once. You can't hear it over and over again. But if there's music then you can listen to them. So maybe we are soft-pedaling on the things that you would say, "Oh, this is a gag." What is a gag can happen once, then you take the surprise from it, and it's not a gag. It's wasted after once. Humor is forever.

People call us many things. It's because we are brothers. They say we are the Ramones. We are the Roosevelts. We are any famous family. We are the Marx Brothers. The Marx Brothers is okay. So long as they don't say we are the Three Stooges, it's okay. Whatever Stooges. I don't mind. Any reference is good. It helps people think about the voice of the group. We are quite amusing.

Another song, "Taxi Driver" is from a man called Bobby Benson from Nigeria. It was a number one hit in Nigeria in nineteen-fiftysomething. We have a kind of bond with taxi drivers, with taxi and there is a theme in it. Throughout all our records there are references to all sorts of different taxi lifeforms.

Yes, the taxi lifeforms. We did "Taxi Driver" for many reasons. Because we like taxi drivers, and because we wanted to work with this man Gaspar Lawal, on the "Taxi Driver" song. He's a Nigerian percussion expert. He's a very, very fine percussionist, and we wanted to have the chance to work with him. We like Nigerian music. We listen to a lot of Nigerian music. Always do.

"Awara" is from the film *Awara*. It's a very famous Indian film. It stars a man, a dead man, called Reg Kapur. Reg Kapur was the father of Sammy Kapur. In Indian films, in Bombay, they have dynasties. They are dynastic. He is a famous actor. Very, very good. Indian films in the fifties brought a lot of new things. He was often playing the little man in a way like Charlie Chaplin, but not a clown Charlie Chaplin. He was bringing sensitivity into the film. The more street man. The pathos. This is the character in *Awara*. "Awara" means rogue. It is a very famous film. A very beautiful film. We learned this song. Everybody learns this song. I think you'll find, outside of the English language, it is one of the most covered songs.

You can investigate deeply, but music is not like, you say in America who is your favorite baseball team. Everybody can say. It's Arkansas Travelers, or whatever you call them. Of the playing Mustaphas, everyone is going to tell you ten different ones every day.

My own, today, I like a kind of music from Indonesia, which is called Jaipongan. I like that very much. I like a man from Nigeria, his name is Barrister. He plays a music called Fuji music. I buy all of his records. It's mainly percussion music. It has Hawaiian guitar, maybe. It's like juju, but it's not juju.

There are many people I like. I like a man D. O. Misiani, from a group called Shirati Jazz, from Kenya. I like him very much. There are many, many people. There's a man called Diómedes Díaz from Colombia, who plays Para Alta music. There are so many.

Indian film singers always make me feel good. I listen to Mukesh or Mohammed Raffi. They are very charming singers. Some Americans. George Jones, he's kind of an American folklore singer, from the south of America. He's very good. I like a man from Washington, Chuck Brown and the Soul Searchers, because I think he's very strong in his tradition. People say go-go is a fad, but he will always play and be strong. He is a good player, and in Washington, they have evolved a music very special for the area. It's strong and I like it. I am very unprejudiced. I will evaluate what you let me hear.

We like Balkan harmonies. People say to us, "Oh, Mustapha, you're very good to sing like that, even though you are not the Trio Bulgarka."

And we say, "That's very observant. We're not. And so that's good. We're better dressed maybe, or at least differently." It's well sung by the Trio.

We sing in more languages than we speak, but we speak quite a few. There are six in the group, and each has a specialty. Myself, I speak two or three. My brother, Kemo, is a specialist in Balkan languages, more than myself. I endeavor to speak courteous language.

VLADIMIR IVANOFF & TANJA ADREEVA | LES MYSTERE DES VOIX BULGARES

Several years ago, the twenty-to-thirty-voice choir, then known as the Bulgarian State Radio and Television Choir, captivated the critical and musical community with their decidedly non-Western diatonic harmonies. Tanja Andreeva is one of the leading vocalists in the group and Vladimir Ivanoff their musical director. They played at the serious concert halls to audiences that included the likes of Jackson Browne and Carly Simon, both of whom would very vocally sing the group's praises. These new fans also wondered where this extraordinary group had been all their lives. In the wake of glasnost and perestroika, people were starting to discover that the iron curtain was hiding more than military secrets: a different sound than most Westerners had experienced lurked just out of earshot. The extraordinary and sometimes unearthly yet earthy harmonies created by these Bulgarian women intrigued and ultimately captivated Western ears as the Iron Curtain began to lift and aspects of Warsaw Pact culture began to come to the West. Yet, in Bulgaria, the choir has existed in one form or another for over three decades. In part, this gets reflected in the group's new name. Le Mystere Des Voix Bulgares was actually the title of the first Western album released by the group. Yet, after the changes in Eastern Europe, the government more or less cut them loose. Ask most people trying to merge creativity with commerce in a free market society, "How's business?" and chances are you'll have to duck a punch. So when those artists whose creative and professional lives were wards of the Eastern European states found themselves cut adrift from the bureaucracies that nurtured them, they faced the tough task of cutting it strictly on their merits.

TANJA ADREEVA: The government was supporting the choir, the government was supporting the culture in Bulgaria, but this support was done for keeping the art and using it for a kind of propaganda for the Communist regime. I think that now the artists feel, for the first time, free to develop, to make their own decisions. Otherwise, in the past, everything was under the control and monopoly of the government.

Now I think a group or choir, well established like our choir is, can earn much more because they depend on what they're earning themselves. The others, under the competition of established choirs, it urges artists to really work hard. All the time, they had to prove what they can do.

We should be considered a choir of the radio, but now with all the political changes and structural changes in Bulgaria, and the possibilities that artists could work freer, the choir is working on its own now.

The choir was established first as a radio choir. It was, for all these years, a radio choir. In the meantime, for organizational Bulgarian, the radio and TV were under one and the same administration, so it was considered for this time the choir of the radio and the TV. Then, when they were split, it was only a radio choir. This happened several times in the thirty or more years.

VLADIMIR IVANOFF: In the old Bulgarian system, the influence of Turkish music, for instance, was very much suppressed. You would have this explanation that Bulgarian music is this very pure music, which is based on the worker's culture and all these things. In fact, Bulgarian music is a very multicultural music. The *Mystere* album tries to show all these influences, from the Ottoman Empire, from the Turks, from Central Asia, urban sounds, rural sounds. I wouldn't think that a record like this would be possible before the mid-eighties. It would have been impossible also for economic reasons, but mostly for political reasons. This is absolutely clear. I mean, a project like this, but also the *Mystere* album, has been possible like this only since then. Not long.

If you listen to sixties recordings with so-called traditional Bulgarian music, you have this kind of socialist-realistic aesthetics.

Let's say, the old style, to do Bulgarian folk music or traditional music, would be with a big orchestra consisting of remade folk instruments. You'd have six bagpipes, fifty singers, like a rebuilt symphonic orchestra. Everything oversized, with a big score, a twenty-voice score done by some composer trying to imitate some type of Wagnerian style.

ADREEVA: In the past, it was really difficult to bring a choir outside of Bulgaria. The first tour we did was in 1987, before some of the soloists who are performing were there, but not the choir performing. It was because of all these democratic changes, the perestroika in Russia. In Bulgaria they didn't take place at the same time. Still, we had the influence and the possibility to travel more freely and perform in the last few years, starting around when the perestroika started happening in Russia, and all the influence towards the new democracy.

IVANOFF: The basic idea is the choir has been doing a very restricted repertoire for a very long time. What we want to do now is experiment with different repertoires, because the choir is capable of doing lots of different things. It's also fun for the singers. They like to do different things. It stretches from, on one hand, doing a Terry Riley composition with the Kronos Quartet. The *Mystere* album is a history of Bulgarian music and anthology of Bulgarian music that starts with pieces that are probably the oldest pieces of Bulgarian music you could find and goes to very avant garde contemporary pieces by living Bulgarian composers.

ADREEVA: We say this is traditional music, but traditional Bulgarian music is monophonic. It is typical for our way of singing, there are only one or two regions where duophonic music is used. This, we have in our program. We say it's an arrangement, but actually it is a composition by a contemporary Bulgarian composer. These should be considered compositions by Bulgarian composers. They use a traditional melody, which is simple, including several songs in it, and they put all this harmony using the special characteristics of the Bulgarian way of singing and using freely dissonance and consonance. These compositions, they keep the main, traditional melodies but add additional harmonies. Their strength and their power are the main melody.

This is a common feature of the Bulgarian music. Even though, geographically and ethnographically, Bulgaria is divided into several regions, this affects the style of the singing in the different regions. There are still common features between all of that. The way the voices are used, the sounds are produced, the timbres and all these features are common.

This is the so-called open throat singing. The sound is produced in the larynx and resonates in the chest, so there is a limited scale, and limited dipthong, but this gives the special quality of the timbre, of the voices.

IVANOFF: In Bulgarian music, you have basically two different styles, apart from the regional different styles. You have urban music and peasant music. Urban music is music based on traditions that go back to the eighteenth and nineteenth centuries. These are usually solo songs accompanied by an instrument, nowadays it would be mostly the accordion, which has taken over the place of really traditional Bulgarian instruments. Then you have the really traditional peasant culture, which consists basically of pure instrumental music. This is usually dance music, performed with bagpipes, different types of flutes. Then you have a cappella music that is performed either by a solo singer or a very small group of either male or female singers. So you have either two to three girls or men who sing either dancing songs or very slow mourning songs. The repertoire of the Mystere is based more on this peasant music.

The urban music is a completely different style. It's quite modern. So, it's based on this a cappella singing that you'll find in small Bulgarian villages. As Tanja already explained, that's mainly one voice singing without harmonies. Then you have two regions in Bulgaria where you have a very special system, which you could describe as diaphonic. One singer sings something like a burden, one or two notes, and the other singer is improvising above this melody.

These harmonies are elaborated in a very modern sense. The composers or arrangers who work for the choir, they are nowadays people and musicians with conservatory training. They take these melodies add this diaphonic system [in] which you can also hear many avant garde influences. There are impressionistic influences, for example. Debussy and Ravel are very popular in Bulgaria. Many pieces are arranged in this style, also. I suppose if you were to hear a piece performed by three peasant girls from a rural Bulgarian village, and then the same piece performed in an arrangement that was made for Le Mystere Des Voix Bulgares, it would be hard for a nonspecialist to recognize that it's the same piece.

ADREEVA: The traditional music, in its pure character, is monophonic. This was the tradition, one singer, one voice. It could be two singers, one voice. Usually, they are accompanied by traditional instruments. What the choir is doing is a different interpretation of the tradition. You can consider this as classical pieces performed by traditional singers or folk singers.

This way of singing, the choral singing, started in the early fifties. Up to that moment, there was no tradition for singing traditional music in chorus. This was not the way they did it. This is a new stage from the fifties for this kind of thing.

IVANOFF: I think I have to explain something very basic, because the Mystere has been mistaken since their beginning for being a traditional ethnic group. There's a very big difference between this choir and traditional recordings. You could go to a good record shop and get ethnological field recordings of Bulgarian music, which is real folk music. The Mystere Des Voix Bulgares is a choir based on folk voices, which later were trained in a normal conservatory. These singers are not only capable of doing Bulgarian folk music, they can do virtually any kind of choir music. So they can combine traditional folk singing with the classical voice training.

That's a very, very important thing. The choir learns its music from scores, so they're reading music. This is composed music. These are compositions by composers. Orally transmitted music is a completely different thing. I mean, the singers from the choir are also able to do, I guess, what you'd call authentic music of the oral tradition, but what they do in the choir is sing compositions.

It has to be like this. The important thing about the choir is that it tries to show different regional traditions from Bulgaria. Really, only traditional singers would sing in the style of Rhodopes or the Shopska Mountains. The same singer couldn't sing more than one style. In the choir, you have singers from all Bulgarian regions, but to put them together, you need some organizational means, which are these compositions. You can give an overview of every possible Bulgarian style, but at the same time, it's no longer pure folk music in the very traditional sense.

That's a big point. A traditional musician is no longer a traditional musician the moment you put the microphone in front of him. You change the whole circumstance of the performance. What I consider to be a living tradition, what are traditional instruments today are . . . I'm traveling a lot in the Islamic countries, and they are now using synthesizers that are built by the Japanese companies which use Arabic modes. They are built specially for the Arabic countries. These instruments are, over the last two or three years, replacing all of the traditional instruments. At the moment, you would find more bands in Arabia using synthesizers and Hammond organs—which were reconstructed to play these modes—than you would find the oud or canun.

Another important feature is the rhythm, which is very special in Bulgaria. This is something that makes Bulgarian music different from any other kind of music. You have what musicologists would call "unequal rhythms" in English. You find these types of rhythms throughout the Islamic community or in the Near East, or also in the Far East.

This is a typical Gypsy tradition again. You would find this type of music also in what is not any longer Yugoslavia or in Romania, played by Gypsies. So this constant change of different meters, like changing from 15/8 to 15/16 or to 11, this is a typical Gypsy style of playing.

ADREEVA: Nobody can say for certain how old this music is. I think it has the influence of Asia. The Bulgur tribes came from Central Asia. They ruled over the Slavic people that were in this land, but the Slavic people assimilated the Bulgurs, so we have the influence of Asia, the influence of Slavic music, the influence of Thracia, Byzantia, Rome, the influence of the Orient because of the geographic situation of Bulgaria. And we should add to this five hundred years of domination of the Turks over the Bulgarians. So it incorporates different influences.

IVANOFF: We tour with four instrumentalists. You have one gadulka player, a gadulka is a bowed stringed instrument. You would compare maybe to a violin, somewhere between a violin and a cello. You have a gaïda, which is a Bulgarian bagpipe. You have a caval, which is an end-blown flute. It's a very difficult instrument. And there's the tanbura, which is a kind of plucked instrument with a long neck, a type of lute. These are basically the most important folk instruments.

Ethnomusicologists in Bulgaria may not personally be happy with that idea, but I think that it's very much influenced by the Ottoman Empire. The tanbura is a big family. The long-necked lutes are a big family of similar instruments, which you'll find mostly from Central Asia to the Near East. But it's also a very Bulgarian instrument, a very important folk instrument in Bulgaria.

You would find the same kind of ensemble playing in Bulgaria, in Yugoslavia, across the whole Balkans, more or less. But you would also find it in Iraq. You would find it in Turkey, throughout the whole Islamic world. I've even seen similar things in southern India. That's a small problem about the history of these instruments. These instrumentalists were traveling a lot, from village to village, from town to town. It's hard to reconstruct the real origins of any type of instrument, the long-neck lute, for instance. Basically, musicologists think that it originated in Mesopotamia, but how it came that you find it today in something like thirty-five countries across the world, that's a very difficult process to reconstruct.

It uses a nontemperment temperment, untempered scales. So you have things which we call quartertones, which is not the right expression because it's not really a quarter tone, but it's like you have intervals like neutral thirds or sevenths which are not exactly tempered. You have not only major and minor scales, you have lots of different things, which you could compare to the Indian raga system. Lots of it must have Byzantine influence, so you have lots of influence by Byzantine church modes. I think the present system is basically a mixture Byzantine influences, earlier Central Asian influences and influences from the Ottoman Empire, so the whole temperament and mode system is quite complicated because it's very mixed. It also changes from region to region, so you find modes in certain regions of Bulgaria that are unknown in other regions.

ALEXANDER (SASHA) LIPNITSKY | ZVUKI MU

Zvuki Mu is one of the few rock bands qua rock band featured in this book, for similar reasons to Tribe After Tribe. Originally banned in the Soviet Union, this Russian rock band shows both how far rock traveled and how it changed as it went through various cultural filters. Taking hold of the anti-establishment aura of the music, although based in Moscow, they initially had to sentence themselves to Siberia if they wanted to play and remain relatively under the radar of the Soviet government. While the only really consistent element in the band has been leader Pyotr Mamanov, when the band came to America in the nineties, longtime bass player Alexander "Sasha" Lipnitsky had the best English, and became the group's de facto spokesperson.

Maybe the most interesting thing about us is that we started to play very late. Pyotr and me, Pyotr Mamanov is our leader, started to play musical instruments after thirty. I think this is a rare case. The members of our band are from very different generations. The oldest, Pyotr, is thirty-eight years. The youngest is twenty-four. We have three generations of rock music. It helps us.

We must talk about the meaning of the word "underground." We are the group with the underground story. But now, the name of "underground band," we cannot use it to describe our statement in Russia. Today, we have no underground rock music in Russia, because now all the bands have the same chances to have recording, to have concerts in the state concert halls.

Certainly it's easier to have recording time in the state studios for the bands who are closer to the officials, and who play more pop music without any political ambitions. But now it is not a big question, and

I'm sure that a band like Zvuki Mu can have a record on our state recording company, Melodya, if we think about it seriously. It's a big line. We have only one recording company, and many rock groups who are waiting for their times to record in the studio. We don't want to worry them, because we have a chance to make a record in the West.

Our American record didn't come out in Russia because they didn't want it, and we didn't want it. The quality of the plastic and the covers of the albums are very weak. Then you have to spend a lot of time in conference with the officials. Then we couldn't have enough money for our record. Even if it were a million kopeks. Because there are no laws to protect the musicians. Now the officials are working on a new law to protect the rights of the musician.

We traveled a lot in the Soviet Union. We've played in very deep and strange places. For me, they were the most interesting concerts of our career. We played in the north of Siberia, and places where people are trying to mine diamonds, like in South Africa. When we went to play there, we were the first rock group to play those places. They had no information before us. We were supposed to play one concert in this place, but they were so curious about us that they asked us to play seven concerts for the same audience. They were very excited. They asked us to be citizens of this cold place forever, but we left them.

We played in Central Asia, in Vladivostok, and the Baltic Republics. Now we're playing in New York. We were walking around Broadway, and I said to my friend, the keyboard player Pasha Hortin, that now we had reached the top of our travels. I think this is the most interesting city for musicians. We heard much music over previous nights at some clubs, and the musicians are excellent.

My first music was Presley, Chuck Berry, Ray Charles. Then the Beatles, the Doors, and the Rolling Stones. The Rolling Stones, I think, were the favorite band of our group, of our leader, Pyotr Mamanov and I. Then it was Hendrix. In the seventies, it was such interesting groups as Can, from Germany, and King Crimson, art rock, Frank Zappa. At the end of the seventies, we were very fond of Captain Beefheart's Magic Band, and some groups of the new wave, Joy Division. I think that's very ordinary. We were big fans of rock music. Maybe we were not so busy as Western people, who worked hard, and we heard everything.

Some of our musicians are big professionals in jazz. Our keyboard player and drummer know jazz music and can play jazz music professionally. Their favorite musicians are Miles Davis and Herbie Hancock. We have very different ideas about music. I think it helps us in our work.

Our drummer learned the art of drums at the special jazz school in Moscow, the Experimental Jazz Studio. Our keyboard player usually plays with some jazz rock musicians from his company. I took part in the very popular Pop Mechanics, which is well known in Russia and in Europe. They work with half jazz musicians and half rock musicians. It is near to the idea of Sun Ra, but more pop.

We have very different music in Russia because we are the biggest country in the world. Our Leningrad rock school is very different from Moscow. Now we have a strong influence from our folk Russian roots. I think Siberia and rock from the Ural Mountains is very interesting, and I hope it will be known in the West. We have lots of rock groups that are unknown in the West from Kiev, the first Russian town.

Boris Grebenshikov is an old friend of mine, and I can't be honest talking about him, because he is one of my best friends. He helped us very much when we made Zvuki Mu, because his band, Aquarium, had a seventeen-year-old story. It's an old band. It's a pity that now the band is ruined because Boris became an American rock star. But his friends from Aquarium recorded a very interesting record two months ago. The band has another name. They were the real heroes in Russia, Boris and Aquarium. They were very popular. I think after the death of Vladimir Vysotsky, the first pop star, Boris was the most popular man in the country.

Vysotsky died of a problem with alcohol. You must know his way was very hard. He was ignored by officials, totally. He had no records. It was a sad story. His wife, the French actress Marina Ladia, wrote a book about his life. I knew him. He was a great guy.

We are very proud that we are playing in New York with such a great band as the Residents. I am a religious man, and it is interesting that the first band that we are playing with in America is our favorite band. The Residents are unknown in the U.S.A., and they're unknown in Russia. But our group knows their art very well. We have all their records. Yesterday, we played the same concerts in performance. We are very happy.

MARCEL | DUTCH ROCK MUSIC FOUNDATION

I've included this short interview to highlight some of the basic differences even Western countries have with the way they deal with youth culture. France, for example, has a government minister of rock and roll. Where in the U.S. pop culture is a business (just like pretty much everything else in the U.S.), in Europe, pop culture is culture. In the U.S., the government holds witch-hunts about porn rock; in Holland, they subsidize the clubs. I met Marcel at the New Music Seminar, where the DRMF had taken a booth for the sixth straight years.

The Dutch Rock Music Foundation is government funded, a government-funded, noncommercial private company. Our aim is to take action for Dutch rock music, to try and promote it. This is our foreign policy, so every year we come to the seminar to promote Dutch rock music.

When we first came here six years ago, it was really almost impossible for a Dutch band to play in the States. It was really something far away. Now we have this action for a couple of years, and now we see that Dutch bands are playing the States. Of course, it's not really our thing, but our action helped a little bit. It was one stone in the whole thing. That's the main reason that we did it. And it worked.

There are several bands playing the States, like Candy Dulfer. She worked with an American producer and American artists on her album. You have the Nits. They played opening night two years ago. You have the Urban Dance Force, also in showcase. Now, the house music is really getting big, and Holland is one of the biggest producers of house music at the moment.

So our action helped a little bit. We also give the stand to other businesspeople from Holland and let them use the stand. We hire the stand, we pay for it, and we let other companies use it, companies that don't have the money to hire a whole stand. That's why Holland is one of the nicest countries in the world.

You have to pay a price for that, but you have other things like our crime rate, our level of development, our level between rich and poor are more equal compared to the States. Here, you have a lot of shit going on. The main reason for all the shit in the States is that you never had a socialist government. In Holland, we have it. That's why there's really relaxed living there. It's very free. Our drug policy is very lenient, but the level of heroin deaths is very low. Here you have strict laws and your amount of deaths by drugs is very big.

I've been told that one of the most important things we do is give subsidies to Dutch clubs. We have forty clubs. Every time they program a Dutch band, we give them a subsidy. That's why we have a very stable atmosphere, where Dutch bands are benefiting. All the Dutch bands can play there. They can play more gigs for better money. We have one million gilders ($500,000) going into the clubs.

ASIA

JAPAN, THE INDIAN SUBCONTINENT, AND "THE ORIENT"

There are salsa bands in Japan, the most notable being Orchestra La Luz. There are also klezmer bands. There are more Beatles cover bands along one block of Tokyo than in most U.S. states. There are *idoru* (idol singers) and many Western acts that could only get arrested at home have rabid followings in Japan. They export cars, toys, and semiconductors, yet much of their music doesn't translate in any sense of the word. Very little Japanese music, be it pop or traditional, finds its way into the rubric of the noise of the world.

Star guitarist Osamu Kitajima thinks he knows the answer, as he spent a great deal of his youth playing shredding, high speed rock instrumental music. He even earned a Western release doing it on the old Antilles label, which also featured such oddities as the Portsmouth Sinfonia (a small orchestra of musicians, including adventurous rockers like Robert Fripp, playing unfamiliar instruments) and such varied music as Steve Winwood's excellent and long-out-of-print *Aiye Keta* album, the Tibetan bells, and several collections of African music. Simply, in the post–WWII environment, Osamu-san opined, "A lot of Japanese things are just no good."

The Antilles collection of Tibetan bell music shows just how broad and wide Asia is, and how diverse. David Lewiston's travels took him through most of what is thought of as "the Orient" from the balmy climes of Indonesia to the icy environs of Tibet, planets apart both meterologically and musically. The Indonesian gamelon became a cause célèbre in the "new music" (i.e., the non-jazz, non-classical music taught at colleges) community among practitioners like Barbara Benary, who practiced an interesting brand of cultural imperialism.

Still, this is the most populous continent on the planet, and it produces an enormous amount of both classical and popular culture.

The Indian subcontinent is rich with both, having the most thriving film community in the world and a popular music cojoined with it. However, the Indian music known better around the world is the centuries-old classical tradition as espoused by Zakir Hussain and Ravi Shankar, to name two of the genres most popular artists in the West. The rigorous training alone makes these musics daunting.

OSAMU KITAJIMA

Osamu Kitajima is the embodiment of East meets West. A guitar hero of huge proportions during his teen years in Japan, he decided to move to California to achieve some personal freedom in his work, unfettered by the demands of being a pop star. He has since developed a sound where kotos and keyboards, synthesizers, shakuhachis and sassaras coexist, a Japanese jazz fusion that could never exist in Japan. This is amply reflected on his humorously titled album, California Roll. *Like the California roll, Osamu's music makes use of conventions from his original Pacific coast and his current one. The pentatonic scales that crop up in his music are not contrivances, however, any more than the use of samples. By just letting them flow through him, Osamu creates compositions that reflect his heritage and his environment naturally. Still, he never seems content to go with what he knows.*

Sushi was originally from Japan, and I'm from Japan, but the sushi California roll was born in California. My music is also born in California.

Because we were born after the war, I grew up in the country, westernized. Even when we were kids we didn't wear kimonos at all. Occasionally, maybe, for New Year's, or something. We grew up sort of like you guys, in a way. Different, but in a Western style. These clothes and cars and tape recorders and TV. A lot of influence from America and Europe.

When I was a teenager, I had a number one hit single with my band, the Launchers. But Japanese pop is different. It's really just for Japan.

A lot of Japanese things are just no good. I think so. That's another reason I wanted to move over here. I could easily make a living in Japan. Maybe more than over here. Here I had to start from scratch again. In Japan, I could earn money, as much as I want to, because I know everybody there. People ask me to write music more and more. But I hated it, because I had to write something I didn't want to write.

Technically, it's easy to write that kind of music, because I know what they like if you want to make a living. If you're really into jazz, you could do it, playing at nightclubs, getting small money at that time. But, because I have the album out on CBS, I can play. In Japan, if you don't have a record deal, you have to keep doing something, playing somewhere. There was no challenge. We have an expression, "It's like being in a lukewarm bath."

The Japanese names you see on my albums, are in my band. They are from Japan, like me. One of them still lives in Japan.

Like I said, I don't try to use American or Japanese. I don't care if they use American or Japanese or Indian.

When I was in Japan, I studied both Western music and Japanese traditional music. I wanted to get something more from the real country. I had never been to the States before I moved here.

I have not tried to do any special thing. When I write music, I don't try to write something special. I always try to just let it come out. For instance, when I write something, starting with keyboards, and I hear some nice chord changes, then I hear melody lines. If it's on a Japanese instrument, then I use a Japanese instrument. If I hear it on violin, I use violin. There is no reason not to.

If I hear it, I use it. Sometimes I start on koto, sometimes just a click track, sometimes a just drum machine, sometimes I start with a keyboard. It really depends.

If you are really into it, writing music happens in seconds. If it takes four minutes, that's a four minute song, from the beginning to the end.

I did some film work for MGM. It was not a big movie. You know Pat Morita? It was one of his movies, called *Captive Heart*. I did the soundtrack for the whole movie. I've done documentaries. I was one of the musicians on *Cannonball Run*, *Sharkey's Machine*.

I was just a studio musician, but I did a lot for *Shogun*. I was almost like an adviser to *Shogun*. Maurice Jarre did the music. He was a great composer, but he was out of his idiom. Whatever he wrote sounded Chinese to me. So every time I'd go to the studio, "Uh, uh. This is not Japanese."

We'd change the notes and stuff. All these gongs. Chinese! I know it's kind of tough for you guys to know the difference between Chinese and Japanese. It's totally different. We use gongs but . . .

It's like food. The difference between Chinese food and Japanese food, there is that much difference.

In terms of food, sushi is pretty new, actually. It's only two hundred, three hundred years old. We have a few thousand years of tradition.

It takes a while for America to understand what the real thing is from Japan. We Japanese have been learning English for over a hundred years. I think you guys should learn how to speak Japanese. Language has a spirit. That's the way you express things.

Japanese is totally opposite from English. It's real hard for us to learn English. You need to know fifteen hundred characters to be able to read a newspaper. My last name is Kitajima. You have to pick the character. You put in the Ki, and you get maybe ten characters.

But I feel the Japanese have been committing cultural suicide for the last hundred and fifty years. Some people have started realizing that. But it's like the energy is plus and minus, like a magnet. Oriental culture has been developed by the spiritual world, or what we call yin, like in yin and yang? Western culture has been developed based on yang energy, which is technology and materialized stuff.

That's the order of the universe. If you look up in space, anywhere in this world, the plus energy and the minus energy get closer, the plus energy pulls the minus first, then the minus pulls in the plus energy. Still, the energy has to be balanced.

DAVID LEWISTON

Chances are good that, if you have dabbled in music from the East or from South America, you have tripped over the work of David Lewiston. Over the last twenty-odd years, he has chronicled the native music of such exotic locales as (break out your atlases) Bali, Colombia, the Himalayas, India, China, Japan, and Iran, making high quality recordings in the field. One of the earliest ethnomusicologists to take a tape recorder and capture the noise of the world, David Lewiston made a career recording the street music of Bali for Nonesuch, refining the methods of field recording along the way. Lewiston has embarked on an odyssey that has resulted in forty-two released recordings from all over the world, with particular emphasis on the traditional musics of developing countries. It all began with a three-week recording tour of Bali and Java in 1966, the year after "The Year of Living Dangerously."

In 1966, when I went to Indonesia, I couldn't find a battery operated stereo machine. The Nagra wasn't invented yet, only the mono. And the Stellavox had not yet come out. That was four or five years down the road. So I had a little 1/2 track 7 1/2 ips mono. But when I was in Singapore, on my way to Indonesia, in one of the electronics stores I noticed something called a Concertone, which looked like a piece of junk, but at least it was battery operated and stereo. So I bought it for something like a couple of hundred bucks and brought it down to Bali. And luckily, it worked just long enough before it expired for me to record music first in Bali, then in Java.

It was an astonishingly brief trip. I spent less than three weeks total in Indonesia, and recorded eight of the major styles. Bali, at that time, was much more peaceful than it is today. There were not many

Westerners on the island, it was the year after the aborted communist coup, and the island was very peaceful after the bloodbath in 1965, and there were not many Westerners there, maybe twenty.

I was very fortunate in having good introductions thanks to an ethnomusicologist friend, Ruby Ornstein, who still lives in New York. Ruby had just returned from two years of field work in Bali, and she gave me introductions.

So with Ruby's introductions, I went in. In the course of two years, she had come to know the best musicians on the island, and the people I met were uniformly helpful. So in something like two weeks in Bali, I came out with lots of material. Hours of recording. On a typical day, one of my friends would join me and we'd rattle around the island in a car. We'd go from one village to another, meet the leaders of three groups and arrange recording sessions for later that day. So we'd do that in the morning, go back at noon, have one session from twelve to two, and then we'd have another in the middle of the afternoon, and once in the evening. That was really incredible, to be able to record so much so easily.

I read a lot of books about Bali, because I had not been traveling. It was my first big trip. I did a lot of reading, so I'd have a certain idea about what to expect, but really, I don't think there's any preparation for the real thing. Just going in and exposing oneself to great art.

Sukarno maintained an uneasy balance between the three centers of power, the army, the Muslims, and the communists. Then a point came when the communists thought they could take over. This was in 1965. But the army's intelligence was very good: they heard about it very fast and launched a preemptive strike. And that was the end of communism in Indonesia. Many people were killed in Java and Bali, certainly. It took a bit of time for things to return to normal. In 1966, things were still relatively quiet. So when I went in with my recording gear, there wasn't much going on in the way of tourists coming in. Bali's been a tourist destination since the 1930s, when people like Charlie Chaplin would go there, spend a few weeks, and have a marvelous time. But there was a lull in that period in the sixties.

I didn't go back for years, because everyone said, "Euuwwgh, tourists! The place is crawling with tourists." That was by no means inspiring. But in '86, after I had been grounded for two years after a bad smash-up on my two-wheeler, I was well enough to start moving around again, so I went back to the Himalayas to see what was doing there, and decided, "Why don't I go back to Bali anyway?" So I did, and was entranced all over again, and saw that the music was not only alive and well, but that it was flourishin, and was worthy of serious efforts.

I think that the energy of the music has changed. It is much more dynamic now. It had been much more tranquil in '66. That may come through if one listens to some of the older recordings and some of the newer recordings.

I found one thing especially interesting in Bali this time around. Women's lib has come to Balinese music. There are now women's gamelans. There's a big thing every year, a competition for the men's gamalons. It's contested quite fiercely. It's a big prestige thing. Women now also have their gamalon competition. And it's equally as ferociously contested. Normally in the village they'll use the same instruments as the men's gamalon. They've become astonishingly proficient, especially in the dexterity at the gansa and the other metal instruments. As proficient as the men in that respect. Also, there are now some women dalangs. The dalang is the narrator or the traditional shadow play, where the puppets are flat two dimentional painted parchment, manipulated in front of a screen, illuminated by a flaring, smokey lamp. Traditionally it has been the men, but now there are a couple of women doing that.

Now, I find it's not nearly so easy for a variety of reasons. People are much busier. They have a lot to do. They have their businesses to attend to, that sort of thing. So it was harder to arrange sessions. We'd have to plan a week or two ahead of when we wanted to record it.

The islands have become very noisy. There are motorbikes everywhere, even on the narrowest lanes. So it's really difficult to find a peaceful place to record. Also, there are packs of wild dogs throughout south Bali, so it's really hard to find a place where you don't have yapping dogs. Which the Balinese don't kill. They're not wild, they're more stray dogs. They're not owned by anybody. But there are so many of them that they get together in packs and render the night air hideous with their howls. It is difficult to find a peaceful place for recording.

When I'm recording festivals, like the Kulu festival in the western Himalayas, I had a couple of mics, separated by maybe twenty feet up on the stage. I was given a privileged position in the pit, right under the stage, to set up my Stellavox, and my other recorder. I used different recorders for the backup. At one point I came to a Sony battery machine, what is that, the 510, 520? A five-inch portable, good quality.

The Kulu festival is really quite wonderful. Kulu is, most of the year, just a sleepy little town in the western Himalayas. It comes alive one week out of the year, and that's for the Dussehra festival, which is the big Autumn mountain bash. Essentially, fifty thousand hill people come down to Kulu for one last week before they are snowed in for the rest of the winter. It's buying and selling, it's trading. You can buy everything from pots and pans to a cow, win a raffle for a car, have your photo taken, lots of grazing. I counted one hundred fifty separate stalls selling food. There are pubs to go and have some rice wine—well, rice beer, actually.

Now there is a big amphitheater, which has been built, because this festival is a big moneymaker for people in the Kulu region, people coming in here and dropping their money for the annual festival. In the amphitheater, you have entertainment that would appeal to the hill people, and that means sophisticated entertainment from Delhi. It means young men playing the most horrible Indian film music on electronic instruments. It's really quite vile and excruciating. It means the worst magician I've ever seen in my life. His name is Ching Fung Lee, and he would stretch out one interminable trick after another. Ballet companies from Delhi performing the Ramayama and other classical stories, bring a little culture and raise the tone of the festivities. And what appealed to me, the best village folk dancing companies from all over Himachal Pradesh [the province].

Typically, they would invite six to ten of the very best every year, pay their expenses, and support them during their stay. Each group would appear two to four times a week during the festival. So that is what I would go for, because during the course of an evening of this unbearable entertainment, there would be these performances of folk music and folk dance. In one evening, I might see two or three groups, and each performance would last for fifteen minutes. So over the course of a week, I could see and hear material that would otherwise take me the best part of a year to record. It's a unique opportunity to get the very best.

Also during the '72 junket, in the pit next to me, were the boys from All India Radio in Simla, which is the provincial capital of Himachal Pradesh. They were really nice, and we collaborated on a bunch of recording projects. They knew many of the fine local instrumentalists and vocalists, and we would record them jointly. That made my job a lot easier. That also meant that I got a much more rounded take than would have been possible with just the dance performances.

In '73 I went back to India from May of '72 through February '73. I went back to New York, stayed for six weeks and deposited enough material with Tracy Stern for four or five albums. I remember going to the studio and laying down two records of Tibetan rituals, one from the Himalayan material and one from the Kashmir material. But there was essentially enough for more in the can, which Tracy later bought. From that period of work, I generated enough material for five LPs.

Then when I was back in India, I'd always wanted to go to Hunza, and I thought, well, good time to do it. I went to Pakistan, went up to Pindi, which is in northern Pakistan, and from there flew up to Gilgit, which is right up in the Northwest Territory, and went up on the recently constructed road up to Hunza. In the old days, it took three and a half days on trails on horseback to get up to Hunza, but on the road which had been made at that time it took only three hours by car or minibus. Much easier. The road from Pindi was not really complete, so that's an extraordinary part of the world. It's arid Central Asia.

When I got to Hunza, it was really incredible. There's Mount Rakaposhi, twenty-five thousand feet, and Baltit, which is the principal village of Hunza, at eight thousand, so you get some incredible vistas. You look down through the terraced hillsides. All the water has to be brought down by irrigation for miles from the glaciers. They have these incredible irrigation works, all built by hand. They bring the water four or five miles from the glacier, and they have this verdant hillside, which is the result of all that labor of terracing the hillsides and building the irrigation. So you overlook that, all the way down to the Hunza River, and then the other side which is Magar, the adjacent state, all the way up Mount Rakaposhi, twenty-five thousand feet. Really stunning.

There, I was befriended by the Mir, the late ruler of Hunza. He was really a genial gentleman. Terribly English, wore beautiful English tweeds that he bought at Savoy tailors by Savoy hotels [where] they spent their winters. He said, "We have not central heating in Hunza, so we spend the winters in Gstaad or in the Savoy at London." He was the ruler; he could do that. Anyway, he was very genial and was pleased that I wanted to record the traditional music, thought it was a worthy project, and sent for the local schoolteacher, who was friendly with the best local musicians. He took me around, so I met the musicians and recorded them. Out of that came the Gilgit and Hunza records.

After that, I went to Gilgit, and the commandante of the Gilgit scouts, who's like the local military formation, was equally welcoming, and arranged for me to record the musicians of the Gilgit scouts right in Gilgit. Out of that, I got enough to make quite a record.

The following year, after recording in '73, I must have dropped those recordings off, and went back again. I was sitting in Delhi when I heard that the Indian government had opened up Ladakh to foreigners. It had been closed for years and years and years. Ladakh is in the western Tibet. You have Kashmir and Ladakh, Tibet proper and Xinjiang up here. I had been wanting to go there for ages, so up I went. Spent three very interesting weeks there, difficult physically because the valleys were at twelve thousand feet, the mountains went up to twenty-two thousand. So a bit of a strain on the system.

There I had equally good luck. I met the chap who was the local information officer. The Ladakhi were really sensible. They didn't appoint some bureaucrat. The chap was the local poet, and really knew everything locally. He wasn't very good at making money, so they appointed him information officer so he would have some income to support himself. He was a really nice guy. He took me around to meet musicians, and from one group I met another group. We would be recording in orchards. Really nice. They also took me over to the All India Radio station, in Leh.

As I recall, Ladakh was the first place I had the Dolby box with me, so those would be the first location tapes made that way, with Dolby A. That would be 1974.

I didn't have enough from Kashmir for a second album, so I went and did another stint in Srinagar. The recordings from that period were done using the Stellavox and Dolby A, which enhanced the sound considerably. Made it much cleaner.

In '67 and '68, I quit my job as a financial editor for a banking magazine, took off for a year and a half and went down to South America. I spent several months in Venezuela, and then I decided, "Well, it's time to see the subcontinent." So I went down the west coast, not the east coast, stopping in some places longer than others. Went to Colombia.

The middle class mode of travel in South America is by what they call a *collectivo*, and that is a taxi, plying for hire long distance, in which one engages one's seat. It's a great way to travel because you get to meet the literate middle class. So you meet really interesting people who know about the local situation. You can have a really interesting discussion when you are with four or five congenial strangers. One person I met was a doctor in a hospital in a remote Pacific village named Guape. To get to Guape, you have to first go to Buenaventura, which is the major Pacific coast seaport, which is out from Cali. This is all in southern Colombia. So you go out to Cali, and you either take a boat or a light plane down to Guape, because there are no roads. Too many rivers coming out from the Andes. I went to Guape, and since the hotel had been knocked down, they put me up in the hospital. I had a man croaking his last next to me the whole time I was in Guape.

So the doctor and her colleagues were delighted to have someone from outside, something interesting for them to do, so they enjoyed as much as I did taking me around to meet musicians. Going around to meet the local musicians meant getting into the hospital's launch and going up- or downriver. The river is the local equivalent to highways. Everybody has dugout canoes. Even the kids have small dugout canoes. It's the local equivalent to the bike. That's how kids go to school. And the houses are on stilts by the side of the river. That's suburbia. So they would take me to meet these families, and they would set up sessions for me. It was there that I learned one of the basic lessons of recording in communities of this kind: you'd better take plenty of booze along, because when the booze runs out, the recording stops. It was local firewater. We'd pick up bottles of firewater.

From Guape, I went back to Cali and was in Papayán for holy week. It's really incredible, physically very difficult for a person with light skin in that part of the world. Buenaventura, for example, is in the torrid tropical zone, and I remember the thermometer being in the nineties, and it raining twenty-two hours out of every twenty-four.

From there I went south to Ecuador. In one community, there's a remote inland valley with a village called Chalguayaquil. There were blacks who were exceedingly poor. Nice people. They received me very warmly. I went there with a chap who specialized in folk music from Quito, and these blacks are so poor, they couldn't afford real musical instruments. They produced notes by blowing across leaves. They blew into calabashes to imitate bass instruments. It was great. I'd never heard anything like that before.

Then I went down into Peru and was most active in Ayacucho, in southern Peru. Ayacucho is best remembered now as the center where the Shining Power guerillas got their start. I was staying with the daughter of one of my friends from Lima, who was the *professora* of music at the university there. Since she was an educated woman from Lima, all of the other young faculty members would be around her house in the evenings. So I got to meet lots of interesting and helpful people. They took me out to meet the local musicians. We would sit around drinking pisco and 7-Up. Pisco is the white grape brandy from Peru. It's really quite good. It was quite cold in the evenings, so we would keep ourselves warm by drinking it with 7-Up. So they took me around to meet the local musicians. I met a marvelous harpist and a group of musicians who made their living as guitar makers. It would take them a week to make one guitar. Not much money to be made with one guitar. They called themselves El Conjunto Dos De Mayo. The Second of May was the name of the street they lived on. They were really good. Sort of rough and raunchy, but really great.

From Ayacucho, I went south to Puno, which is the principal town on the shore of Lake Titicaca, at twenty-three thousand feet. It was close to the border of Bolivia. There they have the pan pipes made from the bamboo tubes. They have two names, zamponia and siku. There was one group that consisted of sixty men playing siku.

I don't know if they're still there, but in La Paz, which is also high up, around twelve thousand feet, I met Gilbert Favre. Gilbert is Swiss, and when I was there in 1968, he was the best player of the Cana, the notch flute. The people in La Paz went nuts over his playing. They liked his playing better than any of the local musicians. He had a *conjunta* called Los Jiras. I wonder if he's still playing. It would be interesting to know. They had the best selling record in La Paz when a best seller was around six thousand.

When I was in South America, fortunately I learned Spanish. Enough so I could get cab drivers to reduce the fare to an acceptable level, "*Señor, no estoy Rockefeller. No se puedo señor.*" As soon as they heard that, they would smile, say okay, and the price would come down by half. I think that's the acid test of one's language, whether one can bargain with a cab driver and win a concession. I'm really glad that my friends in Venezuela taught me Spanish. That was very nice of them. I spent ten months there.

I must confess that I am basically a lazy individual, so I haven't learned Hindi and I haven't learned Tibetan. Fortunately, many Indians are very well educated, and every progressive Indian speaks

English. They think of English as the language of the Jet Age, and Hindi the language of the cart era. Every Indian who considers himself progressive will speak some English, either a little or a lot. My Tibetan friends, because they are refugees, have per force had to become linguists. They've had to learn Hindi because they live in India, and because they want to exchange with Westerners, more and more of them are speaking English as well.

When one is as lazy as I am, one can get by. When I went to Dharamsala, after having been going there since 1972, the Tibetan shopkeepers I do business with look at me in disbelief. They can't believe that after all these years I haven't learned to speak Tibetan. I think they're wondering what's wrong with me. "It's that stupid gray-haired man with the tape machine. Still can't speak Tibetan."

You won't get adventure and derring-do from me. What you will get are practicalities. Travel, in the beginning, is fun. That's why we all begin traveling. But it rapidly becomes something other than fun. A point came, where I began to feel myself like a traveling salesman, felt like I was in the role of a traveling salesman, because every two or three days, it would be, "Well, I'm off to a new place right now. Where am I going to sleep, where am I going to eat? How am I going to meet musicians?"

After a period, the thrill of going to a new place starts to wear away. So while we expect travel to be exciting, what it winds up being, more often than not, is educational. Whether we like it or not. We learn about ourselves in various situations.

One thing travel can do, like anything else in life—for me it's been through travel—is you learn a lot about yourself. Where I'm coming from, and that sort of thing.

Also, travel has its hardships. I nearly always have stomach upsets in these out of the way places, and they can be extremely debilitating. It's really hard to be happy and enthusiastic, getting out there and working with the musicians, when the intestines are acting up.

Photograph: Ebet Roberts, Private Music

RAVI SHANKAR

There is a certain irony to a piece titled "Three Ragas in 'D' Minor" unless that piece is written by the legendary sitarist, composer, and champion of the classical music of India, Ravi Shankar. One of the best-known non-Western musicians in the West— indeed people were listening to Shankar decades before the words world and beat got together in print and record stores—Shankar was at Monterrey, influenced the Beatles (particularly George Harrison) and introduced the world to the wonders of the raga and Hindustani classical music, paving the way for musicians like Zakir Hussain and Ali Akbar Khan, among many, many others. He composed music in the Hindustani classical tradition and merged it with the Western tradition as well.

The classical music has rhythms and forms that stay the same, but we improvise all the time. That's why we have all the new things we do sort of added up on the old style of things.

As far as the classical tradition is concerned, we don't have drastic changes. Maybe some presentation, timing, duration, sophistication, lightness, things like that might change a bit. But as far as classical music is concerned, there hasn't been that much change, but we always go on improving and developing. That's how it has lasted all these centuries. But on the other side, the creative phases of music, there have been all sorts of changes. There are lots of experimentations either in jazz or in rock or even classical. Indian classical music remains the same.

By now I have a lot of experience composing for Western instruments as well. We played the closing of Russian Indian Festival. I was commissioned by the Indian government and also by the Soviet government. It was the special event of closing the India Festival. It was one year that the festival was going on, and this was the closing, the end of it. The piece was made for the Moscow Chamber Orchestra and so we arranged it with them in mind. They were happier, instead of playing very plain musical lines. Some of them had come to India in the initial stage, particularly the conductor and the head of the orchestra, etc. And we had quite bit in Moscow, also. I have been there four times before. All in all, we had eighty-five maybe ninety musicians on stage. In addition to the Moscow Chamber Orchestra, we also had a folk ensemble and our musicians.

I was there first fifteen years ago. Now there was definitely a social difference. There was much more freedom.

Unfortunately, at home, all the people I admired most are dead and gone, but they were great masters. I learned from one of the great masters himself, and there have been few people I admired more.

Among the present group, there are some very wonderful musicians, especially in the field of singing. My contemporaries and colleagues like my son, and people like Ali Akbar Khan.

VIJAY ANAND

While the "classical" music of India, featuring the sitar, etc., is well documented, for decades the true popular music on the subcontinent has been the music that came out of the Bombay film industry. One of the most ubiquitous, if not best known, noises of the world, Indian film music is one of the Asian subcontinent's most popular sounds. The Indian film industry makes Hollywood look anemic in terms of sheer proliferation. For years, Vijay Anand has been among "Bollywood's" most ingenious and adventurous composers. Borrowing liberally from the traditional and classical musics, he makes a sound that pushes envelopes in an often staid and conservative environment, allowing it to compete with the Western music that had become so much a part of the electronic global village. Vijay Anand is one of the genre's most innovative voices.

Here in Tamil Nadu, people have tried producing their own music as an alternative to cinema music, but nothing became a big success. I mean that it didn't become a success commercially. When it comes to Bombay, it is somewhat better. They have become modern enough to take alternative music. In Tamil Nadu and in other states, this has not become a success.

Keyboard is my main instrument and also synthesizer and piano. I entered the music field in the rhythm section, playing triple conga and bongo. That is why you find rhythm very strong in my music.

I've learned Carnatic music (South Indian classical music). I've not learned Hindustani music, but we are using it in our film music. Besides, I have a lot of listening knowledge. So I follow other musical styles. I observe it. After understanding how they are doing it, then I use it in my music.

I learned Carnatic music from Mr. Radha Krishna for two years. I listen to a lot of music. Apart from Indian music, I listen to other countries' music, too.

In classical music, I appreciate G. Ramanatha Iyer. He was in the cine field before Visvanathan. He gave a modern touch to the South Indian classical music. He changed the Carnatic music to a level that could be appreciated by everybody.

One needs a lot of patience to sit and listen to traditional music. If only you have some knowledge, only then will you be able to enjoy it. He made it light and made it possible for a lot of people to enjoy it. He did this maybe in the forties. Then slowly, step by step, the music field started changing.

You know how I learned Western music? There in a center called Musimusical on Mount Road in Madras. The Trinity College of Music in London is conducting classes there. You can appear for exams. The examiners come from London and conduct exams. There are different grade levels. I've done both practical and theory in piano and classical guitar. I did this about five years back. There is up to the eighth grade. I did up to eighth grade, but passed only up to the sixth grade. I could not attend the eighth grade exam because during that period I was very busy in the cinema field.

I will tell you another thing. I told you about Western classical. I have used a lot of modern jazz in my music.

In cinema tradition, the tenor banjo has been used for a very long time. In Hindustani music, they combine sarod and banjo, so this is not something new. I have used it in my songs on the basis of country and western style. I have used very many countries' instruments in my composition. This tenor banjo is disappearing. I am using it in order to keep it from disappearing. In one song, I fed the tenor banjo samples into the computer.

I am using a lot of modern instruments. Whenever an advanced system comes, I use it immediately. I have used keyboards, synthesizers, the latest modules, etc. The cinema audience likes everything. They don't seem to think that is something strange or awkward. They seem to like it when they listen to those songs.

But we use them to the appropriate limit. More than ten years we've been using combo organs. Back then, that was considered to be a big electronic instrument.

Around the forties, G. Ramahatha Iyer used an instrument called Univox. It was small in size. That was the modern instrument of that period. In the seventies, there was the combo organ. In the eighties, there was the synthesizer. In my songs, I have used computers a lot. Now we also have the beat machine and rhythm machine.

The peculiar thing about my music is I mix it up. I would call it a *masala*. In one song, you can see many varieties. You find our Indian traditional music and also the other countries' music. The people like this very much. I will continue to do like this a lot. The way I have used the rap in the middle of the song is peculiar, is it not? When you listen to this song it comes in suddenly. It has a kick as soon as it starts.

In some languages, when you write the words it fits very well. In some languages, it may sound very harsh. It may not suit the music. So, when it comes to the song, if we do anything, it may change the shape of the song and it would sound very harsh. For Western music, English words sound very apt. But if you use Tamil words or other languages' words when the song is set in such pitch, it will sound very awkward. So, with songs, no risk is taken. The same style is followed. But we can differentiate in the arrangement of the music. Words are something that get registered. The meaning should get registered correctly. It should reach the audience. The people should also be able to understand the situation of the song. We don't have to do any daring experiments. That is why it has remained the same. I think that is the main point. If we overdo it, the lyrics won't be understood. The language is like that.

With respect to the voice, it is better to follow the tradition without any change. We should not confuse the audience. Suppose we try some different modulation and splitting the words. This will affect the audibility of the lyrics. Lyrics are very important. People who don't know music, even they are able to enjoy music, if it should reach that kind of audience, we can do anything with the music, but we have to keep the voice the same.

Music is a universal language. I listen to music from all languages. You don't need to know the language to do music. Music is language. It is a common language throughout the world.

When I was a boy around twelve years old, when I was going to school, I had an interest in music. I wanted to learn music. As a kid, I never learned music properly from anybody. I started playing on my own and improved my playing. Gradually, I started playing with music groups, cinema music orchestra, also known as light music orchestra, in contrast to our classical music, and developed my talent. Then, I had my own light music orchestra, called Melody Cans, playing cinema music. Then I started playing background music for dramas. The leader of that drama troupe entered the movies and became a big director. He introduced me to the cinema field.

Nobody can become big without being inspired by somebody. In the beginning stage of my musical career, there were these two music directors named Visvanathan and Ramamoorthy. These two were the melody makers of two decades, the sixties and seventies. In the later part of the seventies, they split, though Visvanathan continues while Ramamoorthry fell out. I always admired their music, and I even told Visvanathan so. He is my mentor. I was very closely following his music. In the beginning, I was so crazy about his music.

There are many musicians I admire from different angles. In the beginning, when I started playing music in my teenage years, I listened to a lot of Western music. I used to like country and western music a lot. I was a fan of Jim Reeves. I have a collection of Cliff Richard's songs. Even then I was inspired by musicians like them. I wanted to adapt their music. Later, many musicians came.

In modern music, I like Chick Corea's keyboard. In modern Western music, they are bringing out new arrangements. If you take my songs, they are simple, but in the arrangements of chords sometimes to a limit, I use the style of Chick Corea. So, I would mention only his name, but there are lots of other musicians.

I am bound to a lot of people—the director, producer, songwriter, distributor, and the audience. I always have to think about their liking. When the film is released, if the distributors come around and say the song is not good, I would lose my market.

At first, the producer may say, "Let us do this nicer orchestration for this song." Later he may say, "Well, we'll try this out with a different song," or "This is what my budget is, you have to reduce the orchestration." So there are lots of complicating details and I have to restrict myself. I have to revolve around a small circle.

If I were a record producer, I would be free to bring out whatever I think. But now, with hands tied, I still manage to do some of the things I want to do. Western musicians are independent. That is a great gift for them. I haven't come across any opportunity like that. Some people tried producing their own music, but they could not succeed. In the West, it is possible for the musicians to produce their own CDs. It is a great drawback here. The audiences are yet to receive it.

Each one has a different style, is it not so? For instance, if you take African music, rhythm is something very special. There is a lot of emphasis on percussion. In jazz there are plenty of good chord arrangements and good harmonies. All together this has some richness. Classical music also has lots of substance. If you take Japanese music, it is peculiar. Japanese music has different sounds. So I cannot say what I like and don't like. Because I am a music lover, I love everybody. In everything we see, there is a different substance. I like to listen to everything, so I cannot say which I like.

I've listened to all the countries' music. I have used some Spanish Gypsy music, but what I have used is little. I have a lot of desire to do different styles. There are different kinds of materials available in a cloth shop and how one would have the desire to get them and stitch them in many different styles is the same way I have the desire to try different kinds of music. I have to do it gradually, into the future.

In Indian films, you have to be very careful. We do things according to the situation. Otherwise it would sound bad. I used heavy breathing in a song sometimes, but if we do this beyond a certain limit, the Censor Board of India won't allow us. There were songs of mine censored by the board saying that they were too much. So the song won't come in the picture. But it will come out on cassettes. A lot of people like it. Some people don't. When you bring out something explicit, you always face such a situation.

At one period, it was okay to be moderate. Now the modern generation, through satellite, watch Star TV and MTV. They are able to see the latest things in foreign countries. Now everybody has cassette tape recorders. People have videos. Even in the village, this has become common. Through TV, they are able to see a lot of other countries' music.

The audience will accept us only if we compete with the shows they see. Otherwise, they will get the feeling there is no improvement on our side. Now the people have understood what is going on around the world. We have to compete with that.

In a way, it may have some effect. But in foreign countries the video has become very common. Still, the movies are coming out.

In other countries, they have problems. We also have the people not coming to the cinema in large numbers because of the TV and video. Whatever you say, you won't get the interest and the same thrill in watching TV and video. Whatever you see on videocassettes, you won't get the impact, the original effect. People are still coming to the cinema.

Cinema is still making a good profit. We can't say no to the arrival of modern equipment. It will be coming all the time. We will have to compete and produce good stuff and only then we'll be able to stand in front of the audience. How long could they go on sitting in their houses watching TV? It is impossible. They need relaxation; they'll have to come to the cinema.

MIDDLE EAST

Again, trouble and strife help perpetuate great art. Throughout the Middle East, vast amounts of great Arabic music, ranging from the traditional Egyptian Nubian music of Ali Hassan Kuban and Hossam Ramzy—the latter noted in the West for his work with Robert Plant and Jimmy Page—to the local classical music of Mohamed Abdel Wahab to rappers like Kat Kut el Amir. This is a very cosmopolitan scene indeed.

However, as in most places outside of the West, the audience is usually not global and not exactly monolithic locally. It is the rare artist making noise of the world on a local, indigenous level—even if he records—who can actually make a living playing music. In Israel, this was once colloquially described to me as, "They are the most popular musicians in the country. They can almost make a living playing music."

OFRA HAZA

No matter what you did to the backing tracks of an Ofra Haza record her voice never lost its singular Middle Eastern quality. As she became an international vocal diva and darling, many of her recordings became as heavily redolent of contemporary dance music as Yemenite coffee is of cumin. Beyond that, once you get behind the beat and the standard midi-samples, Haza kept the indigenous instruments, the brass trays and double reed shepherd pipes as a major element of her music. Yet it brought her fame throughout the world and a number one single nearly everywhere except the U.S. with "Im Nin'alu." The themes, from her songs about the Jews who are still in Yemen—among the worst human rights situations in the world—to slave ships in the seventeenth-century triangle trade to her "exotic oriental love songs," exuded an innocent power and eloquence. Her sudden death from AIDS—an illness hidden until her actual passing—represented another sad casualty in the global health crisis for music fans everywhere.

My parents came to Israel before Israel became a state. It was in 1929, something like that. They came by foot all the way from Yemen to Israel. It was desert in Israel. In the beginning they lived in a tent.

I started performing when I was twelve years old. I was born in a poor neighborhood, Hatikva, in Tel Aviv. I met my producer, Bezalel Aloni, in our neighborhood. He did a workshop theater: protest theater, political theater about the problems we had in the neighborhood. We were people, not professional, just people from the neighborhood who wanted to say something. Instead of demonstrating in the street, we did it on the stage. We sang, we danced, we acted. It was actual things. One day something would happen, we'd see it on

TV, in the newspaper, so immediately we'd change the show. It was like one and a half hours of doing the musical, then a five-hour discussion with the audience about the problems and our view of them.

It was very important theater in Israel. We became very famous and we did records. The first one came without any help from the government, without any help from the mayor of the town, with money. Just people who wanted to say something. Everyone brought from his house whatever he liked. If we had to have clothes, we did it ourselves. We went to paint posters on the street. All the work was done by us. It was wonderful experience. I worked there for seven years.

First of all, it's a poor neighborhood. We didn't have good schools, we didn't have good teachers, because of all the Sephardim from Yemen, from Morocco, from Iran, Iraq, all the countries, we don't deserve to have good teachers and stuff like that. We didn't come from Europe. So we had problems like, we want our rights in many things. We want help, we want support. We wanted to be like everybody. This was only in the beginning.

Now Hatikva is a wonderful place. On the main street there are restaurants that all the people from TV—famous people—come to, because the government and everybody helped the country. We have wonderful schools, the schools are very nice. We have everything like the people from North Tel Aviv, for example. Now the surroundings are wonderful. There is grass, there are flowers, there's a place for children to play after school. There's a place if they need help after school to do homework. It's wonderful. We also said about things, like people would say, "She's from Hatikva. Maybe she's a thief, or something like that." We'd shout about that. Suspect, always suspect.

The first musical we did was called *Plastic Flowers*. The people think we are like plastic flowers, without a soul or anything, because we are very poor. It was so natural. So spontaneous. We were from the neighborhood. We didn't take a teacher, like Bezalel. He was from our neighborhood. He was a director; he wrote the book, lyrics, music. Everything. We did it by ourselves.

Of course, when I was in the theater, we did albums. I was the lead singer and one of the songs went number one in the charts. We were the community theater. After three years, Bezalel changed the name from the Workshop Theater of Hatikva to Ofra Haza and the Workshop Theater of Hatikva. It was wonderful.

I represented Israel in the Eurovision Song Festival in 1983. The competition was in Munich. It was the first time I was in Germany. The song I was singing was "Chai" (Hebrew for life). "Chai, chai, am Yisroel chai" (the people of Israel live). To sing this song in Germany the first time I was there, "Chai, Chai, we are still alive, despite everything."

When we were there, we went to Dachau, and we saw two old people who were in the shoah, in the Holocaust, and they came back. They saw me there and they said, "When you sing, you have to remember us. For us, and for Jews all around the world, what you are doing with this song in Germany is very important to us." We picked the song very carefully.

Actually, everything happens by accident, because when I did the *Yemenite Songs, Fifty Gates of Wisdom* here, I didn't think about Europe, I didn't think about Japan. Just my parents, as a present for them, who gave me this beautiful culture. To please them. And of course the Yemenite Jewish people in Israel. So when I was in the studio, I recorded this album in a different way than usual. I was in the studio with a percussionist, tin drums, percussion and the vocals, like an a cappella.

So, the beginning of the work, we took a cassette home to listen, Benny Nagari and me, and Bezalel's children said to him, "You know, that's wonderful. Why don't you also do a version for us? We also want to have this music."

That gave us the idea to do the disco versions of "Galbi" and "Im Nin'alu," but of course, we finished the Yemenite songs, and only one year later, we did this.

It's wonderful that people who don't understand the language still like the music. That's most important. It's like music is an international language.

The single sold very well here and the album also. Not like Michael Jackson, of course, but really good exposure. America is a bigger market. I'm saying thank you to God about everything. I wasn't expecting too much. For me it's a present, to be in America, to have everyone know me in Europe.

You know, the song "Im Nin'alu" the meaning is, "Even if the doors of generosity are locked, the gates of Heaven are never locked." It's like, open the gates everywhere, all the doors. There's something very symbolic about it. The name of the song and what happened with the song all over.

Since I'm from the Middle East, whenever I go anywhere people ask me about the Middle East, about the Palestinians, about Israel like I'm the prime minister of Israel. But, of course, I'm answering as a young Israeli girl, giving my point of view.

It occurred to me that through music you can do so many positive things that politicians and diplomats cannot, because people are against them all the time. Maybe they are hiding a lot of things; maybe they are saying things and not doing what they say. So from my experience, from my albums *Shaday* and *Yemenite Songs*, I got letters from Kuwait, Egypt, Morocco, and Yemen.

I'm not a folk singer. I don't know if it's "pop." I don't like the word pop. Sometimes for people it means different things. I am doing, as I said, the most important thing for me is to bring messages, to bring something new, even if it's in the music, the lyrics. Sometimes, to your ears, it's pop. Sometimes, like "Kaddish" or "Da'asa," it's traditional. It's excellent that people take my music to them what they want to hear. But the most important is what I did. To do a disco version of "Im Nin'alu" for instance, is just to bring to the people, to the youngest, the culture.

I use my background, my culture, my roots, my education to write songs in order to express more ideas. I expressed things that were very important to me, current and urgent issues about the Middle East. "My Brother Is Out There" is about the Jews that are still in Yemen. The songs were written with Yemenite inspiration, Yemenite influence, Yemenite gripping the center. With each song you can hear the tradition through my melody, rhythm, even the lyrics, even when the majority of the words are in English. I did that because I wanted to bring the messages to an audience in a language that they'd understand. That's what I wanted to achieve, to do something new that I can write about things that I want to say, but, of course, still within my tradition, to bring it to the world with my culture.

In Israel, everyone likes to sing. There are a lot of singers. Some of them are very famous and they have a day job, and they have money. Some of them are trying to find themselves and do special things and sometimes the people don't receive them as well. Like anywhere. I mean, we are a small country, which means we are a small market. It's funny, one channel on the TV, that's what we have. That's it. It's not like here in America, where you have all the possibilities. You can have success just in New York and not have it in Los Angeles. It's very different.

In Yemen, by the way, they presented me like the national singer of Yemen. And I can't go there, because I have an Israeli passport, and it's a hostile country and we don't have relations between Israel and Yemen. But the music is so strong, that people know everything about the Yemenite songs, that I'm Israeli, of course, and they sent me letters, that they appreciated it: "We didn't believe that someday this music would be very famous all over."

If you want to bring a message, you can do it with the album, when they are sitting at home after a hard day, listening quiet, without any advertisements, like the TV. Something very personal. I believe that a peace will come. I believe that there is something happening, and people are more open, and will think very positive things.

Just because they saw Israel on the TV, it's hard. It's hard for me. I'm traveling and I turn on the TV and I see about Israel, what's happening in Israel all the time. People are sitting at home with remote controls and charging Israel all the time, because it's on the TV. It's not fair. Everyone knows what the media can do. I'm not saying there are no problems, because there are. But, if people want to charge Israel, they should come to Israel, to see what's happening in Israel.

Two journalists, one from England, one from Germany, they came to do a cover story in Israel, and I took them to Jerusalem, to the markets. They saw the Arab people say, "Hello, how are you?" in Arabic. "I hope you have success all over. We're very proud."

The journalists said, "You talk?!" And I said, "Of course we talk." And one of them said, "My friends told me, 'Don't go to Israel, there are bombs on the street.' And it's so wonderful!"

I took them to the Kotel, and they changed their mind. They said, "Oh, it's not like what we see on TV."

I said, "There are places, and there are problems, like everywhere. But it's not what you think. It's what the media want you to think."

It's so important to me that now everybody knows about Yemenite Jewish songs. Before, nobody knew there was Yemen, the country. Nobody knew what is Yemen. People knew about Spanish music, French music, Italian music, Brazilian music, because there were nightclubs and groups. Everybody knew about it. But Yemenite songs are so far away, nobody knew about it. That's a big success for me. People now talk about Yemenite songs. They know what they sound like.

SIMON SHAHEEN

An Israeli Arab, Simon Shaheen is a virtuoso on the violin and the oud. He has been a major mover and shaker in a movement to bring together Arabs and Jews musically, working with Frank London of the Klezmatics on a number of projects. But in addition to being an amazing soloist, a doctor of music, and a celebrated composer in both Arabic and Western contexts, Shaheen is a prime collaborator, working with artists ranging from pop star Sting to new jazz pioneer Henry Threadgill to writer William Burroughs.

In Middle Eastern music, you have three aspects of the music. Three elements that are very rich and very powerful. The first is the melodies. It's very linear, and because we have this microtonal quality, these quartertones, we have almost endless possibilities linearly speaking. If I improvise, I never repeat any pattern or any melody that I used before. I just keep flowing with more and more melodies. And what makes it interesting is all this built up tension and the release and the rhythmic counterpoint which I carry into the improvisation.

Then there are the rhythms that we use and the kind instruments that we use, like the riqq, which is similar to the tambourine, or the frame drum. We have more than ten kinds of frame drum, and the boukar. That's the most famous in America.

The third element would be the embellishment, all the designs that I use around the melodies, like the slides and trills and many small different patterns that I use to decorate the music. These three elements are very essential and very powerful in Middle Eastern music. When I play an improvisation, you can sense these three elements very much.

If you take the album I made of the compositions of *The Music of Mohamed Abdel Wahab*, the Island recording, you'll notice that it's a larger ensemble and it is very rhythmic. The energy is in the melodic counterpoint that we created. With this recording, first of all, it's classical Arabic and Turkish music. It's a smaller group playing more intimately. The music itself is more classical. It belongs to the Sufi concept.

Many of the pieces I play are called "sama'is" and "bashrafs". These are compositions that are used by Arabs and Turkish for religious services. For example, when there is a dervish, the religious group called dervish, they dance on these pieces. The bashraf is a very long slow composition. The sama'i are still slow, but they have more movement. Then I put a longa in there, which is anther Arabic/Turkish composition that is very vital and fast. So, these compositions in the fifteenth, sixteenth, and seventeenth centuries were very much in use in the religious services. These are ritual music. So this is the relation, and for me at least, when I listen to a bashraf, especially the way we played it, it has a great deal of depth in terms of the sound, the long notes. It's very calming.

"Bashraf Kurd," for example—the name "kurd" is the name of the mode or the maqan. The kurd is comparable to the frigean mode, where the first and second notes have half intervals.

The connection between this, Turkish, Gypsy, and flamenco is great. This is why I'm thinking of working on another recording that would use both instruments, the oud and the guitar, the Spanish flamenco guitar in its oldest form possible. In fact, I'm talking to Paco de Lucia among others. He is a connoisseur of the oud: He likes the oud. He himself plays the oud. This idea came when I was in Spain, actually, in 1986, recording for RCA Ariola with Fantanita, one of the most famous flamenco singers in Spain.

You know, this thing is happening a lot, this fusion. It is not my intention, just to pick up things from here and there and put them together. I am writing original compositions for oud and guitar, where I want to utilize both instruments to the best of their ability. Many people are pushing me to do that, especially in terms of the marketing and the amount of people who listen to it. It's huge. I'm thinking about this in the jazz field.

I am trying to bring these other musicians, as much as possible, to this concept where you are free to improvise with the flow of melody, especially if they are going to have some inquiry into Middle Eastern modes and try to use quartertones. I think this will be a new thing that's meant to happen.

This is why I'm mentioning jazz. Henry Threadgill and Butch Morris and Bill Laswell is always behind this. We were thinking of writing things and recording together. This is exactly the point, where we have a kind of free improvisation without being committed to very tight harmonic progressions. This is exactly the concept.

Since I come from both worlds—I grew up with Western classical music and Arabic classical music and traditional music, and also I grew up listening to jazz. So since I come from both worlds, I'm trying to create a crossroad here or to try and create a kind of marriage from both sides.

We treat the music as Middle Eastern music, just like classical musicians treat classical music like European music. This is the same concept. Don't forget, the Arab world and Turkey exchanged a lot of music, some of it for good reasons, some of it because of bad reasons, like the occupation of Turkey and of the Arab world for five hundred years. Whether they liked it or not, they had to exchange ideas. If you are talking about Morrocco, you have something that's called "elba."

Morocco, Tunisia, and Algeria share very much in terms of classical tradition. It's when it comes to folklore that they differ. The Turkish influence on these countries was stronger in the beginning of the nineteenth century and at the turn of the century, because they were never under direct occupation of the Turks. The countries that were under direct occupation were Syria, Lebanon, Egypt, Palestine, Jordan. These were what we call the Eastern Mediterranean countries.

The Turkish repertoire became part of the general repertoire of the region, including Egypt. Because of the standing of Egypt as the heart of the Arab world, all of these countries like Morocco, Tunis,

Algeria were very much influenced. And part of this rich tradition they borrowed or learned was Turkish.

I play the violin in the Arabic style. It's a Western violin, but I tune it differently, G-D-G-D. The reason we changed the tuning, first of all, it's much easier for the left hand to play the quarter tones when it's tuned this way, the same way as the arpeggios fit the fifths in Western classical music. Also, for the ornaments. With the ornaments that accompany the melody, they fit very well. When I play Arabic music in Western tuning, G-D-A-E, it's kind of, you don't feel comfortable with it. It's more difficult. In terms of playing and sound, it is the same. Of course the colors are totally different.

The oud goes back. It started to be used initially in the fourth and fith century in Arabia. Actually it's an ancestor of the lute, not fretted at all. This is how we get that microtonal quality.

At that time, it used to be different than now. It went through a lot of changes. For example, the top used to be made of leather, now it's made of wood. Very hard leather. We still have one instrument that is very old. It is an ancestor to the European viola and the violin. It's called the "rabada." It is an Arabic violin. It has two strings and the top is made of leather. It's got a square body with a long round fingerboard. When you play it, you sit down and put it on the leg like a cello.

Many African instruments, like the kora, they have this leather concept.

The oud used to have two or three strings, now we have five double strings and a drone in the bass. It's tuned, from high to low, C-G-D-A, and the low string can be tuned to a G or an F and the drone, the single sixth string, can be tuned D or E. It depends on the mode I chose. Then I tune the fifth or sixth string.

I started to learn to play classical Western violin when I was seven. Then I went to the academy of music in Jerusalem, and finished a performance major in violin. Then I came to the Manhattan School of Music where I graduated with a masters in violin performance and then I went to Columbia.

I do perform a lot. We do a lot of chamber music, and I do have time in the concerts to play half classical Eastern music, half classical Western music. When I do this, I choose things that, for some reason, relate. For example, I gave a concert a few months ago in San Diego. I played half of the program of classical Western violin with a piano, and I chose Béla Bartók. Then I showed, in the second half, how Béla Bartók was very much influenced with the modern music of the Middle East.

HANK BORDOWITZ

One of the first journalists to take world music seriously as a genre and as a sound that Western audiences would care about, Hank Bordowitz has been writing about the noise of the world through four decades. His work on non-Western musicians has appeared in such diverse publications as the men's magazine *Gallery*, the *B'nai B'rith Jewish Monthly*, *All-Star*, and in the regular Cosmopolitan column that ran in *Jazziz* for over ten years, among dozens of other periodicals that included his features on artists and music from South Africa to Siberia. He has contributed to *The Rolling Stone Jazz and Blues Record Guide*, Musichound World, Baker's Biographical Dictionary of Musicians, among others.

He is the author of *Turning Points of Rock and Roll*; *Every Little Thing Is Gonna Be Alright—The Bob Marley Reader*; *The Bruce Springsteen Scrapbook*; *The U2 Reader: A Quarter Century of Commentary, Criticism and Reviews*; and *Bad Moon Rising: The Unauthorized History of Creedence Clearwater Revival*.

In addition to these publications, for the last six years, Hank has programmed the world music service for Music Choice Digital Cable radio. Hank served for four years as the co-chair of the National Writer's Union Music Writers Caucus, organizing his fellow entertainment journalists.